THE

Creative

PROFESSIONAL

THE
Creative
PROFESSIONAL

A SURVIVAL GUIDE FOR THE BUSINESS WORLD

Howard J. Blumenthal

EMMIS BOOKS

For further information, contact the publisher at

Emmis Books
1700 Madison Road
Cincinnati, OH 45206
www.emmisbooks.com

Library of Congress Cataloging-in-Publication Data

Blumenthal, Howard J.
  The creative professional : a survival guide for the business world / By Howard J. Blumenthal.-- 1st ed.
      p. cm.
  Includes bibliographical references.
  ISBN-13: 978-1-57860-245-2
  ISBN-10: 1-57860-245-9
  1. Creative ability in business--United States. 2. Artists--United States--Finance, Personal. 3. Small business--United States--Finance. 4. Self-employed--United States--Finance, Personal. 5. Career development--United States. I. Title.
  HD53.B586 2005
  650.1'02'47--dc22
                                        2005013668

Cover and interior designed by Andrea Kupper

For the many creative professionals with whom I've worked, this book is my way of saying thank you for the laughter, the long hours, the pursuit of excellence, and the good work.

Table of Contents

INTRODUCTION

The good news is, you are not alone.

By my count, there are at least ten million of us, and by some counts, over thirty million creative professionals in the United States alone.

We effortlessly recognize our own unique traits in other creative professionals: curiosity; unconventional thinking; openness to experience; tolerance of ambiguity;[1] superior communications skills; passion; and perhaps, an unconventional sense of humor.

When we're at work with other creative professionals, we place demands on one another that distinguish us from amateurs. We show up everyday, and we stay all day, no matter how we feel or what we are required to do. We rely on our mastery in order to survive, and we get paid because we're good at what we do. We work full-time (or as close to full-time as we can get); we accept criticism as part of the job and make the required changes to get the job done right. Our work matters, but the best of us do not define ourselves by our careers.[2]

We are professionals with a legacy dating back at least 500 years, working in careers no less legitimate than those of accountants, lawyers, doctors, or merchants. Our jobs offer one benefit that none of these careers can supply: the opportunity to make magic.

As advertising executive Jack Keil wrote in *How to Zig in a Zagging World*, "Everyone can come up with a gem every now and then. But the professionals know how to come up with great stuff, time after time, regardless of the restrictions, regardless of the deadlines. And that's

---

[1] SOURCE: ERIC EDO-CE-99-204 — "Creativity in Adults" by Sandra Kerka; C.E. Adams-Price, editor, *Creativity and Successful Aging*, New York: Springer, 1998; R.S. Albert, 1996 "Some Reasons Why Childhood Creativity Often Fails to Make It Past Puberty in the Real World," from *Creativity from Childhood Through Adulthood: New Directions for Child Development* no. 72 edited by M.A. Runco, pp. 43-56. San Francisco: Jossey-Bass, Summer 1996.

[2] SOURCE: Steven Pressfield, *The War of Art*, pp. 68-70.

the difference between the amateurs and the pros. The big difference is discipline."[3]

We share at least some common traits, beliefs and habits, including the feeling that every one of us is extraordinarily unique.

A large percentage of us work and live in San Francisco, Boston, New York City, Seattle, and in smaller cities where talent congregates: Austin, Texas; Portland, Oregon. We're also drawn to communities that are tolerant of alternative lifestyles, where theaters, ethnic restaurants, technological innovation, and quality of life are above par.[4]

We tend to avoid mainstream attractions. We view shopping malls, Disney World, Las Vegas, the spectacle of major sporting events, and most prime time television shows with a critical eye, even irony and disdain. These seem to be for others, not for us. Instead, we see nothing wrong or incongruent with our own "individualistic" stereotypes: poking around comfortable old urban bookstores; listening to world music or blues or other alternative music. We're more likely to spend a Sunday afternoon riding a Cannondale or Trek bicycle than watching a pro football game with a Bud (American beer? Sorry, I only drink American beer made by a microbrewery!). We seek high ceilings and natural light, appreciating the north light favored by artists even though we're staring at a computer screen all day. We represent a high percentage of Apple computer users. Foreign films; long working hours; a working style defined by sprints, not marathons; boundless curiosity; a desire and capacity to learn, discuss, and delve deeply into new domains and ideas are us. We have minimal desire to work with anyone wearing a suit, and scholars are beginning to understand what we've known all along: Creative professionals behave differently from the rest of the population.

We cause change. We probe emotional nerve endings, trying to

---

[3] SOURCE: John M. Keil, *How to Zig in a Zagging World*, Wiley, book on audiotape (draft script).
[4] SOURCE: Richard Florida, *The Rise of the Creative Class.*

provoke a reaction. That's what we do all day every day. Change makes some people nervous, but it's the lifeblood of the creative process. Our tendency to dissect, interrogate, twist, and push makes some people crazy, but we can't work any other way. We need to know what "works." Creative people question, explore alternatives, wonder what would happen if.... We do that better than anybody, and we ought to be licensed to do so. (More on that later.)

Defining Creative People

Who are these creative professionals? Artists, writers, musicians, producers, directors, performers, designers, and others with similar job descriptions are among the most obvious answers. In fact, the list is longer, as creative professions embrace not only those who develop ideas and products, but also those who market, analyze, and improve upon them. Take a moment and explore the long list of creative professions. Add more if you like.

Creative Jobs

ADVERTISING AGENCY
Creative Director
Art Director
Designer
Illustrator
Photo Researcher
Copy Director
Copy Writer
Account Manager
Commercial Producer
Commercial Director

PUBLIC RELATIONS
AGENCY
Executives
Agency heads
Writers
Designers
Producers

PROMO AGENCY
Creative Director
Art Director
Writer
Producer

MUSIC INDUSTRY
Songwriter
Lyricist
Composer
Musician, Performer
Record Producer
Stage Show Director
Choreographer
Arranger
Promotion Manager
Publicity Manager
Art Director
Music Journalist
Music Photographer

Event Producer /
Promoter

RADIO
Radio Programmer
Performer
Producer

THEATER
Producer
Director
Performers
Designers (Set,
    Wardrobe, Lights)

OTHER PERFORMERS
Dancers
Storytellers
(Stand-up) Comedians
Performance Artists

EDUCATION
Teachers
Curriculum Designers
Learning reformers
Principals
Producers of
    Educational Materials

CIVILIZATION
Museum Designer
Museum Producer
Transportation Planner
Public Space Designer
Park Designer
Historian

ARCHITECTURE
Architects
Draftspeople

**INTERIOR/EXTERIOR
DESIGN**
Garden Design
Landscape Design
Interior Design
Room Decorating
Specialty Home & Office
  Designers

MEDIA SPECIALISTS
Comic Book Artists and
Writers
Toy and Game Designers
Public Speakers
Creative Consultants
Documentary Producers
Jugglers, Puppeteers,
  Magicians
New Media Innovators

**NON-MEDIA
SPECIALISTS**
Executive
Chef
Travel Packager
Entrepreneur
Community Activists

TELEVISION
Program Executive
Development Manager
Executive Producer
Producer
Head Writer
Writer
Production Designer
Art Director
Prop Master
Animation Director
Animation Artists
Music Director
Music Composer
Musicians
Wardrobe Designer
Director
Casting Director
Actors
Other Performers (news,
  sports)

On-Air Promotion
Off-Air Promotion, Events
Advertising Manager
Public Relations
  Manager

MOTION PICTURES
Program Executive
Development Manager
Executive Producer
Producer
Director
Production Designer
Screenwriter
Music Composer
Music Producer
Musicians
Publicist
Advertising Manager
Marketing Manager
Performers
Effects Artists and
  Producers

ART AND DESIGN FIRMS
Industrial Designer
Brand Identity Designer
Restaurant Designer
Retail space Designer
Publication Designer
Interior decorator
Jewelry Designer

PHOTOGRAPHY
Fashion Photographer
Product Photographer
Portrait Photographer
Travel Photographer
Stylist
Makeup Artist
Model

FINE ARTISTS
Illustrators
Painters
Sculptors
Calligraphers
Fine Art Photographers
Specialty Artists

CRAFTSPEOPLE
Decorative Artists
Furniture Design
Needlecrafts
Textiles, Rugs, Weaving
Quilters
Glass and Pottery
Woodworkers

WEB AND INTERACTIVE
Site Architecture
Site Strategy
Site Design
Content
Partner Marketing
Promotion
E-commerce
Video game Designer
Software Developer
Interactive Producer
Web Community Leader
Game Producer
Viral Marketer

COMMERCE
Retail Merchandiser
Consumer Advertising
New Business
  Development
Franchise Development

MAGAZINE PUBLISHING
Editorial Director
Editors
Designer
Art Director
Marketing Manager
Writers
Artists and Illustrators

BOOK PUBLISHING
Editorial Director
Editors
Book, Cover Designers
Art Director
Marketing Manager
Authors
Artists and Illustrators

**NEWSPAPER
PUBLISHING**
Editors
Reporters
Writers and Columnists
Cartoonists
Advertising Artists
Advertising Managers
Marketing Managers

FASHION
Designers
Marketing Managers
Advertising Managers
Special Event Producers
Special Event Designers

CORPORATE
Public Relations
Event Planning
Consumer Marketing
Sales Training
Employee Training
Employee
Communications
Investor Relations
Advertising
Design
Business Development

DIRECT MARKETING
Catalog Editor
Marketing Manager
Catalog Designer
Production Artist
Catalog Copy Writer

**SPORTS & SPORTS
MARKETING**
Venue Promotion
Venue Special Events
Team Promotion
Licensing
Licensed Product
Development
Public Relations
Advertising

B2B MARKETING
Journal Editors
Trade Show Producers
B2B Promotion
Managers
Patents and Unique
   Processes
Relationship Marketers
Industry Events
Speeches

**GOVERNMENT &
POLITICS**
Campaign Management
Campaign Promotion
Speechwriting
Voter Communication
"Brand" Management

LARGE SECTORS
Finance

Individual Investor
Media
Financial Advertising
Web Promotion
Pharmaceutical/Medical
Direct to Consumer
Patient Communications
Doctor Communications
Sales Training

Dictionary definitions provide little more than synonyms, suggesting that creative people "produce something through imaginative skill." Psychologist Teresa Amabile[5] judges a work to be creative if it is both novel and an appropriate, useful, correct, or valuable response to a task that requires a degree of discovery or learning." That definition roughly parallels Laurie Anderson's brilliant summation, "Writing about music is like dancing about architecture."

A closer look at the habits, styles, and attributes typically associated with creative professionals at work may mirror your own way of working.

1. Intense Focus

The best creative work demands an extreme amount of attention paid without regard to time, relationships, or other real-life priorities. Quoting Edison: "Godlike genius! Godlike nothing! *Sticking to it* is the genius!"

2. Self-Motivation

Creative professionals make a project their own. Money is rarely the primary driver. More often, the primary drivers are personal adventure or challenge, the opportunity to collaborate, the opportunity for reinvention or rejuvenation, and/or satisfaction.

---

[5] SOURCE: *The Social Psychology of Creativity* by Teresa Amabile as quoted in *Creativity in Business*, Michael Ray and Rochelle Myers, p. 4.

3. A Sense of Humor

Most creative work is fun, or ought to be. Humor may be lighthearted, but it is often dark, cynical, or razor-sharp. If a creative workplace lacks laughter, something is fundamentally wrong.

4. Taking Breaks

In one office, this materialized as a daily nap break for the writing staff.[6] Breaks relieve the pressure and allow ideas to simmer on a back burner.

5. A Need for Feedback

Creative work benefits from early input from others and from peer review. Feedback late in the process is not as productive or useful.

6. Passionate Self-Confidence

Most creative professionals are driven by a clear understanding of their own capabilities and value. Nevertheless, we all dip into the stereotype from time to time, becoming fearful, insecure, and overwhelmed. Once the curtain goes up, stage fright vanishes—or we don't remain creative professionals for long.

7. A Highly Personal Sense of Time

Creative people may perceive time differently. When a project is in active production, hours pass quickly, days and nights may blend, and sleep may be scarce. Work may be done at odd hours; tasks planned for hours may require days. Ideas may require decades to move from concept to completion.

8. Individuality

Among the endless manifestations: odd choice of clothes, hair styles,

---

[6] This daily routine was key to the creative success of *Where in the World Is Carmen Sandiego?*, a PBS series that I produced. The writers napped around lunchtime; the associate producer's job was to manage the phones so the writers would not be disturbed.

hair colors, word choices, perceptions of the world, places to go on vacation, ways of decorating a work space. We may be colorful just for fun, or monochromatic for the same reason. Or, we may have reasons that you really don't want to know....

9. A View of Society Based on Merit and Quality of Contribution, not Power or Authority

From a creative perspective, the ones who do good work are the ones who deserve praise and recognition. Those who ascend without superior talent or better-than-average output are regarded with suspicion. Creative people think about power as the ability to garner resources to do good work; they tend not to relate to power over people for its own sake. Similarly, those in authority over creative professionals should approach governance with an enlightened outlook, or serve a rabbinical role as guide or teacher. Authority figures who serve in power positions without these attributes are often vilified or ignored by creative people. Richard Florida wrote, "Casual dress gradually crept in partly for the simple reason that it's more comfortable, but also because creative work came to be more highly valued in our economy. No longer did status accrue from being an officer, or at lower ranks, a good soldier. It is accrued from being a member of the creative elite—and creative people don't wear uniforms....They dress as they please."[7]

10. "Networks of Enterprise"

Biologist Karl Pfenninger noted that creative people tend to build and nurture their own communities. Members may provide resources, business contacts or advice, feedback, suggestions for improving work, recommended reading, or perhaps most commonly, cool ideas that might be pursued by the community itself, by members, or by individuals.

---

[7] SOURCE: Richard Florida, *The Rise of the Creative Class*, p. 119.

Physicist Freeman Dyson confirms,[8] "Science is a very gregarious business. It is essentially the difference between having this door open and having it shut. When I am doing science, I have the door open....You want to be, all the time, talking with people. It is essentially a communal exercise...."

Intelligence expert Howard Gardner studied several of the world's best-known creative professionals and recalled, "Picasso particularly appreciated the companionship of poets and writers, whose interests and skills complemented his own. They helped him articulate what he was trying to accomplish, gave him suggestions about where to direct his considerable energies, informed him of the world of ideas, and promoted his work to the rest of the world...."[9]

Myths about Creative People
Many of these myths are centuries old. They are perpetuated by the media, by characters in the movies, and by the woman in the next cubicle who is the embodiment of every stereotype pinned on creative people.

1. Creative People Are Smarter Than Other People
Many creative people are skilled in scanning the environment, synthesizing information, and communicating ideas. The combination of these three skills can make us seem more intelligent than other people. Quoting Howard Gardner, "Creativity is not the same as intelligence... an individual may be far more creative than he is intelligent, or far more intelligent than creative."[10]

2. Creative People Are Disorganized
We're no more organized or less organized than other people. Why won't this stereotype go away?

---

[8] SOURCE: Mihaly Csikszenmihalyi, *CREATIVITY.*
[9] SOURCE: Howard Gardner, *Creating Minds*, pp. 149-150.
[10] SOURCE: Howard Gardner, *The Unschooled Mind: How Children Think and How Schools Should Teach* (Basic Books, 1991), p. 20.

3. Creative People Are Crazy

There's a difference between (a) being paid to challenge society's norms, and (b) exhibiting neurotic or pathological behaviors. Despite volumes of scholarly work connecting mental health issues with creativity (see chapter six), most creative people have never visited Vincent Van Gogh's planet. However, many of us also live in a world that feels different from mainstream America.

4. Creative People Tend To Work Alone

This simply is not true. Some creative work is done by solo practitioners, like writers or designers. One in four creative professionals works as a freelancer; the others work as traditional company employees.[11] Creativity at work is almost always a collaborative process, but portions of each project are done by individuals or small teams.

5.You Can't Learn Much About Creativity by Reading a Book

True enough. You can, however, learn to become a more successful and happier creative professional if you read and follow the advice in this particular book. It will force you to see yourself as others do. It will help you to fit into the business world, on its terms and on your own. It will help you to make (and keep) more money and to stay out of trouble. And it will address the deeper issues that creative people ought to talk about more often: What happens when the muse just isn't there; what happens when you're old and in the way; what motivates us all to do good work.

Finally, there is a business book written for creative professionals.

—Howard Blumenthal,
Summer 2005, The South of France[12]

---

[11] SOURCE: Richard Florida, *The Rise of the Creative Class.*

[12] (Don't I wish!) The book was mostly written in my home office, a large converted bedroom located above the garage in a suburban housing development. As I dream of Provence, go ahead and read the first chapter.

CHAPTER 1–YOU

This is a business book written for creative professionals: creative people who work, full-time, as a career, in creative jobs.

Sometimes, amateurs perform similar tasks, but there is a qualitative difference between a creative professional and an amateur. Screenwriter Steven Pressfield captured the thought beautifully: "The word amateur comes from the Latin root meaning 'to love.' The conventional interpretation is that the amateur pursues his calling out of love, while the pro does it for money.... In my view, the amateur does not love the game enough. If he did, he would not pursue it as a sideline, distinct from his 'real' vocation. The professional loves it so much he dedicates his life to it...."[1]

A creative *person* may exist in his or her own space, undefined by market demands. A creative *professional*, however, is a creative person *and* a participant in a marketplace.

Your marketplace may be an old-style market fair, perhaps selling your own photography or crafts; the record or book publishing industry; or a corporation where employees vie for resources and recognition. Your role in the marketplace is not fixed; it will change over time. When he was a freelance artist working for Children's Television Workshop

---

[1] SOURCE: Steven Pressfield, *The War of Art*, pp. 65-66.

(now Sesame Workshop), Jim Jinkins conceived *DOUG* as a newspaper comic strip or a book character. In the early 1980s, Jim was freelancing as a Nickelodeon art director when the network asked him to develop *DOUG* as a potential cartoon show. The resulting animated television series became a bona fide brand and a huge success. There were picture books, toys, a second TV series called *Disney's DOUG*, and eventually, a motion picture. The marketplace first perceived Jim as an artist, then as an art director, then a producer and leader of his own production company. Successful creative professionals know that the market changes constantly, and that adaptation is a key component in winning the game, or at least, staying alive long enough to remain a player.

Marketplace Behavior: The Rules

The rules of the creative marketplace are generally fixed, but there are so many exceptions that one can't help but wonder whether there are any rules at all. In fact, there *are* some rules, and they're worth memorizing:

1. The marketplace values experience. For every executive or manager who approves a creative endeavor, there is some risk. The risk may be associated with reputation; with the company's money or other resources, such as time and support; or with the people who have been selected for the project. The best way to minimize risk is to bet on a creative team with experience—creative professionals who have done similar work in the past. Often, experience carries a higher value than originality. The television industry, with programs produced by long-time network prime-time veterans, provides ample evidence of the experience-over-originality phenomenon.

2. Reputation matters. A creative professional who delivers work with minimal hassle, on time and on budget, will typically work more often than one who is perceived as "high maintenance," or misses deadlines or over spends the available budget.

According to author Kenneth Atchity, "In Hollywood, it is said that four things guarantee your success, in this order: perseverance, connections, being fun to work with, and talent." One word summarizes his comment: "reputation."[2]

> *3. Nothing matters except success—or the potential for success.* Here's the rule that breaks the others. The marketplace is always greedy for the next big idea, the next breakthrough, the next creative wizard whose idea can make millions. Most fail, but the few that succeed drive the market. Here, neither experience nor reputation matters—both can be hired in order to supplement and/or support the potential fortune maker.

The teen music marketplace of the early 2000s is one of many examples. Britney Spears is a talented performer, but her career was manufactured by the experienced professionals at Jive Records. With the Backstreet Boys and N' Sync selling millions of records, Jive was well positioned to market Britney to teens. Without Britney, Jive might not matter. And without Jive, Britney might be singing to small crowds in Louisiana. The long list of people and projects developed without meaningful professional experience or reputation is long, but the vast majority of creative professionals have nothing to do with this game. Most of us simply work for a living, managing to find enough work to remain self-sufficient or even prosperous. Some of us become rich or famous, but fate is both unpredictable and fickle.

Your Valuable Assets

Basic economic theory: Every worker exchanges time and skills (their assets) for various forms of compensation (money, personal advancement, sense of accomplishment, interaction with co-workers, etc.). According to one survey,[3] the top ten skills sought by employers are:

---

[2] SOURCE: Kenneth Atchity, *A Writer's Time*, p. xvi.

1. Ability To Get Things Done
2. Common Sense
3. Honesty/Integrity
4. Dependability
5. Initiative
6. Well-Developed Work Habits
7. Reliability
8. Interpersonal Skills
9. Enthusiasm
10. Judgment Skills

A creative worker promises all of these skills, plus several more:

1. Situational Understanding
2. Ability to Synthesize Ideas
3. Superior Communications Skills
4. Collaboration; Ongoing Learning
5. A Sometimes Magical Connection to Human Emotion

These are the ones worth looking into.

Situational Understanding

"As the human race moved from its earliest ancestors, two basic types of cultures evolved. In the areas which were lush with plant and animal life, and had a low human population density, hunters and gatherers predominated," Thom Hartmann wrote. Hartmann details mental and physical characteristics of successful hunters, then parallels archetypical hunters with contemporary people labeled with attention deficit disorder. As it happens, Hartmann's list also applies to creative people. He

---

[3] SOURCE: Study conducted by Michigan University Placement Services; data were compiled from a survey of 500 U.S. employees and reported in *Zen and the Art of Making a Living*, by Laurence G. Boldt, p. 492.

describes an unusually acute monitoring capability, along with an instinct for changing strategy quickly as the environment requires. This knack is apparent in quick-witted comedians. Robin Williams is the embodiment of what a psychologist-researcher might call a comedian-hunter. Carl Reiner and Jonathan Winters share similar skills. So do improvising jazz musicians. The finest sales people "read the room," sensing a potential customer's inner thoughts.

Many creative people develop their situational understanding skills through natural observation. Others learn with a partner, sometimes analyzing behavior after a meeting. ("I knew we had him when he stopped using the word you and started saying we instead....")

Synthesizing Ideas

One deep, dark secret is shared by many creative professionals: We're not creative per se. That is, we don't actually invent anything new. Instead, we're extraordinarily resourceful. We scan the environment for useful stuff, tie it together with a marketplace need, and create something "new." The process may be perceived as magic. We know it's usually nothing more than craft.

Corporate trainers are fond of playing games that test this capability. At a large corporate meeting, a pile of LEGO bricks is placed on each of twenty tables, each with a dozen employees. Each table is told to build an object that represents, for example, the company's future. The creative professional quickly assesses the available bricks and simply "knows" how the bricks can be put together to make just the right statement. Perhaps most telling, the creative professional also plays back the trainer's very specific instructions to determine whether there are any rules that might be creatively broken.

Some creative professionals can synthesize ideas with astonishing speed and efficiency. The keys: a sense of humor, which helps distance oneself from what was yesterday's passion; a high comfort level with change; a willingness to work hard and work fast; and a responsiveness to cues and clues. An experienced team also makes the difference.

A few years ago, my company[4] produced a television series for cable's Food Network. The show was not a hit, but the network asked us to build a replacement series quickly and without spending much money. A goofy pop culture stage set with columns made from giant corn cobs and a host podium supported by an oversized banana peel was quickly reconceived as a classy, subdued environment. The offbeat host was replaced by a food expert. Questions about marshmallow Peeps and TV Dinners were replaced by smarter ones about *tarte tatin* and the Scoville Scale (which measures the intensity of hot peppers). The set, the format, and the entire series were transformed within weeks—and we spent very little money for the changeover. The transformation worked because of the experience of the people involved.

A Clear Understanding of Group Dynamics

Back to the table full of LEGO bricks. The creative professional has subverted the rules and is now returning from the kitchen with enough brandy to douse his LEGO tabletop rodeo in preparation for its flambé. At that defining moment, when the group looks at the creative person as if she is completely out of her mind, we pick up the discussion of group dynamics....

Our brandy-wielding perpetrator is faced with several possible paths: (a) simply laugh the escapade off as a silly idea; (b) sell the flaming brandy as the only possible solution; or (c) fast-talk a compromise acceptable to the group. No clever Churchill she, the perp instead studies the group and rethinks her options. With every pair of eyes avoiding contact with our creative idiot, she can (a) quietly proceed, complete the project with or without group participation, and either give or take credit for the success or failure; (b) try to pry at least one potential co-conspirator from the group; (c) discard the idea and move along with the group; or (d) leave the group in disgust (this is best staged in a colorful, memorable way, preferably with

---

[4] Glow in the Dark Productions, jointly operated by five producers.

great anger and an acidic exchange of devastating accusations).

None of these solutions is perfect. And at this point, the crazy creative must somehow figure out how to participate as a productive team member. Doing the project alone (a) does not improve working relations, but it's not half as bad as the final solution (d). Both (b) and (c) are compromises.

Compromise is good because it builds trusting relationships and often allows for satisfactory resolutions. Compromise is bad because it often subjects the idea or its execution to less-than-optimal results.

Or, as artist, author, and world leader Winston Churchill said: "Never give in, never give in, never, never, never, never...."

A seasoned creative professional (almost) always makes the right decision.

Interpersonal Communication

College may offer only limited education to a young creative professional, but I do recall the day I learned about *The Shannon-Weaver Model*. This communications model was developed by Claude Shannon at the old Bell Labs to improve telephone signals, then expanded by Warren Weaver, who more broadly applied the model to interpersonal communications. Decades later, the Shannon-Weaver model is used to explain all forms of communications (and not only human communication at that).

Shannon-Weaver Model

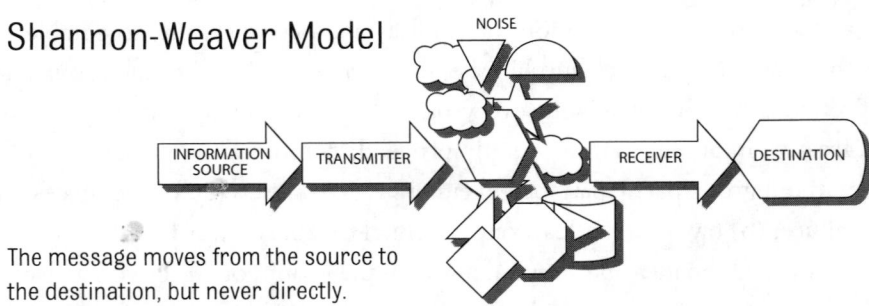

The message moves from the source to the destination, but never directly. A transmitter and receiver are required, and these often encounter noise along the way. After the message reaches its destination, the model reverses, so that the destination becomes the source and the source becomes the destination. The message encounters noise on the return trip.

The objective is to efficiently move a message from sender to receiver with a minimum of clutter or distraction. As it happens, this model becomes an ideal checklist for every creative pitch and presentation.

The message itself must be specifically crafted for the target audience. If the message is too complex, or presented without sufficient context, its value will get lost in the model. The message must be delivered with sensitivity to the receiver's perceptions: The person who presents must dress the part; and the physical materials must be appropriate to the venue. A PowerPoint is fine for a conference room, but a poor choice for a pitch meeting at a busy restaurant. Noise is always a factor, and not just the ambient noise that a restaurant pitch must overcome. Noise might also come in the form of prejudice; a few key words might cause the listener to associate the new concept with one that was previously pitched. If a room is too dark, too bright, too cold, too hot, or too crowded, these factors also add noise to the communications cycle. Study the Shannon-Weaver Model and put it to use, and you'll quickly understand that the model is not a line but a circle. Feedback completes the circle, and all aspects of the pitch must be altered, in real time, to respond to input from the receiver. Once again, this is about "reading the room" and picking up cues that move the pitch into a dance that engages each party in equal measure.

Clarity of Expression

It is not unusual to find creative people who express their ideas clearly and with style. Superior communications skills often come as part of the package whose components include self-confidence; natural talent for engaging others in conversation or for engaging an audience; and some education or training, perhaps in acting classes. We are schooled in writing and speaking in public. We learn from coworkers, who freely provide pointers and more formal training. We think through the presentation. We live inside the project, we write proposals and plans, and we rehearse. By the time we're ready to present an idea, the professional patina is in place.

We also obsess about the details, so their understanding and ease in explaining a project, its parts and its likely consequences also contribute to the perception of superior communications skills.

Admittedly, creative ideas can be difficult to explain. Most creative professionals have spent a lifetime trying to capture other people's imaginations. We battle noise, poor listening skills, lack of attentiveness of those who simply care about a project or an idea less than we do, and life's other distractions. With practice, we learn to overcome these obstacles, and so we learn to become superior communicators.

At some point, when they're still not getting it, you need to pray to the gods. One of the gods, Louis Armstrong, had this to say: "Unless you know what it is, I ain't never going to be able to explain it to you."

Nobody needs to know about your fear of being laughed at, of rejection, of losing what you've got, of the unknown, of being exposed for who and what you truly are. Instead, when you come at an opportunity to present yourself, your adrenaline is at work and you can't help but present your best possible self.

Inviting Collaboration

Composer Philip Glass once said, "My goal in life was to reach a point where I could collaborate with anyone I wanted.[5]

For some, collaboration is instinctual. Why do the work yourself when you can share the fun, frustration, and creative process with others?

For others, collaboration is counterintuitive, particularly in the early stages, when a concept requires quiet contemplation. Why spend the time listening to others when the idea is not fully formed in your own head?

For most people, most of the time, collaboration begins because you're assigned a team or partner, because you need help, or because it just "feels right." Perhaps a concept emerges from an informal conversation; subsequent conversations add depth and dimension, and the conception takes shape as a collaboration. Or, the creator considers a new idea and decides that it would be improved through collaboration with a specific

---

[5] SOURCE: Shira P. White with Patton G. Wright, *New Ideas About New Ideas*, p. 200.

contributor. A team coalesces around an idea.

A while ago, I collaborated with writer Dorothy Curley and artist Brad Williams on a book about time travel.[6] We began by accepting the premise that time travel was possible Then we created the essential tourist guidebook for time travelers. As a girl, Dorothy dreamed of earning her doctorate in time travel; she studied physics and taught herself relativity theory. Brad's youth was spent reading science fiction. Remarkably, when we approached Brad about the project, he happened to be building a full-scale model of a time machine for a children's theater production. I knew almost nothing about time travel. When Dorothy explained relativity theory to me on the back of a napkin in a Japanese restaurant, I knew we could create a wonderful book together.

Our collaboration was intense—one of the greatest creative experiences I've ever had. We all lived together for weeks, with papers spread all over the floor of my home office. Waking up in the morning to wrestle through the ideas for each chapter, we then separated to write (Dorothy wrote first drafts, I rewrote); design (Brad illustrated and art directed while I laid out pages); and review (each of us commenting on the other's work until it was truly the best work of the group). Several days into it, we were easily completing one another's sentences. Two weeks into it, we hardly needed to speak at all—we knew what each other was thinking.

When she reads the book today, Dorothy claims she can separate one person's idea from another. I can't. It's all a wonderful blur to me. What's more, this was the project that taught me that a good group collaboration was generally superior to the work that one person could do on his or her own. This revelation changed my way of working.[7]

Understanding and Appreciating Synchronicity

"Synchronicity" is a word I learned while time traveling. Synchronicity is

---

[6] The book was called *The Complete Time Traveler: A Tourist's Guide to the Fourth Dimension.*

like coincidence, but better, richer, and deeper. It's the kind of coincidence that seems to grow from a sixth sense, one that makes higher-level connections in the universe while the rest of your mind and body is busy with day-to-day activities.

How was it that Brad was building a time machine at the very moment when I called him about a time travel book? None of us had ever done a time travel project before, and none of us has done anything related to time travel since. We used Brad and his time machine on the cover of the book. Was the universe watching out for us, knowing that we needed a terrific image for the cover? Or did this "just happen by coincidence"? Coincidence seems too random; these kinds of situations happen too often to me and to other creative professionals to dismiss them as a result of random events.

Dorothy ends her e-mails with: "Life's a journey. Enjoy the ride." You never know who is traveling the road with you, but you are rarely journeying alone. Creative people learn that lesson time and again. It is *never* just a coincidence. "Just a coincidence" dismisses any possibility of magic associated with a journey. Creative people know that magic makes the journey possible *and* worth the time and trouble.

Non- creative professionals also benefit from synchronicity. Still, I like to believe that the god of synchronicity favors our people just a bit more than the rest. I wish I knew her name, but when the time comes, I will.

Concept to Completion: How Work Gets Done

It's astonishing how quickly everything can come together in your mind.

---

[7] To complete the story: *The Complete Time Traveler* was the worst-selling book I've written. Dorothy and I remain friends and collaborators. In fact, much of what we learned about creating a fantasy world became the basis for the popular PBS series, *Where In the World Is Carmen Sandiego?* which we co-created (with producer-director Dana Calderwood). I do not believe Carmen would have been possible had Dorothy and I not previously traveled through time. Sadly, Brad died in a car accident shortly after the *Time* book was published.

In an instant, your mind forges a connection that wasn't there before. An idea materializes where there was none. And then there's this inexplicable arc, a kind of instantaneous rainbow—a clear route from concept to completion, a complete model of necessary resources, required staff, a timetable, and a list of potential challenges. In just minutes, your mind lays out the basics, and the project that didn't exist an hour ago begins to take control of your life.

When you speak of this phenomenon, others may become concerned, awestruck, or just plain annoyed. Thinking six steps ahead comes naturally to you, but others may not synthesize information so quickly. They may be struggling with the initial problem statement while you're already hiring half the staff and planning the ad campaign. When you work this fast, others will either blindly follow or instinctively challenge your assumptions and your plan. Either way, if you handle the magic wand carefully, it will not fail you.

Recognize your initial assessment for what it is—preliminary! Analyze it; just because an idea arrived quickly doesn't mean it's good. Some ideas are just plain stupid. No matter how attractive your rainbow arc may be, you should filter everything through trusted advisors to make sure you're on the right track.

Then, go for it! If you're clear on the destination, and reasonably clear on the roadmap, then you should lead the way. Others will follow.

Are creative professionals more capable of moving a project from concept to completion than other professionals? Probably not. All dedicated, hardworking people with remarkable passion and focus and a natural inclination toward projects with clear beginnings, middles, and ends will find results in a substantial number of projects conceived and completed each year.

Ongoing Learning

Right now, I'm interested in: drawing; watercolor painting; pastels; medium-format photography; black-and-white photography; remembering what the world looked like before everything became commercial and modern; designing Web sites; raising capital and building a foundation for a new business; teaching; some aspects of cognitive learning; childhood education; Japan; France; the effect of light on shadows and color; some aspects of mythology; a wide range of topics related to food and cooking; architecture and indoor spaces; human anatomy (to improve my drawing skills); travel; U.S. and English history; how children learn and why adults forget how; foreign cultures; the future of television; and a long list of other topics that could keep me busy for a very long time.

I pursue some interests by walking around and observing. Others, I learn about by reading books and articles and poking around Web sites. When I have the time, and I can find an appropriate course, I enroll at a local college to learn a new subject or to study more about a topic that interests me. I talk to friends, visit art museums, go to concerts, and travel whenever I can. And when I think I'm beginning to understand something, I try to find some way to write about it.

In an effort to make this book more about you than about me, I've scattered a series of exercises throughout its chapters. This first exercise is straightforward: Make a list of things, places, people, and ideas that interest you. Someday, you'll have the time, energy, resources, and/or inclination to dig deeply into most of them.

Your Personal Interests

At first, this exercise may seem pedantic or touchy-feely. Try not to resist. Instead, take fifteen minutes and complete the exercise. If you're stuck for ideas, enlist the help of friends or family members. People who know you since childhood will be most helpful; they will remember your long-forgotten interests, the ones you've discarded in favor of adult pursuits.
There are a total of thirty-five blanks. Be sure to complete every blank for thirty-five total interests. If you have more than five interests per section, jot them down beside the list, but the exercise is not complete until you have at least five items per section.

Interests I Pursued as a Child

1.
2.
3.
4.
5.

Interests I Pursued in High School

1.
2.
3.
4.
5.

Interests I Pursued in College

1.
2.
3.
4.
5.

Adult Interests I Regularly Pursue

1.
2.
3.
4.
5.

Adult Interests I Pursue When I Have The Time

1.
2.
3.

4.

5.

Interests That I Would Pursue If I Had The Time, Money, Skills, etc.

1.

2.

3.

4.

5.

Interests I Might Pursue When I Retire

1.

2.

3.

4.

5.

How to Know Yourself

In pursuit of self-knowledge, some of us reach out to self-assessment quizzes, like personality or IQ tests. Those are fun, but there's something better. Many human resources professionals, executives, and just plain folks have found useful information about themselves and others by using the Myers-Briggs Type Indicator. (MBTI is based on Jung's ideas.) Alternatives are also popular, such as *The Herrmann Brain Dominance Instrument* and other tools.

Robert Todd Carroll, who bills himself on the Web as the "MBTI Skeptic,"[8] wrote: "Psychological typology did not originate with Jung, of course. Remember the four temperaments? Each of us, at one time, would have been considered to be either *melancholic, sanguine, phlegmatic* or *choleric*. These classifications go back at least as far as the ancient

---

[8] SOURCE: *MBTI Skeptic,* http://www.SkepDic.com, Robert Todd Carroll, 2003.

physician Hippocrates in the middle of the fifth century B.C. He explained the four temperaments in terms of dominant 'humors' in the body.... Hippocrates was simply adding to the ancient Greek insight that all things reduce to earth, air, water, and fire.... A person's physical, psychological, and moral qualities could be easily understood by his temperament, his dominant 'humors,'... This ancient personality type-indicator 'worked' for over a thousand years."

Carroll continues: "Some think there are only *nine* basic personality types and follow the enneagram. As Jung said, there could be any number of types, even 360, if we wished. Who is right? Maybe they're both wrong. Perhaps we need only think of two types, those from Mars and those from Venus, as John Gray, Ph.D., claims."

There are many theories about how and why we behave as we do. I like Einstein's assessment of his own discoveries: "How did it come to pass that I was the one to develop the theory of relativity? The reason, I think, is that a normal adult never stops to think about the problems of time and space. These are things which he has thought of as a child. But intellectual development was retarded, as a result of which I began to wonder about time and space only when I had already grown up. Naturally, I could go deeper into the problem than a child with normal abilities."[9]

Myers–Briggs Type Indicator (MBTI)
The MBTI provides a useful means for understanding how you work, and how other people work. A self-scoring version of the test may be available to company employees, on request from the human resources department. Alternatively, several books provide enough useful information to develop some fair assumptions about the four letters that indicate your preferred way of working, or, to put it in MBTI terms, your "temperament."

Personally, I find the MBTI useful in understanding how I work on my own, how I work with others and how to best build teams. I also use the tool to understand and cope with people who present challenges or

---

[9] SOURCE: R.W. Clark, *Einstein: Life and Times*; New York: World 1971, p. 10.

obstacles. I never use MBTI results exclusively; instead, I allow the results to infect the more general range of my thinking.

Meanings of the Single Letters

Spend some time exploring the letter combinations below. Most likely, you will identify more strongly with one letter than the other. Jot down the result. If you feel equally connected with both letters, see if one dominates. If not, just jot down both letters.

E vs. I

E's will often think aloud; talk too much; deal well with distractions elsewhere in the workspace; pick up the phone even if they're engaged in another conversation; speak up during meetings; don't always listen; and prefer groups.

I's are not as comfortable presenting ideas in public, so they may rehearse or write them down, or send a long memo or e-mail; may seem to listen well; feel most comfortable in ones or twos or threes, not in larger groups; don't say much during most meetings; and need quiet time to center themselves.

S vs. N

S's spend their lives in current time, not dreaming much about what could or ought to be; they'll drift toward facts, figures, and what's "real" rather than get caught in a conceptual discussion; insist upon details in order to fully understand; and tend to view the world quite literally.

N's multi-process; think constantly about the future and its possibilities; take pleasure in figuring things out, and in twisting the world or someone's world view for the sheer pleasure and complexity of the experience; and find details tedious, bothersome, and needless except in very specific situations.

T vs. F

T's value fairness and justice; they can view any situation with cold practicality and develop a logical course of action; may not take other people's feelings into account (and may not understand why feelings even enter into the discussion); and remember facts and figures but forget names and situations.

F's often wonder why T's are allowed to make decisions at all; everything is about people and feelings, subjective reactions, the heart and soul of the matter; they may avoid difficult topics, and generally drive toward balanced group harmony; they do not always stand up for themselves, and instead overinflate the value of others.

J vs. P

J's cannot understand why the world does not operate efficiently, why meetings begin late, why deadlines are such a difficult challenge; they plan; they know what happens to every minute of every day; they manage resources and stay organized; and always work to completion.

P's are far more organic in their thinking, their lifestyles, their sense of organization, work, play, relationships, deadlines, style of dress, and so on; they're easy to distract, and fun to bring along on tangents; and they keep their options open because something better might just come along.

Multiple-Letter Combinations

Double-letter combinations are extremely instructive. NT's, for example, are wonderful team leaders because they can plan, they treat people fairly, and they surround themselves with competent players. If you want to get work done quickly and efficiently, a team full of NT's isn't the best choice: They can be dodgy on details; they can get very caught up in any complexity of their own design; and they tend not to be team players—unless they happen to be the person in charge. An NT teacher will expand students' minds and implement all sorts of curriculum improvements—but don't expect much compassion if you're the student who doesn't get it, or doesn't hand the homework in on time. If you're looking for compassion with a teacher who is more likely to complete the term's curriculum but not a lot of frills, seek out an SJ teacher instead. Looking for a teacher or mentor change in your life? Find an NF.

If you'd like to know more about the double-letter combinations, refer to one of the books in the appendix. More likely, you'll be interested in the four letter combinations, detailed briefly in the sidebar.

MBTI – Four Letter Combinations

The most interesting results of the MBTI are the four-letter combinations. It's most instructive to see yourself in these descriptions—and to see what you're not. (The "not" part may help to explain why you are uncomfortable in certain work situations.)

Common Creative Professional Combinations:
ENTP:People who tend toward non-conformity, quickly analyze and synthesize ideas and produce new results, and deal well with theoretical problems: actors, advertising executives, mathematicians.

INTJ: Independent thinkers who cannot help but improve upon the present situation, regardless of the skepticism they frequently encounter: photographers, architects, engineers.

INTP: People who are endlessly curious and combine introspection with a clear style of thinking and communicating: scientists, designers, philosophers.

ENFP: Problem-solvers who are also very people-oriented. Need to work at their own pace, with their own rules and their own schedule: journalists, filmmakers, musicians (particularly composers).

INFP: People generally perceived as "on the quiet side" with a need for self-expression, minimal rules, and an emphasis on nurturing potential in themselves and often, in others: college professors, ministers and other religious guides, some health care workers.

Sometimes Associated With Creative Professionals:
ISFP: People who strongly value harmony and compassionate relationships: gardeners, interior designers, nutritionists.

ENTJ: Confident and competent leaders: general and departmental managers.

ENFJ: People who exercise a high degree of control while interacting with many types of individuals at very different levels and phases of their lives: politicians, many social workers, public speakers, and expert consultants.

INFJ: People who cause change, often for the public good, but go about it in a gentle, considerate, organic fashion: career counselors, religious leaders, teachers.

Not Typically Associated With Creative Professionals:
ESTJ: People who follow the rules: accountants, bank officers, military officers, police officers.

ESFJ: People who enable, serve, or help others: nurses, religious and restaurant workers, teachers, and physical therapists.

ISTJ: People who are precise, detail-oriented, careful, and whose work is based in facts, figures, research, accurate analysis: Opticians, librarians, auditors, pharmacists.

ISFJ: Similar to ISTJs, but with more of a service or helper orientation: dieticians, religious educators, veterinarians.

ESTP: People who are strongly results-oriented: professional athletes, stockbrokers, salespeople.

ESFP: People whose jobs involve engaging the interest and imagination of others: teachers, travel agents, real estate agents, athletic coaches.

ISTP: Observation leading to action: firefighters, financial analysts and the family doctor.

Herrmann Brain Dominance Instrument (HBDI)

If the "left brain-right brain" model seems like a silly oversimplification to you, you're not alone. In the 1970s, Ned Herrmann, then a management education manager with General Electric, considered the available research and developed a better model. Instead of two halves of the brain, Herrmann envisioned Left/Cerebral, Right/Cerebral, Left/Limbic, and Right/Limbic modes. And rather than plotting results in letter combinations, Herrmann used a circular chart with four quadrants.

HBDI Plots

The Hermann Brain Dominance Profile (HBDI) is easiest to understand if you compare two or more plots from people whose talents and working styles differ. On the next page, the plot on the left shows the test results of a creative professional, and the plot on the right shows the results of a professional middle manager.

In general, the creative professional's plot shows a high score in typically creative endeavors. The person is an artistic, big-picture thinker who is strong in conceptualizing and, in a word, envisioning "futures." The result, however, is not absolute. The plot also shows competence and ability in logic and analysis (upper left) and also in humanistic "touchy-feely" work styles. Bear in mind, however, that these plots represent an averaging of multiple choice answers related to a particular quadrant. A very high analytical component score within the upper left and a very high score for expressiveness in the lower right increase the overall value of the scores in these quadrants. Still, the overall pattern is instructive.

HERRMANN BRAIN DOMINANCE PROFILE

HERRMANN BRAIN DOMINANCE PROFILE

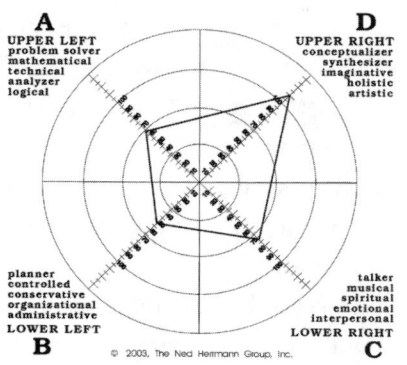

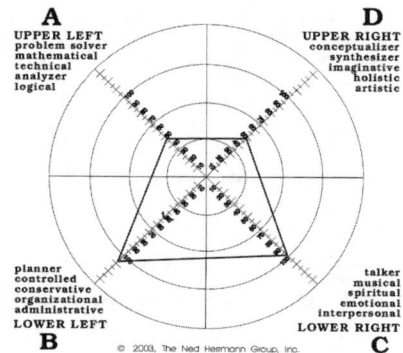

And when the two patterns are compared, it's immediately clear that the middle manager's profile is very strong not in one, but in two quadrants. She overindexes equally in both the "feelings-based" area (the lower right) and the "sensible" area. Once again, the details behind the overall scores are telling: very high scores in the organizational and planning components within the "sensible" quadrant mask a very low score for administrative ability.

Incidentally, the creative professional plot is my own. The manager's plot belongs to my wife, whose background is editorial production management.

All of this is explained in considerable and often fascinating detail in Herrmann's book, *The Whole Brain Business Book* (McGraw-Hill, 1996). In Herrmann's model, the upper left (Left/Cerebral) deals with logic, facts and analysis; the upper right (Right/Cerebral) is concerned with synthesis and integration, as well as intuition and a range of other creative activities; the lower left (Left/Limbic) deals with planning, details and organization; and the lower right (Right/Limbic) is about emotions and personal relationships. These concepts expand upon left/right brain research done by Roger Sperry and others in the seventies.

The HBDI's circular plots are helpful when comparing one person to another, or one person to a norm. Herrmann has used the model to test over a million brains, including many creative and business people. He also pointed out that different tasks require different types of thinking. Writing the company's vision statement, for example, strongly emphasizes the upper right, while the company's operating plan would naturally employ the more analytical lower left. Obvious? Consider the following:

In Herrmann's extensive research, BMW owners tended strongly toward the upper right, while Mercedes owners tended to cluster in the upper left (logic, facts), and Toyota owners gathered mostly around the lower left. What's more, freshmen entering a college engineering program were relatively even in their distribution in all four quadrants. The faculty, however, was powerfully represented in the upper left, and very weakly represented in the lower right (emotions, inter-personals). The good (or bad) news: The same class, at the start of their senior year, demonstrated a pattern that was very nearly identical to the faculty. Therefore, education succeeded in changing thinking. Sadly (but no big surprise here), the creative quadrant was far less pronounced than it was before education occurred.

Team-Building

Having the ability to analyze and understand yourself and the people you work with will help make you a better team member and team leader. The first thing to remember: As much as you may think of yourself and your own abilities, you should not put together a team of people who are like you. Instead, you want to cast team members who will work well together, while simultaneously approaching situations with very different temperaments, work styles, and perspectives.

For example, if you are an INTJ—as some creative people are—then you've probably got the theoretical problem-solving activities covered. You are likely to be weak on the operational details and the people skills. And you may not be the best salesperson, and perhaps not the choice to present your own ideas or results. *Seek out your opposite*: an ESFP for the sales and people skills, plus an ISTJ to handle the details and make sure the material is acceptable to any possible audience. Round out the team not with problem-solvers but with detailers and workers who are "good with people." Your team will succeed because of its blend of different working styles.

A Quick Exercise

Many creative people require little motivation for self-exploration; we're famous for "navel-gazing." Actors and directors joke about "what's my motivation?" before shooting a used-car commercial. There's some truth in the joke: Self-knowledge is a key component in any creative professional's bag of tricks.

Complete the next exercise, but don't do the work in the book. Instead, make copies. You'll need them now and in the future.

Your Work Style
Circle the answer that most often describes your/his/her preferred way of working:

Involving Others
   A. Alone
   B. With one other person
   C. With two other people
   D. In a small group
   E. In a mid-sized group
   F. In a large group
   G. With as many people as possible

Mood of Workplace
   A. A silent environment
   B. With some soft natural noise
   C. A generally quiet environment
   D. A typical office environment
   E. A lively office environment
   F. An energized work environment
   G. A place that's completely crazy

Developing Ideas
A. Take time to consider the challenge before developing any ideas
B. Slowly write down a few ideas for subsequent discussion
C. Generate a reasonable list of ideas and perhaps get some feedback
D. Freely discuss a few preliminary ideas
E. Get started with any sort of idea discussion, preferably one that's robust
F. Brainstorm ideas
G. No-holds-barred idea jam

Structure
A. Very tightly organized, planned, structured
B. Well-organized
C. Reasonably well-organized, but with plenty of room for change
D. Organized, but flexible
E. Flexible, but generally organized and together
F. Not very together, but some hints of structure
G. Chaos

Office Organization
A. Meticulous and antiseptic
B. Neat and tidy
C. Everything in its place, but it's clear somebody works here
D. Nothing much to say; neither organized nor messy
E. Professionally cluttered
F. Messy
G. A jungle

Gathering Facts and Information
A. Meticulous, well-classified research
B. Frequent reader, collector of useful information
C. Keeps what's useful
D. Research combined with interpersonal feedback and conversation
E. Discusses what he/she reads or sees

F. Listens to other people, forms opinions organically
G. Mainly operates by instinct and feeling a vibe

Attentiveness
A. Highly responsive
B. Good listener; responds with understanding and empathy
C. Pays attention
D. Pays attention, but gets distracted
E. Hears what he or she wants to hear, may not have impact on action
F. Does what he or she wants, regardless of what is said
G. Why bother talking to him/her?

Details
A. Never misses a detail
B. Remembers most details, delegates others
C. Misses on occasion, but gets just about everything right
D. Relies upon an organization system, like a task list
E. Writes the task list, but rarely looks at it
F. Somehow, everything gets done
G. Details aren't nearly as important as the big picture

Now ask several friends and coworkers to complete a blank form as they believe *you* would fill it out. Compare the results, and you will learn a lot about yourself and how others perceive you.

Incidentally, this exercise can be useful in group team-building. Start by making one form for each team member, with the person's name at the top. Then make one copy of each person's form for every member of the team. Each member then (anonymously) fills out the form for everyone else on the team. Each form goes back to its owner. Allow fifteen minutes for reading the forms and quiet reflection, followed by a group discussion. Keep the conversation light; discourage any negativity.

Your Style of Working

No single style defines the creative professional at work. Some of us work alone; some work in temporary or permanent teams; some work with multiple collaborators. Some of us move into management, and some of us move back into the creative side. Some of us shift our modes often, and others stick with a particular formula.

Working Alone

The tradition: Authors, illustrators, playwrights and other creative thinkers require time in their own heads, truly creating something from nothing. This tradition is at least a thousand years old and remains a viable option for those who work outside the traditional business community. This style has also been adopted by an Internet-enabled work force of writers, researchers, market planners, and others who decide to work alone for personal or family pleasure, to eliminate a commute, or because it's simply easier to work on their own.

The classic Thoreau quote still rings true: "If a man does not keep pace with his companions, perhaps it is because he hears a different drummer. Let him step to the music he hears, however measured or far away."[10]

The really *good parts of working alone:*

1. If the creative work is great, you get lots of credit (external gratification).

2. If the creative work is great, you know that you made it happen (internal gratification).

The good parts of working alone:

1. There's nobody to bother you, or tell you what to do or how to do it.

2. You get work done faster because there are fewer distractions.

3. You get work done your way, because your way is best, most efficient, or otherwise superior.

4. You set your own working hours. As long as you meet the deadline, your time is your own.

---

[10] SOURCE: Henry David Thoreau, *Walden.*

The bad parts about working al
1. It can be lonely.
2. Your ideas don't benefi
3. You can become overp
your creations.
4. Potential clients and
5. You may always be pe
player.

The really *bad parts about*
1. You're not creating and nurturing new
this reality will decrease your workflow and cause you to either accep
lesser work or to figure out how to fit back into the normal working
world (the more time alone, the more difficult this can become).
2. You can develop really bad habits in terms of working hours, and
spend too much time alone in your own head.
3. If your computer crashes at 3 A.M., you'll have to fix it yourself.

Working with a Partner or Collaborator

The tradition: Mostly a twentieth century phenomenon, unusual before the
days of songwriting (one lyricist, one composer); performance (a duo),
advertising (one writer, one designer). Comic acts were often collaborations
(e.g., Laurel & Hardy, Abbott & Costello, the Marx Brothers), but these are
less common today. Pairings are made for movies, but the performers don't
otherwise work together: Tommy Lee Jones and Will Smith in the *Men in
Black* films, for example. Collaboration was perfect for songwriting (Gilbert
& Sullivan; Lennon & McCartney); Broadway (Rodgers & Hammerstein,
Lerner & Loewe), but creative/business partnerships are common in all
media, including television (Klasky-Csupo; Carsey-Werner-Mandabach);
and motion pictures (Coen brothers, Farrelly brothers).

Comedy and music groups sometimes become a collaborative unit
and work together for a long time. Examples include the Monty Python

46

performers and many
Dead to Phish and
More often
projects or g
Charlie Ka
and Ad
that

rock bands, from the Beach Boys and the Grateful
Radiohead.

in today's world, collaborators come together for specific
groups of projects, but also work on their own. Screenwriter
ufman and director Spike Jonze collaborated on *Being John Malkovich*
ptation. These were specific, short-term projects in the midst of careers
also involved other types of projects with other creative people. Kaufman
so wrote for television and other movies, and Jonze directed music videos and
other motion pictures. Jazz musicians have played on one another's recordings
for decades; the practice keeps the musicians sharp and the music fresh.

Collaborators may deeply affect one another's work, even if they
don't work together directly, as Howard Gardner[11] explains: "In a word,
Picasso and Braque invented cubism.... For many months, the two men
were virtually inseparable. They painted during the day and then, at night,
came together and studied each other's works. At times, their works
were so similar that only an expert can tell them apart....The two men
appreciated one another's company; they jokingly referred to themselves
as 'Orville and Wilbur Wright.'"

The really *good parts about working with a partner or collaborator:*
The best collaborations turn out far better work than either partner
could or would contribute on his or her own. If the work is good, then
the team gets the credit, and because the team is small, the credit and
gratification can be huge.

The good parts about working with a partner or collaborator:
1. You're not alone. Somebody is there to encourage, cajole, criticize,
stroke, and make it happen alongside you.
2. When one of you is down, the other may be up. That allows you
to work more productively and to neutralize the inevitable depressing
moments that accompany any creative adventure.

---

[11] SOURCE: Howard Gardner, *Creating Minds,* p. 161.

3. It's fun. A lot of fun when it's going well. Far more fun than working alone.

The bad parts about working with a partner or collaborator:
1. You're going to share the money. Teams are not often paid as two people, but instead as an expanded version of one.
2. You're reliant on another person to do the work. Nobody's perfect. Some people are difficult, unreliable, crazy, out of step, erratic, or simply unsuitable partners. Finding a good fit can be challenging.
3. Both parties must be committed to the marriage. If the commitment is out of balance, then problems can pile up quickly—and these problems might directly affect the work.

The really *bad parts about working with a partner or collaborator:*
1. In today's world, the partnership or collaboration ought to be defined in a legal agreement. That means roughly that a business negotiation must occur before the creative work can begin. There's no better way to ruin a beautiful relationship than to start out by discussing what happens when things don't work out.
2. Few partnerships last forever. When things don't work out, the hurt can be long-lasting.

Working as Part of a Team

The tradition: The circus, the *commedia dell'arte*, and the performances of Shakespeare's plays at the old Globe Theater date back several hundred years. Teams were led by a director, or the equivalent of a director. Theater carried on the tradition, which informed early motion pictures, radio, and then television, advertising agencies, and Web development shops with similar ways of working. From the start, some aspects of the process were more team-oriented than others. Some tasks were always solo acts and always will be. Others require the entire company on stage.

You're part of the team, but you are hired with specific responsibility for costumes. You're the music director, but you also play an important role in shaping the entire creative presentation. You're the writer on this campaign, but the client is looking to you *personally* to provide the appropriate attitude. Junior people may not be assigned specific roles. More experienced hands train the young ones. It's always been that way; it's how we pass on the tradition.

The really *good parts about working as part of a team:*
   1. If it doesn't work, it's nobody's fault (and everybody's fault, but that never matters).
   2. If it works, you're a hero, and you get to share the joy with a lot of other like-minded people. (This is team sports for creative people.)
   3. On a really fine team, the work is shared, and the result is far greater than any one could have done on their own.

The good parts about working as part of a team:
   1. You really are a part of something greater than yourself.
   2. You learn a lot about working with other people, and how you fit in.
   3. You figure out some interesting things about yourself ("Why am I always the first person to speak up?" or "Why don't I ever speak up?").
   4. You learn some interesting things about other people ("I never realized she was so critical"; "I never thought of him as a natural leader").
   5. You learn soft and hard lessons from other team members. Team members take the time to nurture one another's skills and contributions. When it works, this is just wonderful.

The bad parts about working as part of a team:
   1. You might end up on a lousy team.
   2. You might not fit into the team, regardless of its quality.
   3. You might screw things up for the team (on a really good team, everybody covers, so this isn't much of a problem—unless, of course, you screw up more than once).

4. Regardless of how much you contribute, you will never get the credit. For some people, this is a big issue. For others, it's a nice break, and for others, it's a far more comfortable way to work.

The really *bad parts about working as part of a team:*
None, really. There isn't much personal risk when you're part of a team.

Leading a Team

The tradition: The Greeks did not build their theaters and temples through pure teamwork; someone was in charge. The Sistine Chapel, the Pyramids, every great architectural endeavor was built by workers who followed a visionary, a manager, one who kept his eye on the entire enterprise and (either directly or indirectly) managed the details. Centuries later this model has not appreciably changed. It remains the job description for the architect, the theater and film director, the orchestra conductor, the animation director, the executive producer in television, the record producer, the Webmaster, the headmaster of an innovative educational institution.

Tim Burton commented: "To be a director, you can't have any fear. At best, you probably have to have a very healthy balance of not being an egomaniac, but with enough security in yourself to just go for it."[12]

What makes a creative leader?
1. A thorough understanding of the market, the project, the production process, the available resources, and the capabilities of the available people.
2. A relatively clear vision of the end product.
3. Some reasonable means for planning the steps between concept and completion, and for the required actions.
4. Some degree of either attention to detail or a strong talent for delegation.
5. A quick mind that can size up current progress and make in-course changes.

---

[12] SOURCE: *Burton on Burton*, p. 49.

6. Good relationships, all around.

Dag Hammarskjold, one of the United Nations's more creative, inspiring leaders, said of a colleague, "He broke fresh ground—because and only because, he had the courage to go ahead without asking whether others were following or even understood. He had no need for the divided responsibility in which others seek to be safe from ridicule, because he had been granted a faith which required no confirmation—a contact with reality, light and intense like the touch of a loved hand: a union in self-surrender without self-destruction where his heart was lucid and his mind was loving."[13]

The really *good parts about leading a team:*
1. Leading a successful creative enterprise is an incredible high. It just feels great.
2. In many parts of the creative world, you'll get paid well for doing the leadership job effectively—and you'll be asked to do it again and again.
3. Your stature within the business will grow, so your project range will become more varied, more interesting, and ultimately, you will have more control over your career.
4. Other cool people will want to work with you.

The good parts about leading a team:
1. You get to train the next generation of talented people, to have some positive impact on other people's lives.
2. You get to do the right projects in the right way, which makes everyone on the team feel wonderful.
3. You can handpick the people with whom you work closely.
4. You make most of the big decisions.
5. You gain enormous self-confidence.

---

[13] SOURCE: Dag Hammarskjold, *Markings*, translated by Leif Sjoberg and W.H. Auden from the Swedish, New York: Alfred A. Knopf 1970, pp. 97-98.

The bad parts about leading a team:
1. Everything becomes your problem.
2. If you make a bad choice, you can cause an avalanche.
3. It's lonely; there aren't many people (in or out of the business) who understand what you do.
4. If you mess up more than once, it's tough to find work further down the ladder.
5. You can do everything right and the audience could still hate the end product.

The really *bad parts about leading a team:*
1. You have the power to screw up people's minds and careers, sometimes without realizing that you said or did anything at all.
2. You can become a target for crazy people.
3. You can become a target for lawsuits or other nasty stuff.
4. You might not be anywhere as good as you believe yourself to be. That's a devastating lesson to learn.
5. You might lose your friends, your family, or your self-respect while on the way to the top, or while trying to remain there. You might find success, but lose your way.

Moving From Leadership to a Specialist Role

You can shift from a leadership position to a more specific creative role and back again, but you must be mindful of what you're doing, and you must think about how to present this duality to the marketplace.

If you are a longtime creative and you've simply done some career-enhancing management stints, nobody will be confused or think twice. However, if you are a long-time creative who has substantially shifted her career into a clear management direction, particularly a senior management direction, you must move carefully. It's okay to be an executive vice president and also write music or children's books, but remember: Every bit of your creative work now becomes part of your resumé. In the midst of interviewing for a job, someone will find material that you created earlier in your career and toss it into your resumé file. Which, of course, raises the question: "Do we really want our new executive vice president of finance to be the same person who wrote the best-selling preschool book, *Everyone Farts?*

There's nothing wrong with being prolific. I'm a senior executive, and I've written about twenty books and I've also produced hundreds of hours of television. The package makes sense, in part because I've learned how to tell my story to highlight consistent themes of management, leadership, and a record of project-oriented accomplishments. Generally, it's okay for me to be an individual contributor (an author, for example), or a consultant (often as a portable executive or a creative team leader or guide), or a senior-level producer. The marketplace will not allow me to take a job writing copy or designing ads because I'm considered to be overqualified. That said, I am taking drawing classes at a local college to improve my skills. You can build a similar model for your own resumé.

Management of Your Personal Brand

The poet T.S. Eliot wrote, "There are only two ways a writer can become important—to write a great deal and have his writing appear everywhere, or to write very little.... My reputation in England is built upon one small volume of verse.... The only thing that matters is that each of these should be perfect in their own kind, so that each should be an event."[14]

The fundamental concept of branding is not complicated, nor has it changed much since Eliot's time.

A brand is the commercial representation of you and your work in the marketplace. That is to say: You are not your brand. You-the-person and you-the-brand are not identical. You are an individual human being, presumably one with a life. Your brand is your commercial presence.

[14] SOURCE: Vivien Eliot, *The Letters of T.S. Eliot,* Volume 1, 1898-1922, Harcourt Brace N.Y., 1988, p. 126.

Celebrities jealously guard their personal lives. When the demarcation between one's life and one's brand blurs, coping can become a challenge.

Brand Definition

From a marketer's point of view, a brand is a collection of subjective and objective attributes that describe a product or service and distinguish it from competitive products or services. Generally, *brand value* equates with a reduction of risk in a purchase decision. Those risks may be financial (not worth the price); functional (doesn't work properly); social (results in embarrassment); and so on. These risks are also considered when hiring a person: A new employee or freelancer might simply not be worth the money, or may not do the work properly, or may be a complete disaster, resulting in embarrassment or even career damage to the hiring manager.[15]

Brand Equity

Branding is not synonymous with marketing or advertising. Branding is not about presentation, it is about performance. Honda automobiles outsell other brands because they offer a superior ride and require minimal service. A student who regularly participates in class, does her homework, and doesn't disrupt the teacher will gain a better reputation over time than a slacker. This reputation will be communicated among teachers, and over time the child's *brand identity* will become as significant as her actual academic performance.

There are at least four ways to define a brand.[16] One is descriptive, simply using words to define the brand. A second is functional, explaining

---

[15] This is based upon an article entitled "Consumer Ranking of Risk Reduction Methods," by Ted Roselius, which appeared in the Journal of Marketing, and was reworked for a textbook entitled *Strategic Brand Management: Building, Measuring and Managing Brand Equity* written by Kevin Iane Keller and published by Prentice-Hall.
[16] If you are interested in reading more about brands, I recommend *Building Strong Brands* by David A. Aaker, published by Free Press, or *Strategic Brand Management: Creating and Sustaining Brand Equity Long Term* (Second Edition) by Jean Noël Kapferer, published by Kogan Page.

how the brand is used by consumers ("new, advanced sudsing ALL laundry detergent"). A third is competitive, examining the ways in which the brand is similar to, or different from, related brands ("Choosy moms choose JIF"). Fourth, a brand may be defined in terms of its perceived personality ("the Energizer bunny… it just keeps going and going and going").

Apple Computer has provided endless case studies in superior brand management. The company's brand equity extends well past the reliable, clever technology that makes the G5, iPod, and other products possible. Apple does not sell technology; instead, the company sells design, reliability and creative potential. The simplicity of its "Why Switch?" campaign, aimed at Windows users, is one of many examples of Apple's understanding of itself and its market. (The top ten reasons to switch include: "It just works," and "it doesn't crash," and "works effortlessly with PCs" and "it's beautiful." The other reasons refer to ease of use and capabilities related to digital music and digital photography. Apple doesn't spend much time explaining why or how technology has enabled these features. Instead, it presents a clean, clear, trustworthy, state-of-the-art image to the marketplace.) Visit an Apple retail store, or Apple's Web site, and you'll see a consistent display of brand equity over a large number of products and services. All are based, ultimately, on performance.

Your Brand Equity

One of the tough problems associated with being a creative professional, and establishing your own personal brand is the similarity of our resumés and our accomplishments. Every creative professional's resumé is filled with terms like "wrote," "designed," and "created." Every creative professional's resumé says that the person was "directly responsible for" and "won awards for." So how do you distinguish yourself?

Bearing in mind that brand value is based upon performance, not on spin, you must differentiate based upon qualitative distinctions. Begin with your brand definition. Try to define it in terms that the marketplace understands.

Very quickly, you'll realize that the work you do in the office does not provide sufficient differentiation. But why limit yourself to working in the office? Do some freelancing. Pursue your own interests in historical re-creations, extreme sports, or teaching English as a second language. Hiring managers will check for the essential job requirements, but they'll *remember* you as the woman who made a film about transforming neighborhood danger zones into pocket parks.[17] Take some chances. Get involved with some projects or with some people that might be described as crazy. One New York City writer decided to launch his film writing and directing career with a documentary on a century-old sport that was once on par with baseball and football, but somehow fell out of favor. That sport was, of course, pillow-fighting.[18]

A complete understanding of your brand equity is just the first step. The second is messaging. Most creative professionals rely upon a resumé or a biography and a sample (a demo reel, a portfolio, etc.). Although some designers cleverly present their employment and project history in a fascinating package, most hiring managers are unimpressed by fancy wrappings. Although this direction may seem contrary to presenting your brand in all its glory, it's best to stay on the conservative side. Don't take out advertisements, don't sing and dance outside the hiring manager's office. A resumé and a professional sample kit will do.

Brand Direction Over Time

Over several months, you can't do much to control your career. Over several years, however, you can transform yourself and really improve the way your brand is defined and perceived.

---

[17] I have a specific person in mind here. Her name is Tamra Raven, and she produced a lovely small film called *Rats to Roses*. This accomplishment separates her, in my mind, from dozens of other NYC production staffers with more-or-less interchangeable backgrounds.

[18] Actor and writer James Greenberg, who wrote much of the material for Lynne Thigpen's "Chief" character on the *Where in the World Is Carmen Sandiego?* series conceived and produced this unlikely documentary. The very idea made people laugh.

Several key factors that will affect your brand over time include the following (numbered in order of their importance):

1. The size and depth of your personal network.
2. Your personality.
3. The vibrancy of your industry sector.
4. The amount of time and energy you devote to career advancement.
5. Your status within the industry: articles, awards, gallery showings, personal affiliations.
6. The quality of your work.
7. The kinds of freelance projects you do.
8. Your perceived age, and your actual age.
9. How long you stay with a particular job.
10. How long you stay with a particular company.

Many of these factors are discussed in detail later in the book.

Being Present

From the Japanese way of the warrior, known as *bushido*,[19] we learn three keys for making aggressive energy serve our creative visions:

- Be present
- Be concentrated
- Be strong

I think of this in more pedestrian terms. In order to succeed, you must do three things that most people do not bother to do.

First, you've got to *show up*. It's amazing how many people don't show up, don't show up on time or don't show up prepared for work. If you do these simple things, you will be ahead of a surprisingly large number of competitors (and pretenders).

[19] SOURCE: Laurence G. Boldt, *Zen and the Art of Making a Living*, pp. 63-64.

Second, you've got to *pay attention*. Showing up isn't enough. Listen carefully. Take notes (no, you won't remember everything, and taking notes is one way to teach yourself to listen critically). Make your presence known by asking questions, or thanking your host in person after the meeting or presentation. If you show up but don't make your presence known, that's tantamount to not showing up at all.

Third, *do what you promise*. Try to leave the meeting with a specific promise to follow up. This promise will increase the odds of continued communications, and possibly, a future relationship. Then, follow through. If you promised to send information, or a way to get in touch with an associate, provide the information in a prompt, professional way. Do this often enough and people will notice. Don't do this with any specific hope of a returned favor. Just believe that as you help others, others will help you, too. This is not opportunistic behavior. Instead, you are encouraging everyone to be their best possible self.

The Wrap-up: Adaptation

After a few years of managing your career, building intellectual property assets for yourself and for other people, and trying your best to earn a living, you eventually come to a singular realization: The real work of a creative professional is creating and developing your own career. Your specific contribution to a given project might help you get your next job, but the sum total of all of your jobs, plus your personality and perspective, add up to something much more valuable than technical or managerial expertise.

The whole package, in its fully adaptive glory, is the creative professional's greatest asset. The way your career is constructed, the way you add to it, the ways you communicate what you've got, the new paths that you teach your brain and body to follow—this is what you are bringing to market.

Chapter 2 – The Marketplace

There are three ways a creative professional can earn a living. Each is steeped in history. Each is entirely practical, or impractical, depending upon who you are and how you look at the world.

Working for an Employer

This is what most people in the western world do every day. They work for one company, or for several companies within one industry, typically for years. The work is done on behalf of the employer, and the work is owned by the employer. There isn't much freedom, but there is a steady paycheck, plus health benefits, camaraderie, and resume-building power that comes with a job title linked to a bona fide company name.

The idea of a company, led by a boss or a board of directors, did not take shape in any meaningful way until the industrial revolution in the mid-1800s. At that time, most companies were manufacturing concerns, often with factories, long hours, lousy working conditions, and virtually no one resembling a creative professional. At this time, there were a small number of book, magazine, newspaper, journal, and game publishers, and an equally small creative community of authors, writers, and artists. Most workers provided hands and strong bodies to do the work; few workers were employed to think or to create.

By the late 1880s, reliable mail service enabled the shipping of goods nationwide. Catalogs and national brands brought about an advertising and marketing industry, and creative people were needed to write and illustrate marketing messages. In the cities, larger retail emporia employed creative professionals to display and promote their merchandise. Theater—opera, vaudeville, and burlesque houses—provided work for musicians in the pit band, performers on stage, artists who designed handbills and scenery. These new jobs fit neatly beside the emerging music industry, where songwriters, song pluggers, and music publishers were among the first to sell intellectual property directly to the public. By 1915, movie studios were regularly employing actors, directors, artists, producers, and promotion men. A decade later, radio networks provided regular employment for actors, comedians, musicians, and producers who could put together programs and commercials.

Throughout the twentieth century, the media, entertainment, sports, and retail industries provided the majority of jobs for creative professionals.

At the start of the twenty-first century, the media and marketing businesses had become large enough to employ more than five million workers worldwide.[1] A century ago, the idea of any respectable person working with stage performers, or radio people, or (perhaps worse yet) advertising people would have been unthinkable; certainly a well-bred lady would not mention these people in polite conversation. Today, there are few colleges or universities without multiple majors to prepare young creative professionals for careers in the arts, marketing, or media.

---

[1] According to the U.S. Census Bureau, over 1.5 million people are employed in specific media professions; add support and management staff, plus the many self-employed who are not counted in that number. Similarly, there are over 200,000 marketing managers in the United States, plus an additional 100,000 advertising and promotion managers, and about 150,000 people selling advertising. Add media buying, management, public relations, plus 10,000 art directors and nearly 50,000 artists, and the numbers suggest about two million professionals in the U.S. marketing business. The world total is probably twice that number.

Working for Clients

Here, the tradition is longer, and the history is richer. The scene is the drawing room in a musty castle. The year is 1533, and the place is Saxony. A patron has hired an artist to paint a beautiful portrait of his ugly daughter. The artist begins by sketching, then the only means of capturing an image. Slowly, and with seemingly magical skill, the artist applies paint to canvas, and the lovely princess comes to life. By his hand, she is preserved for all time, and beautiful. He is paid with room and board and royal gifts. The patron is pleased; there is another assignment, this time a rotten-smelling prince, and then the king, who is to be preserved not in oil but in stone.

To be an artist or a musician, a patron was required. Some lived by the patronage of the royals, or through fees paid by wealthy merchants. Others lived by the good graces of the church, with difficult, demanding clients whose critical comments were often backed by God's will.

Starving artists were common. For every musician who could earn a living, hundreds could not. Writers were few, as writing did not fit comfortably into a patronage system. Performers were temporary inhabitants of the town or kingdom, always moving on to the next promising opportunity—and often as far away as possible, lest the townspeople catch up with them, for they were often scoundrels, or at least, scandalous in words and deeds.

Once again, it's not until the twentieth century that a client-based creative services industry emerges. In 1904, Collier's signed illustrator Charles Dana Gibson to a six-figure contract to supply the magazine with a regular supply of captioned illustrations called "The Gibson Girl."[2] There was merchandising of The Gibson Girl on the level of Mickey Mouse or *StarWars*. Large-size books ("table albums," they were called), china plates and saucers, ashtrays, tablecloths, pillow covers, chair covers, souvenir spoons, screens, fans, umbrella stands... all bore the image of Gibson's

---

[2] SOURCE: http://www.mutoworld.com/Gibson.htm.

creations. Other illustrators of the time were as famous: Norman Rockwell, whose work eventually graced 324 covers of the *Saturday Evening Post*; and James Montgomery Flagg, whose illustration for the "I Want You" for U.S. Army poster was one of many paintings and drawings he created for magazines.

Performers worked for a variety of clients on radio, on stage, and in the movies. (Even the Hollywood studios' "star system," which provided contract employment to many famous names, allowed performers to separately work for radio and on stage.) The New York writing establishment was populated with the likes of writer Dorothy Parker, whose various staff jobs were outnumbered in years by time spent freelancing. (Parker wrote for *The New Yorker* and other magazines and wrote several plays and screenplays, including "A Star is Born.")

Freelancing wasn't any easier in the 1920s, 1930s, or 1940s than it is today. Parker was one of NYC's best and best-known writers, and despite an impressive catalog of short stories, essays, books, plays, and articles, she found it difficult to earn a living.[3] Nearly a century later, freelancers are still trying to figure out how to piece together a sufficient income from client-based work.

Ditto for Philip K. Dick, now a familiar name because of movies based upon his short stories (1982's "Blade Runner," based on Dick's "Do Androids Dream of Electric Sheep"; 1990's "Total Recall"; and 2002's "Minority Report"). "He hand-to-mouthed it in the 1950s as a genre writer, churning out a couple of novels and reams of short stories each year, all for paltry sums.... Blade Runner provided the artist with a small measure of financial security, and after five marriages and spates of garret-style artistic poverty, it appeared as if the author was about to emerge from the sci-fi ghetto. But he died the year the movie was released."[4]

---

[3] Parker also suffered from depression and a generally unstable personality, she was a poor financial manager, and she was an alcoholic. But she was also one of the century's best writers.

[4] SOURCE: BOOK Magazine, July/August 2002, page 34; published by West Egg Communications LLC, N.Y.C., N.Y.

Not all stories are so dramatic. Many creative professionals do earn a living through clients, some for a very long while. For most freelancers, it's a tough road, and when the journey hits the inevitable skids, coping can become a challenge.

Selling Work Directly to the Public

Writers are not publishers, and publishers are not writers. Artists rarely own galleries, and gallery owners rarely paint. It's difficult to play both sides: different skills, training, and orientation are required. Still, there is a long history of selling creative work directly, beginning hundreds of years before the Internet.

An eighteenth century English artist and printer named William Hogarth worked in the same London that spawned Daniel Defoe, John Gay, Jonathan Swift, and Henry Fielding. Hogarth was drawn to London's street life and produced a series of engravings about the life of a prostitute. A Harlot's Progress (1732) was positioned as a cautionary tale. Hogarth sold his cards directly to the public. The cards sold well enough to justify a sequel: the story of a male street hustler called The Rake's Progress (1735).

Nearly 300 years later, selling work directly to customers remains challenging, but it has been adopted by a variety of creative professionals, particularly craftspeople like jewelry designers, as well as photographers, watercolorists, furniture makers, potters, pewter figure modelers, and metalworkers whose work is often seen in street festivals and arts fairs.

Hogarth was a significant artist and storyteller; some consider him a founder of the modern comic industry and credit him with the first graphic novels. But that's not the reason why you ought to frame a picture of William Hogarth above your desk.

As the story goes, Hogarth's prints were unusually successful. And, as was common practice in Merry Olde England, other artists and printers ripped him off. They made copies of his work and sold the prints to unsuspecting consumers. Instead of accepting the practice, Hogarth got angry. He petitioned and then badgered Parliament to do something about what he considered to be property theft. Remarkably, in 1735, Hogarth got his law—referred to as Hogarth's Act, or the Copyright Act—and so began the legal history of copyright protection. Subscribers to The Rake's Progress were informed that "Mr. Hogarth was... oblig'd to defer... Delivery of... the prints till the 25th of June next, in order to secure his Property, pursuant to an Act lately passed by both Houses of Parliament... to secure all new invented Prints... from being copied without Consent...thereby preventing a scandalous and unjust Custom... of making and vending base Copies of original Prints, to the manifest injury of the Author, and the great Discouragement of the Arts of Painting and Engraving."[5]

Selling Work to the Public through an Agent, Publisher or Distributor

Rascals abound! You're an artist or a writer who has spent months, perhaps years, perfecting a creation. A publisher agrees to pay for printing and distribution. The work is published—but your name is nowhere to be found! Or you're a songwriter. It's the 1970s, not so long ago. You write a song, sell some rights to a publisher, sign a contract that's been approved by a bona fide music industry lawyer. Somehow, you find yourself with a co-writer, who happens to be the producer's sister-in-law or your manager's cousin. Your cowriter will share half of your royalties forever.

Florence Ballard, whose name you may recall because she was a member of The Supremes, was on welfare when she died. Because she wasn't a credited writer on the many Motown hits, her royalties from one of the world's best-selling catalog were minuscule.

Merle Haggard enjoyed a string of thirty-seven top ten country singles, including twenty-three records that went to Number One in the 1960s and 1970s. Yet he never received a record royalty check until 2002,

---

[5] SOURCE: http://www.haleysteele.com/hogarth/plates/rake.html.

when he released an album on the indie punk rock label, Epitaph.

Here's where the myth of "the artist will never be a businessman" takes flight. Creative people are treated as innocents, bumpkins, naifs who cannot read contracts and cannot count their own money. The creative person spends his time making things, not selling things. She develops only a vague sense of the marketplace. He collects unreliable data and wonders why the artist seated at a nearby café table claims far fewer francs per painting than does the painter dining on oysters at the next table.

Not every artist is a fool! The model in which the artist and his fame begin to overtake any specific marketer or publisher takes shape in the latter half of the nineteenth century, with Mark Twain in the United States and Charles Dickens in England. Twain, or Samuel Clemens, was first published in a local newspaper at age thirteen, and he continued to write articles while exploring the West, prospecting for gold (and quartz, which at least paid the bills), hanging out in Hawaii, and more. Eventually, Clemens realized that he could speak in public as well as he could write. He lectured extensively, beginning at age thirty and throughout his life. His speaking engagements made him rich and allowed him to travel on somebody else's nickel. Shortly after Huckleberry Finn was published in 1884, Clemens formed a book publishing company for his own and other writers' work (one author was U.S. Grant).[6] Dickens started out writing serialized short stories and character studies for the weekly and monthly newspapers, and then packaged his popular work as novels.

In today's world, every deal the creative professional makes is no longer the equivalent of buying a used car off the lot. There are now standard agreements to be signed, standard clauses that every contract ought to include (see chapter seven), state and federal laws to protect

---

[6] Ten years later, Clemens bankrupt the company with an investment in new typesetting equipment. Disappointed, and suddenly in serious debt, Clemens packed up the family and moved to Europe. By 1898, the publisher, author, and lecturer had paid back every penny he owed.

both parties to any agreement, legal recourse, and a variety of other mechanisms to minimize fraud and illegitimate dealings. Some dark traditions remain—the net profit definitions in some entertainment contracts, which virtually assure that no money will ever be paid to the creator—but the creative professional has never been in a better position to reasonably expect honest, truthful reporting and reliable, accurate, timely payments. There are books on the subject,[7] some quite specific about the appropriate rates to be charged, and other significant deal points. And thank goodness, there is e-mail and the Internet, so every creative person can compare notes with a worldwide community of like-minded people and anonymously ask for help in evaluating deals before signing anything!

For businesspeople whose trade involves the exploitation of creative works and creative people, it's rarely about the art. Sometimes it's about inhabiting a world filled with creative people, and sometimes it's about the fame and clout that comes with association with celebrities. Mostly it's about the money. The next time you make any kind of deal for yourself, remember that.

A creative person whose work generates significant value in the marketplace is likely to be surrounded by business associates and advisors, such as an agent, lawyer, accountant, and in some cases, a business manager, whose job is to protect assets and increase market value. Unfortunately, few creative people reach this level, and only a small percentage stay on top for any meaningful period of time.

What then? Well, honey, you might consider actually getting a job and working for a living....

How Companies Work

Whether you're working as an employee or a contractor or simply selling

---

[7] One is the *Graphic Artist's Guild Handbook of Pricing and Ethical Guidelines* (tenth edition); another is *All You Need to Know about the Record Business* by Donald S. Passman.

your wares, it's important to understand how a typical company operates. Companies can be mysterious, opaque empires where even long-term employees don't completely understand how or why things work the way they do.

Company Goals and Planning

Most companies do their planning "from the top down" and also "from the bottom up." Top-down planning is typically organized by senior management, which restates the company's vision, reviews its vision statement for the next few years, and outlines the company's annual goals. Individual departments develop the next levels of the plan: specific goals and targets, followed by a handful of strategies to achieve the goal, and various tactics to transform each strategy into reality. Typically, employees are evaluated and rewarded upon the successful achievement of departmental goals. Managers are evaluated and rewarded based upon the achievement of departmental and company goals.

The "bottom-up" approach is less common for establishing goals, but more common for budgeting expenses. Each department submits an operating budget, based mostly on the past year's work plus some added projects or new hires, but the interdepartmental coordination of small, medium-sized, and larger goals can be complicated.

The top-down goal-strategy-tactic approach is extremely common. Most companies use this planning process far more than a general guide. They work out their budgets with this plan, and although they might allow for some unknown projects, most expenditures are locked in place at the start of the fiscal year, when the new budget is approved and new monies are available.

As a creative professional working as a company employee, your job is to support the plan. In fact, everyone's job is to support the plan and to make the necessary course corrections when things don't work out as anticipated. There may or may not be any connection between the company's goals and your personal goals. You may not be assigned to specific projects that advance your career. That's not the company's problem! You are being paid for your services; the company is paying you because it requires your skills, talents, knowledge, passion, and ability to execute the plan. Read this paragraph over again, just to avoid confusion. The company sets the rules, and you are employed at their pleasure. Not the other way around.

That said, you do matter. As a person and as a professional, you can exercise tremendous impact on the planning process and the way the plan is executed. Those who exert the right kind of positive influence get noticed, get promotions, get raises, and may get a voice in future planning. Those who fight the plan play a risky game. Sometimes they win, but usually they lose against the stronger force of the plan's own momentum and the power of multiple levels of coordinated management.

Company Hiring Practices

A department's budget and headcount is usually prescribed by the plan and approved by management. In most organizations, senior management meets every few weeks to review all aspects of the company's operations, including finance, legal/deals, sales, distribution, marketing, advertising, technology/operations, development and human resources. If the meeting brings doubtful or troublesome information, then the human resources discussion often includes a recommendation to slow down the hiring. Immediately after the meeting, any open job requisitions are either collected from individual departments or placed in a folder on the boss's desk, or in a holding file in the human resources department. Regardless of the process, the result is the same: The job opening that existed this morning no longer exists, at least in the short term. Individual department heads might negotiate for specific new hires or replacements, often with some budgetary horse-trading ("I can cut $50,000 from the new promotion if I can hire the new assistant next month"). Most open jobs either remain on hold indefinitely, evaporate because the work is already being done by the existing staff, or become irrelevant because once-important projects are not pursued. And as for the $50,000 cut from the new promotion, that may be the cause for an uncomfortable call to the marketing communications agency that was relying upon the fee to pay its people or its rent.

There is nothing evil or unethical about the process. It's simply the way that companies are managed today, and, often, it is the creative professional who is affected. Why? Because it's the new creative hires who do the new work, create the new products, design the new campaigns, architect the new environments, compose the new music. If something is new, it's likely to involve some sort of a creative professional. And if it's new, it's often the first thing to be cut from the budget and/or the plan.

Why They're Not Hiring You Full-Time

Most companies keep a careful eye on headcount. As Jerry Johnson, the vice president of finance at CDNOW/Bertelsmann used to say, "Every expense comes marching into my office on two feet." Hire fewer people, he preached, and the company will spend less money.

The more one digs, the truer Jerry's mantra becomes. Check out this comparison:

Let's say the company adds a public relations manager. This job could be added as a staff position, or the specific functions could be reworked into a public relations consultant role instead.

A suitable public relations consultant agrees to work in her own home office (more comfortable, more productive, no child care issues). She'll work two-thirds time, but because she's well-organized and not often interrupted by meetings or people popping into her office, she'll complete her task list every week. That's the deal, and she's willing to flat-rate the job at $1,000 per week. She wants a guarantee of a full year's work, a total of $52,000, plus a contract. This figure is relatively high for an employee salary, but the company prefers the arrangement and is willing to sign an agreement. The consultant is also pleased because the remaining one-third of her time can be sold to another client, perhaps two, with potential for future business.

The salaried public relations manager position is budgeted at $40,000—but that's misleading. Add 25 percent for federal and state employment taxes, social security, and health benefits, and the total is now $50,000. The employee needs space to work, plus office furniture, a telephone, and a computer with a small percentage of someone's salary to keep the equipment working and to keep the office clean. True, these costs are already being paid for the other employees, but each additional employee accounts for a percentage of the bill. The cost of the office setup is several thousand dollars; the other stuff might top the whole annual bill at $5,000. So now we're at $55,000. As soon as the employee starts working, additional costs mount: subscriptions, organization memberships, office supplies, lunches, late dinners, cabs, local travel, and, of course, the wonderful new projects that this new employee is bound to generate. Some new projects may generate additional revenue; all will generate additional costs. The new manager will interact with the company's decision-makers daily, so her likelihood of getting projects approved are greater than the consultant who shows up once a week. Conservatively, the cost of the inside public relations manager will be $60,000-$100,000 more than the contractor. If the manager is effective, the costs are more likely going to be more than $100,000. (Yeah, but...)

Spending a few thousand dollars more per year won't break any substantial company. The new manager may add value where the contractor might not. The inside manager could take on other tasks, perhaps train other people, could someday become a director of the department. (If you're cynical, you might also point out that the inside manager could do a crummy job, and have a negative impact, and then could be difficult to fire because of restrictive employment laws.) Of course, the contractor can always be offered a job, when the time is right.

Companies as Clients

Although you may work closely with company employees, there are substantive differences between being an employee and being a freelancer (or contractor, or consultant, or whatever the company calls you). For one thing, you cannot work for one company full-time. To do so calls your independent contractor status into question and might, under certain circumstances, force the client company to treat you as an employee (which involves taxes and benefits). Even those who work part-time for a single client may find themselves in a similar situation (see chapter seven for details).

As a contractor, you will not be considered a part of the company. You may not participate in certain company activities. And, generally, you will not be able to control the direction of your work.

As a creative professional working outside the company, it is vital that you understand the company's planning cycles, as well as the company's or department's strategies and/or tactics. It's unlikely that you'll see a formal document (these are generally regarded as competitive information and are often confidential), but you can ask about priorities at any pitch meeting and get at least a partial answer. Observe the company's behavior— particularly its advertising and public relations activities, new product launches, and the way people behave at meetings—and you'll surmise many of the strategies and tactics.

Let's pick up the story of the public relations department once again....

It is three months later. The independent consultant is working hard, producing excellent results. A letter from the COO congratulated her on the superb effort and positive effect that she's had on the company and its employees. Still, it's been a shaky quarter. No new hires have been approved, and nobody has been hired to replace seven people who have left the company for other jobs. Sales projections aren't promising. Further cuts are necessary. The COO is the first to suggest that some, or all, consultants are eliminated. Someone at the management meeting speaks out in favor of the good work done by these consultants, and another argues that the company couldn't get along without them. Another logically points out the situation's inherent unfairness: First, we replaced the new hires with consultants, and now we're eliminating the consultants. Everyone agrees the solution is imperfect, but the meeting ends with a promise from every executive to at least review their department's current consulting agreements. No decisions are made....

...until the following morning, when one more kernel of bad news causes the e-mail: Please negotiate out of all consulting agreements. The COO willingly meets with any departments for whom this is an insurmountable problem, but approves only one contract extension, and that one for only two months. Every other agreement is to be terminated immediately, with sixty days additional goodwill payment.

From a strictly business perspective, all of this makes some sense. Many companies do not work this way—particularly media companies. Instead, they're less rigorous, more lenient about expenses because they know that a sudden success can change all of the rules. When will that hit come? Nobody knows, but we'd better be ready when it does... and so, expenses are higher than they ought to be. As Anne Kreamer and Jim Cramer pointed out in December 2002, "When you're an entertainment exec, it's entirely possible to suspend all rigor and get away with it."[8]

How This Affects You

First and foremost, it's almost never personal and it's almost never about the quality of your work. For most companies, cutting contractors is less painful than cutting employees. Cutting projects is even less painful for the company manager—it means less work for you, which means money for you, but it also means less work for the employee, who will, in fact, get paid regardless. (The employee might pay a price in terms of career development, or in terms of their ability to get things done regardless of available resources, but most employees can deal with these concerns in other ways.)

---

[8] SOURCE: Anne Kreamer & Jim Cramer, "Culture" column, *Fast Company*, December 2002, p. 78.

Second, your own success as an independent contractor demands stupendous flexibility. The best way to achieve that flexibility is to develop many client relationships. You must have multiple points of contact at each client company. A one-company, one-client strategy is dangerous because your contact might leave, change roles, or need to ditch you because of his own job situation. You must maintain regular communications with other potential clients. You must publicize your work and your ideas to the industry, either through personal appearances, speeches, convention attendance (and "schmoozing" at each booth), or through articles, Web sites, writing books, or other similar means. If you are not willing or able to do these things, you should try your best to avoid building a career dependent upon clients.

The point is vitally important, so I'll repeat: Do not build or maintain a business with a single client. What's more, do not allow any client to occupy more than about two-thirds of your time. Try to maintain three clients at all times; if the number drops to two, get to work finding the third.

Special Problems Related to Client Work

A good client is one who keeps you busy and productive—and pays your invoices on time. If the client is keeping you so busy that you are unable to pursue other work, then you have a problem. Several problems, in fact. Once again, you might resemble an employee and not an independent contractor in the eyes of the IRS. Also, if you are very busy, then you are probably not seeking out new work, and I guarantee that this will become a problem in the future. In addition, the client might develop problems, and your single source of income could unexpectedly evaporate.

Some creative professionals are full-time consultants or project workers. Others are simply biding their time, waiting for the next full-time gig. Which are you?

Be honest with yourself. If you're pursuing another job, then you're a job hunter. If you are pursuing multiple clients in order to change the way you live and work, then you are a contractor.

For many of us, fear or discomfort plays a role. Taking appropriate action can be tough. Sure, another client would be wonderful, but how the heck do you get the client? Not everyone is comfortable schmoozing. Not everyone can just pick up the phone and ask for a new gig from someone they've never met, or figure out how to meet the right people. It's a scary world out there, especially when your self-image is deflating due to lack of cash, clients, or prospects.

A contractor or consultant without clients is a sad affair. The situation can become desperate, both in terms of available cash and a sufficiently positive outlook to find work or get the existing work done. The best solution is advance planning—months before you believe you'll need the work, get out and meet people, write articles, send e-mails, make phone calls—and seriously cut expenses. Weeks before, keep a log to track your follow-ups and new prospects. Manage your cash and your emotional well-being.

If this becomes a recurring pattern, consider resetting your priorities, or taking a job—any job—to keep yourself afloat. If you do this, do not wait until the last minute, and be sure you understand and remind yourself constantly that the situation is temporary while you continue to pursue work to nourish heart and soul. Please do not wait until the last minute to solve a problem that's months in the making.

What about speculating your time on the next potentially big project? Your first responsibility is to pay your bills, to generate the cash necessary to survive. Do this diligently, but allow yourself sufficient time to plan whatever project you please. But don't reverse the order. If you spend most of your time pursuing a speculative project, and things don't work out, you'll be in more serious trouble than before.

Avoid the inclination to say "yes, but..." or "this time, it's different" or "you don't understand." I do understand, I've been there, I've seen lots of other people there, too. Get yourself some cash flow. And then, God bless, I hope your big project makes you a fortune!

Where You Work: Company Size

Companies of every size offer potential advantages and disadvantages.
Here's a rundown:

Very Small Companies

Let's say, up to five or ten people. Everybody knows one another's name,
schedules, boyfriends, girlfriends, (most likely) salaries, frustrations,
desires, and so on. It's a tight-knit team, which is good for working
quickly and delivering with a remarkable, single-minded focus on quality.
Typically, these companies are design firms, music or video or television
production companies, PR firms with limited client lists, book packagers,
and other specialists. Most very small companies struggle with limited
resources. They're built around the special talents of one or two people;
other employees are usually helpers. Substantial growth is rarely a part of
the plan; very small companies tend to remain very small, perhaps adding
an employee or two each year.

Positives:
1. Lots of involvement in every project.
2. Phenomenally good opportunity to learn.
3. (Usually) the hours are flexible.
4. (Usually) the atmosphere is loose.
5. (Usually) personal contributions are valued.

Negatives:
1. Everybody knows too much about you and your life.
2. Projects may be limited or similar to one another.
3. Roles may be firm and rigid; it's difficult to advance or learn.
4. Resumé value may be limited, unless it's your own company (and even
so), or unless the very small company provided your early training.
5. There is limited opportunity to meet new or influential people.

Small Companies

Let's define a small company as one with up to a few dozen employees. These are often preferable for those who seek informality and flexibility, and prefer to avoid the politics and complexity of larger companies. Some of the positives and negatives of very small companies apply:

Positives:

1. Potential for involvement in most company projects.
2. Stability; if the company has grown larger than a dozen or two dozen people, the people in charge probably know how to manage the company's finances.
3. Relatively steady project flow, with multiple projects simultaneously in development, production and various stages of completion.
4. Good opportunity to learn and meet new people (steady flow of employees, contractors, freelancers, clients, affiliated companies).
5. Good combination of personal recognition and opportunity for rapid advancement.

Negatives:

1. A great deal depends upon your own personality; if you fit in, you'll do well, and if you don't, the disconnect will be noticed and corrected.
2. Most likely, the company grew to its present size through specialization. If you enjoy the specialty, great. If there's not much learning or growth, the job could become tiresome.
3. Resumé value might still be limited, unless you happen to be with a hot company.
4. Hot companies go cold, sometimes much faster than anyone anticipated.
5. Often funds are tight, so salaries might be on the low side (a community effort and a promise of excellent future projects help compensate).

Mid-Sized Companies

For our purposes, a mid-sized company employs roughly fifty to 150 people—just enough for clearly defined departments, and too many for everyone to know all the names. In anything except a dot-com business environment, growth to four or five dozen employees suggests a solid financial plan, perhaps backing from investors, a list of solid long-term clients, decent or good salaries, reasonable health benefits, offices that feel somewhat permanent—in short, a "real" company.

Positives:

1. If a company has grown this large, it's probably well-known in the industry. That's helpful for the resumé. Certainly in media businesses, this would be a company with a steady flow of products; in the public relations business, there would be plenty of contracts, clients, and projects.

2. There will be interesting people to meet, learn from, and perhaps who can provide a path to the next job.

3. There's a steady flow of varied projects and the opportunity to advance without too many other people thinking exactly the same way.

4. There's recognition, for the company is still small enough that individual contributions really matter.

5. You'll find potential for personal, professional, and company growth.

Negatives:

1. When a company becomes as large as fifty people, two things happen. First, the people in charge must spend more time actually running the company and less on the work itself. Second, layers of management and individual departments emerge. In the best situations, this additional administrative veneer provides much-needed organization and stability. In many cases, the additions just make life more complicated for the person whose job is getting the company's work done.

2. Smaller work and social groups emerge. If you're part of the right

clique, you're in good shape. If you're not, it's tough to know what's happening, why it's happening, and how you fit into the plan.

3. If the company has grown quickly, there will be some pain due to disorganization, lack of systems, or lack of seasoned management. These problems are often bothersome and time-consuming, and may in some cases become serious.

4. You will not know everybody's name.

5. You will not be able to control or define your own work.

Large Companies

For our purposes, large companies employ about 150 or so people, and up to about 300. There are clearly defined departments, with value being generated every day, a national or international product line, a regular flow of new products and opportunities, and often a long list of people who previously worked at the company.

Positives:

1. By now, the company should be reasonably well-organized. If you need supplies, you probably need do nothing more than fill out an intranet form. If you need information about vacation time, there's an employee handbook detailing policy and procedure.

2. The company is functional, probably as a result of five or ten individual departments having learned to work together.

3. The company is working to an annual budget and some sort of written operating plan.

4. The company's structure can be explained on a single sheet of paper: an organizational chart, detailing who is in charge, who works for who, and who is responsible for which activities. This organization chart is most likely tied into individual job descriptions. People will leave, and others will replace them or build new initiatives. You'll meet lots of people who can help you later on.

5. Your own work group gets the job done. The staff is experienced,

capable, fairly compensated, and well adjusted to working in a group situation.

Negatives:
1. The company is now managed by department heads, who may or may not cooperate.
2. You will not know everybody's name, and most likely you will not be entirely clear on the role or value of some departments.
3. You will know only what you hear in the hallways, or what you happen to be told by the boss or coworkers. It will be difficult to gain any meaningful "big picture" unless you are part of senior management—except when the problems are so severe that they cannot be easily corrected without major change.
4. You will work on the projects that you are assigned, or on ones that you manage to sell to clients or to management.
5. You cannot change the company, and you probably can't change your department.

Very Large Companies
Advertising agencies, television networks, and some magazine publishers employ hundreds, even thousands of people. Pros and cons:

Positives:
1. The company's name looks great on the resume, especially if you're in a position of authority.
2. You will meet lots of people and gain a broad view of the activities of a larger company and its industry.
3. There's plenty of opportunity for new jobs, both up and laterally.
4. The pay is usually good; the benefits are even better.
5. You'll have access to people in other parts of the larger company.

Negatives:

1. You become reliant on senior management and exercise relatively little control beyond your very specific area.

2. Although you will meet lots of people and you'll be exposed to many projects, your personal involvement with them will usually be small.

3. Political intrigue will be a way of life.

4. Substantive changes will be made every year or two or three, sometimes with a deep impact on your job. You will not be consulted, unless you are at the highest level or your participation is essential to the new scheme.

5. It's easy to lose yourself in the work and the people and the benefits. It's also easy to get lost and forgotten by all but your coworkers.

Non-Profits

Non-profit companies, or not-for-profits, vary in size, shape, and orientation. Non-profits with a strong imprint in creative endeavors include: performing arts organizations; fine arts organizations; museums; public television stations; and educational institutions.

These particular organizations share several fundamentals:

Often, they operate with other people's money. They are constantly preparing grant proposals, marketing to foundations, pursuing corporate money, and enticing private donors. A high percentage of their annual budget, and an equally high percentage of their project list, is defined by available contributions.

They are conservative, a style preferred by donors and civic organizations.

They tend to be managed by people who specialize in non-profits. This assures a steady flow of incoming contributions and an appropriate slate of current and legacy projects. Most non-profits are not managed by traditional business people, so traditional business thinking may not apply. Awards and community involvement might attract funding; an asset positive balance sheet might not.

Non-profit companies in the arts and education often attract very bright people with little interest in commerce. They work in the arts because they want to work in the arts. This can be confusing for a creative professional accustomed to commercial rules. The long-term political value associated with a particular project might be more important than the immediate concerns of a production—a philosophy radically divergent from the media and marketing world.

Government Organizations

Look carefully, and you'll find some government organizations involved in creative endeavors, marketing, and innovative community development. Education can also be a creative field.

Working for the government is radically different from working for a commercial concern. Government organizations are managed either by political appointees—who will remain for as long as their party is in power—or by long-time public servants. Either way, their behavior and decision-making will be unrelated to the profit-and-loss paradigms associated with commerce. Projects are instead guided by long-time contributions to the community (by building a monument or renovating a public space); political expediency (a particular publication, poster campaign, television, or public relations effort defined solely by its agenda); or simply communicating the essence of particular laws or regulations to particular constituencies.

That said, there is another motivator: doing the right thing. That's what drives teachers and, under the best circumstances, school administrators and school boards. Given relief from political pressures and budget headaches, many government officials will move in a similar direction. They can be dedicated people who work hard to do something positive for their constituents—regardless of the hurdles. These efforts make news, build resumés and serve communities. Also, you'll meet some very influential people and gain plenty of insight about how the world really works.

Types of Companies[9]

"The output of goods and services produced by labor and property located in the United States"[10] is known as the gross domestic product (GDP). In recent years, our GDP has hovered around ten quadrillion dollars (a quadrillion is a trillion times a thousand). Roughly 20 percent of the GDP is related to the broad category called "services"; and roughly the same amount is generated by "finance, insurance and real estate." Just under 10 percent comes from the retail trade, and another 6 percent comes from wholesale trade. State and local governments account for another 8 percent. Those are the largest categories; they account for about two-thirds of the U.S. economy.

The GDP segment known as "communications" accounts for nearly 6 percent of the US economy.[11] What's more, during the period 1995-2000, the communications segment was our second-fastest growing area, second only slightly to the construction segment. The communications industry grows by 7 or 8 percent per year, making it several times more robust than traditionally rich industries like power, agriculture, mining and manufacturing. Communications includes several subcategories:

• Advertising: $177 billion.
• Marketing services and specialty media: $128 billion.
• Consumer end-user spending: $139 billion.
• Institutional end-user spending: $122 billion.

In comparison, mining contributes just over $110 billion to the GDP, less than consumers spend on communications/media products and services. Ditto for the $125 billion agriculture, forestry and fishing segment. Our advertising sector alone is nearly as large as telephone and telegraph, at $200 billion, and nearly as large as electric, gas and sanitary utility, worth $209 billion. The communications segment is also larger than the federal

---

[9] SOURCE: U.S. Department of Commerce, Bureau of Economic Analysis.
[10] SOURCE: Veronis Suhler Communications Industry Forecast; July 2001.
[11] SOURCE: Veronis Suhler Communications Industry Forecast; July 2001.

government ($370 billion), and transportation ($312 billion).

Consumers spend about 3,500 hours per year, or nearly ten hours per day, with media products. Half this time is spent watching television, and it's no surprise that the fastest-growing activity is the Internet. (And, while television, video games, and other screen-based activities are up, older media are declining: Newspapers, books, magazines, recorded music, and radio have all lost hours of attention, typically at a rate of about 1 percent per year.)

According to the same report, the top seventeen communications industry segments were:

1	Newspapers	$66 billion
2	Entertainment	$65 billion
3	Cable & Satellite Television	$63 billion
4	Business Information Services	$48 billion
5	Direct Mail	$45 billion
6	TV Broadcasting	$42 billion
7	Professional, Education & Training	$39 billion
8	B-2-B Promotion	$39 billion
9	Consumer Promotion	$36 billion
10	Consumer Magazines	$21 billion
11	Consumer Internet	$20 billion
12	Radio Broadcasting	$19 billion
13	B-2-B Communications	$18 billion
14	Consumer Books	$18 billion
15	Yellow Pages	$13 billion
16	Sponsorships	$9 billion
17	Outdoor Advertising	$5 billion

You might also consider the size the specific sectors within the creative media and marketing industries (and no, the numbers don't quite match up; the sources calculate their totals differently).

Core Industries of the Creative Economy
by market size in billions of U.S. dollars 1999[12]

Sector	Global	U.S.	U.S. Share
R&D	545	243	44.6%
Publishing	506	137	27.1%
Software	489	325	66.5%
TV and Radio	195	82	42.1%
Music	70	25	35.7%
Film	57	17	29.8%
Toys and Games	55	21	38.2%
Advertising	45	20	44.4%
Architecture	40	17	42.5%
Performing Arts	40	7	17.5%
Crafts	20	2	10.0%
Video Games	17	5	41.7%
Art	9	4	44.4%
TOTAL	**2,240**	**960**	**42.8%**

One way to determine whether a company is likely to be a creative company is to compare R&D budgets (it's not a pure test because so many line items might be included within the R&D category). Compare the company's R&D expenses with sales, profits, percentage of sales spent on R&D, and dollars per employee spent on R&D. For help, make a friend who works in corporate finance.

Standard Industrial Classifications (SIC) Labor Statistics
The Department of Labor uses many of the same classifications as the Department of Commerce. If you're patient, you can learn a lot about the specifics of many jobs within the communications industries. Vast data are available on the Occupational Employment Statistics (OES) section of

---

[12] SOURCE: U.S. Department of Commerce, Bureau of Economic Analysis.

the Department of Labor's Web site at www.bls.gov. How many creative professionals work in the United States? Based on the SIC charts, and my own analysis, I'd estimate around ten million.

SIC CLASSIFICATIONS

SIC Classification	Job Title	Workers	Mean Annual Wage
27-2011	Actors	94,470	$36,790
11-2011	Advertising & Promotion Managers	85,850	$64,690
17-2011	Aerospace Engineers	74,380	$71,380
13-1011	Agents and Business Managers of Artists, Performers, and Athletes	10,270	$62,480
39-2011	Animal Trainers	6,860	$27,280
27-3010	Announcers (Radio, TV, PA)	50,420	$27,590
17-1011	Architects	84,980	$59,590
25-1031	Architecture Teachers, Postsecondary	4,960	$58,070
25-1062	Area, Enthic, and Cultural Studies Teachers, Postsecondary	5,070	$59,650
27-1011	Art Directors	20,880	$65,570
25-1121	Art, Drama, and Music Teachers, Postsecondary	55,540	$51,100
25-1051	Atmospheric, Earth, Marine, and Space Sciences Teachers, Postsecondary	7,630	$64,210
25-9011	Audio-Visual Collections Specialists	10,320	$33,750
19-1021	Biochemists and Biophysicists	16,130	$61,680
25-1042	Biological Science Teachers, Postsecondary	38,580	$64,410
51-5012	Bookbinders	7,500	$27,550
27-4031	Camera Operators, Television, Video, and Motion Picture	22,040	$34,180
25-1052	Chemistry Teachers, Postsecondary	16,610	$58,390
19-2031	Chemists	84,870	$55,880
27-2032	Choreographers	12,660	$32,750
19-3031	Clinical, Counseling, and School Psychologists	95,640	$53,500
27-1021	Commercial and Industrial Designers	33,600	$52,410
25-1122	Communications Teachers, Postsecondary	18,110	$50,640
15-1021	Computer Programmers	501,550	$62,890

SIC Classification	Job Title	Workers	Mean Annual Wage
25-1021	Computer Science Teachers, Postsecondary	29,690	$53,790
15-1031	Computer Software Engineers, Applications	361,690	$72,370
15-1032	Computer Software Engineers, Systems Software	261,520	$74,490
15-1011	Computer and Information Scientists, Research	25,620	$76,970
19-1031	Conservation Scientists	12,750	$49,640
27-2031	Dancers	17,010	$28,770
43-9031	Desktop Publishers	34,860	$33,380
27-3041	Editors	105,130	$44,910
25-1081	Education Teachers, Postsecondary	40,480	$50,680
25-2021	Elementary School Teachers, Except Special Education	1,452,160	$43,320
17-2081	Environmental Engineers	48,700	$62,640
25-1053	Environmental Science Teachers, Postsecondary	3,630	$61,240
19-2041	Environmental Scientists and Specialists, Including Health	57,430	$50,700
27-1022	Fashion Designers	8,890	$56,340
27-4032	Film and Video Editors	13,750	$42,010
27-1013	Fine Artists, Including Painters, Sculptors, and Illustrators	9,710	$38,330
27-1023	Floral Designers	69,660	$20,490
25-1124	Foreign Language and Literature Teachers, Postsecondary	18,590	$49,130
27-1024	Graphic Designers	13,470	$39,670
21-1091	Health Educators	43,890	$38,040
25-1071	Health Specialties Teachers, Postsecondary	85,220	$66,850
25-1125	History Teachers, Postsecondary	16,710	$54,010
27-1025	Interior Designers	39,340	$43,080
25-2012	Kindergarten Teachers, Except Special Education	161,610	$41,100
17-1012	Landscape Architects	17,980	$51,640
39-5091	Makeup Artists, Theatrical and Performance	1,240	$32,050
11-2021	Marketing Managers	189,140	$78,410
17-2141	Mechanical Engineers	204,310	$63,530

SIC Classification	Job Title	Workers	Mean Annual Wage
13-1121	Meeting and Convention Planners	29,560	$39,680
27-1026	Merchandise Displayers and Window Trimmers	49,520	$24,570
25-2022	Middle School Teachers, Except Special and Vocational Education	57,100	$43,750
41-9012	Models	2,930	$22,600
27-1014	Multi-Media Artists and Animators	30,530	$46,700
27-2041	Music Directors and Composers	7,020	$39,330
27-2042	Musicians and Singers	55,100	$46,690
27-3020	News Analysts, Reporters and Correspondents	64,130	$37,800
17-2161	Nuclear Engineers	14,180	$80,200
25-1126	Philosophy and Religion Teachers, Postseconda	14,000	$52,080
27-4021	Photographers	61,250	$27,940
19-2012	Physicists	10,880	$83,750
25-1054	Physics Teachers, Postsecondary	11,830	$65,050
25-2011	Preschool Teachers, Except Special Education	377,540	$20,940
27-2012	Producers and Directors	52,130	$57,160
25-1066	Psychology Teachers, Postsecondary	24,850	$57,140
11-2031	Public Relations Managers	64,920	$64,280
27-3031	Public Relations Specialists	132,390	$45,240
39-9032	Recreation Workers	263,460	$20,270
25-2031	Secondary School Teachers, Except Special and Vocational Education	980,730	$45,370
25-3021	Self-Enrichment Education Teachers	130,440	$32,180
27-1027	Set and Exhibit Designers	7,840	$35,960
25-1067	Sociology Teachers, Postsecondary	12,890	$54,600
27-4014	Sound Engineering Technicians	9,350	$42,300
25-2042	Special Education Teachers, Middle School	87,330	$43,040
25-2041	Special Education Teachers, Preschool, Kindergarten, and Elementary School	211,240	$44,900
25-2043	Special Education Teachers, Secondary School	123,570	$45,670

SIC Classification	Job Title	Workers	Mean Annual Wage
27-3042	Technical Writers	45,900	$51,650
27-3043	Writers and Authors	40,980	$48,120
	TOTAL WORKERS	7,676,690	
	(excludes self-employed)		

Companies with Many Creative Professionals

Fast Company, a magazine that describes life among creative, innovative, new economy companies, profiled designer and architect David Rockwell. The article described the workplace: "At…designers' desks are packets of Crayola crayons, mini-models of NASCAR racers, Buddha prints, Japanese transformer toys, and stacks of reference books. It all adds up to a workplace of 'messy vitality'… where the designers' inspirations are drawn from pop culture, film, and craft."

Apart from the very smallest boutiques, few companies employ exclusively creative professionals. Even the smallest typically employs a non-creative manager or support staff. As companies grow, the ratio favors non-creatives. In most larger companies, departments are set up for creative endeavors, alongside legal, finance, sales, and so on.

Companies whose employees and vendors are likely to include a relatively higher percentage of creative professionals include media firms (book and magazine publishers; television and radio outlets; advertising and public relations agencies), some types of education, and training specialists; Internet publishers and Web developers; some aspects of direct marketing; and event planning and production.

Also: companies that design fashions, toys, games, jewelry, accessories, plus industrial designers. New consumer products are regularly developed and marketed by such giants as Procter & Gamble, Johnson & Johnson, and many smaller companies, too.

Companies with Some Creative Professionals

Many companies or industries employ creative specialists: travel and lodging (particularly upscale destinations, including theme parks and specialty hotel environments); restaurants (both as designer chefs and restaurant designers); retail (merchandising, product selection, design of physical spaces); education (curriculum design, issues related to learning and physical environment); environmental sciences; and product design.

Sony has succeeded on the strength of its innovative products. "If Sony is going to be different from all of the others, it really has to step ahead. We are always trying to come up with something new, to create innovative products. That's basically Sony's DNA. The path is not always smooth. But if you lose your mission, your DNA, you lose your reason for being. Sony's reason for being has always been to create something new, to create more dreams, to make things fun."[13] However, most of the people who work for Sony are not employed in traditionally creative or innovative roles.

Companies (and Industries) with Fewer Creative Professionals

Industries with a limited consumer facing typically offer fewer opportunities for creative people. Still, just about every company maintains some form of marketing department, and within these departments there might be one or several relevant jobs. This is generally true of finance, insurance and real estate (although certain aspects of marketing communications present opportunities). The same thinking applies to government employment. You won't find much opportunity in the agriculture, forestry and fishing sector, nor in the power area, except in marketing. The situation does change from time to time. The long-moribund telephone sector is now a big spender on marketing, in part because of deregulation and the resulting opportunities, and because of the massive marketing push behind cellular phones and Internet connectivity. Transportation periodically becomes an opportunity area, albeit a minor

---

[13] Kunitake Ando, president, Sony Corp., *Fortune*, November 25, 2002.

one. These days, direct-to-consumer pharmaceutical marketing has also created substantial opportunities for creative people.

Beware, however, of making judgments without first understanding the company. Some companies in "non-creative" industries can be very creative. Marketing wizard Seth Godin[14] muses: "How did Dutch Boy stir up the paint business? It's so simple, it's scary. They changed the can. Paint cans are heavy, hard to carry, hard to close, hard to open, hard to pour, and no fun. Yet they've been around for a very long time, and most people assumed there had to be a reason why they were so bad. Dutch Boy realized that there was no reason. They also realized that the can was an integral part of the product: People don't buy paint, they buy painted walls, and the can makes that process much easier. Dutch Boy used that insight and introduced an easier-to-carry, easier-to-pour, easier-to-close paint jug. "People wonder why it took so long for someone to come up with the idea, and they love Dutch Boy for doing it," said Dennis Eckols, group vice president for the home division of Fred Meyer stores.

Creativity and Innovation as an Economic Engine

Former U.S. Secretary of State William Bennett reflected the widely held government and business view of creativity's place when he wrote, "The arts deserve serious attention. True, learning about them is not as essential as knowing how to read, write, add, and subtract when it comes to earning a diploma or landing most jobs. That's why our utilitarian society neglects arts. But they are important for all our children in other ways. A fully educated person knows something about them because many magnificent expressions of the human intellect and spirit lie in this realm."

When the discussion turns to the importance of creative people in the economic arena, I endorse the views of Richard Florida,[15] as he links the deeply related concepts of technology development, tolerant

---

[14] SOURCE: From "10 Ways to Raise a Purple Cow" by Seth Godin, *Fast Company,* February 2003.

[15] SOURCE: Richard Florida, *The Rise of the Creative Class,* pp. 249-266.

communities, and the likelihood that such places will draw progressively larger populations of talented people. Immigration statistics, the gay population (ties back to tolerance), Florida's Bohemian index (a count of artists, musicians, etc.), and diversity also impact economic growth. Simplistically: San Francisco, Boston, Seattle, Los Angeles, and Atlanta are "more creative" than Detroit and Buffalo. Cities on the edge are recognizing the importance of attracting and keeping people like us.

For example, an organization called Innovation Philadelphia is attempting to enhance "the global innovation economy of Philadelphia" through increased entrepreneurial development and early-stage investment; support of university research; strategies to reduce "brain drain" by assisting in "the development of a world-class, lifelong learning environment;" and enhancing "the global image of Philadelphia as a leader in the knowledge economy."[16]

Why Creative People Aren't Businesspeople

Apart from some very specific types of companies or departments where creative people are likely to work, most companies tend not to hire more than a small number of creative people as full-time employees. This tendency exists, in part, because creative people are generally perceived as employees who are hired to serve specific business functions (and these functions can easily be outsourced to an individual contractor or an agency). In the business world, a life sentence as a creative professional may not be such a wonderful thing. And an employer who hires a creative professional for a traditional role ought to have his or her head examined.

Creative People Are Unfamiliar With Business Realities

Creative people in a business setting? Bad idea! A business book for creative people? Now there's a great idea—I can just imagine some creative ding-dong running, and ruining, General Motors. They'll change every rule,

---

[16] SOURCE: http://www.ipphila.com.

insist on painting every car orange or purple; rewrite the warranties so that they're fair to everyone; then never show up for work on time. It's chaos, I tell you! A bona fide Wall Street disaster!! And please don't show them the numbers. They'll never understand them anyway....

Folks, we've got a big problem here. Business people—real business people—don't trust us, and would prefer that we remain as far from the kitchen as possible.

What makes creative people and business people think of themselves as so different from one another? To explore, I've set up this chart. Note the differences in short- and long-term thinking, and in narrow vs. broad thinking.

TOPIC	Traditional Business People	Creative Professionals
Business Structure	A constant, a reliable foundation of any business.	A variable, useful for only as long as the system works.
Change	Generally undesirable, except to correct course in a conservative, well-planned manner.	Essential to the life and growth of any business endeavor.
Organization Chart	Provides leadership and direction from the top down.	Useful only if those at the top provide clear guidance and resources to those throughout the organization.
Business Purpose	Generate profits.	Generate value, which is measured by more than simply quarterly profits.
Sales	Sales is the most important aspect of any business.	A business is a holistic system. Sales will succeed if the entire system works properly.
"Cool Company"	Building and maintaining a "cool company" is secondary to mainstream business concerns.	A business is only as good as its people, and the coolest people are likely to be attracted to the coolest companies.
Monthly and Quarterly Numbers	Monthly and quarterly numbers matter more than trends.	Trends matter more than quarterly numbers.
Managing Expenses	The place to save money is to cut headcount.	If a business's only option is headcount reduction, it has been poorly managed.
Measurement of Long-Term Value	Best measured by analyzing its numbers.	Best measured by its overall impact on the marketplace.

To observers of contemporary business, the second column might seem old-fashioned and conservative. In the third, seeds of the epidemic that destroyed the dot-coms and other fast companies can be detected.

At one company, the head of sales presented weekly and monthly sales numbers in spreadsheet form. When sales were down, someone on the management committee would inevitably ask how much was sold in the same week of the previous year. The team wanted a clearer picture of what was happening, and why. More data were produced, but sales continued to falter. How bad was the problem? Were sales down at our company, or throughout the industry? Were we actually selling more than before, but at a greater cost?

Trend analysis was part of the finance group's responsibilities, but that group was reluctant to take on the additional work. Other departments took the data and built their own trend charts. The management team began using them. Here, the creative and technical teams conspired to get the information out, and in time, the trend charts became an important management tool.

The trend charts came about, in part, because the creative people were struggling with complicated spreadsheets. They wanted a picture, not a matrix of numbers. It turns out that other departments and managers found the picture valuable, too. This is why I'm advocating an enlightened form of teamwork, where MBAs and creative people are valued in equal measure. Utilize the drive and global thinking associated with creative professionals, and encourage them to better understand the intricacies of financial and operational details.

To be more specific, it now becomes our responsibility to understand their world. Every creative professional should learn how to read and understand financial reports—balance sheets, profit/loss statements, cash flows, budgets, and sales reports. Creative managers should insist on attending meetings related to these issues, at first to learn, then to contribute. Going out on sales calls, spending time in the customer service center, even taking a few management courses and reading some *Portable MBA* books (see page 366)—all of these ideas pave a road for yourself and for future creative professionals to take more of a role in the business community.

Creative people who prefer to work only in their own creative domains, learning little about business, might seal their own fate. Business people control the budgets and, in today's economy, they also control the size of the company's payroll. In the eyes of a hard-nosed business person, a creative professional who takes the time to understand the company's operations and manages his projects accordingly will be far more likely to win the business game than a creative who simply writes or designs with talent and skill.

Creative People Care Only About Creative Projects

Creative people are paid to develop and produce creative projects—that's how we spend our time and that's why people pay us. I'm certainly not suggesting that anyone "phone it in," but I am asking that we get our head out of the sand from time to time and look around.

Creative work can be all-consuming, intense, and great fun. There's nothing better in this world than going to work every day in an expensive car, heading into an office with far too many toys and fun people, and writing jokes for *The Simpsons* all day. For a very tiny percentage of creative people, that's all they want to do, all they'll ever want to do. And many of them will be extraordinarily successful by any measure.

Most of us aren't sufficiently talented to write for *The Simpsons*, not funny or clever or quick-witted or savvy enough, or willing to relocate to Los Angeles, etc. Instead, more of us work in more commonplace jobs, often the coolest jobs in the company: designing ads and marketing campaigns; working out innovative retail environments; figuring out how to sell more products from the first three pages of next month's catalog; inventing new animated characters for video games; or coming up with innovative ways to engage young minds with educational products that are both silly and remarkably effective.

How about exerting a higher level of control over the work you do?

Choosing or managing the team? Controlling what actually gets made, and how it gets made? There's a conceptual and motivational leap from sitting at a computer designing all day (which is great fun and a wonderful creative challenge, not to minimize that sort of work in any way) and sitting in meetings. Admittedly, many meetings are non-productive, boring, and a waste of time. Some meetings, and your continued participation in them, perhaps in place of doing creative work in your own small work space, can really open your eyes to the possibilities and to the broader range of options available to many creative people.

Lack of Involvement With Other Aspects of Business

It's interesting to observe employees at lunch in a company cafeteria. The financial people sit at one table, the customer service people at another. Management sometimes sits with the workers, but more often they flock together at their own corner tables, or huddle in their private offices. Party tonight? You can invite people you work with. Problem with another employee or with a boss? You might communicate first with the coworkers in your department, then maybe escalate the issue to human resources. Working at home? Check your e-mail list, and aside from family members and old friends, how many people on the list do more or less what you do every day?

Creative professionals: We all need to get out more!

Creative People Don't Follow Business Logic

To some degree, creative professionals work for different reasons than other people. This is perceived by business leaders, and might go to the heart of the problem.

Certainly, most employees who work for companies of any size do so for the paycheck. But that's an oversimplification. Daily employment means a place to go every day, an opportunity to interact with others in a community. Apart from money, belonging is probably the greatest need satisfied by the contemporary workplace. Creative people exhibit belonging needs, but our needs only begin at the belonging level of Maslow's Heirarchy of Needs (see below). Creative professionals regularly exhibit three additional needs that are not as often central to the lives of other workers. We overdose on cognitive needs—the need to know, to understand and explore—and often, we are quite public in exhibiting this need. We are also mystified and sometimes dumbfounded when others question this need. Aesthetic needs are fundamental to our work; we hold ourselves to a high standard and constantly learn to improve our technique and our skill set. Many creative professionals also equate their work with some form of self-actualization; we are sometimes unable to separate our work from our lines, and we sometimes derive at least part of our self-image from the work we do. Others do this, too, but creative professionals obsess about it, and often.

For your reference, here's Maslow's heirarchy:

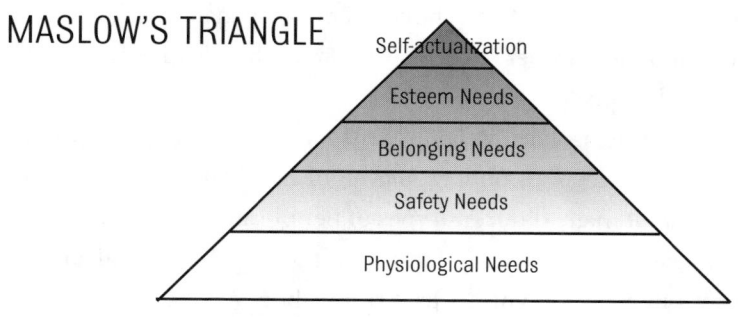

The Benefits of Creative Leadership and Management

"The guy's a genius! If he can produce a blockbuster motion picture, he can certainly run this studio!"

Well, sometimes it works (Walt Disney) and sometimes it doesn't (best left unmentioned). Very early in our careers, creative people are taught to take responsibility for our work. We're taught that quality matters. That cooperation among peers is the way to get things done. That the big picture matters more than any individual detail. That constant learning is vital. Some of us take on enormous responsibility at a relatively young age; it's unusual to place complete project responsibility on a young lawyer, for example, but it's not uncommon to find a twenty-nine-year-old producer in charge of a new MTV series. We learn valuable lessons early, lessons that other people never learn, or seem to forget on the way to the top.

There are plenty of good reasons why traditional executives ignore or dismiss professionals who came up through the creative side. And plenty of ammunition, based largely on the reinforcement of stereotypes that can keep us away from just about every management job, at every level. We're flaky; we lack the proper college degrees; we're outspoken, improperly trained, unreliable, too liberal, and unlikely to focus on any truly important topic for more than a few minutes—you know, we all have ADD, and we all suffer from short attention spans. What's more, we don't understand the numbers. And if we elevate the creative leader, who is going to take her place?

Well now, this is hardly fair. Management of creative projects requires a very high level of understanding of many disparate parts, and the coordination of many different types of people and skill sets. We learn responsibility early, and we understand what accountability is all about— we do not let our team down, it's part of our honor code. Can we learn the numbers? At first, the numbers might seem boring, and certainly the way that they are presented would put just about anybody to sleep. In order to succeed in management, though, you must understand how the numbers work: revenues, cost of sales, budgeted expenses, depreciation, valuation of assets, and so on. None of this is impossible to learn. You can read, learn from others, and/or enroll in an MBA program. The only really tricky part of the formula is the replacement factor: You won't get the management job if the company believes that you are essential to the creative process. You must take the risk, and hire the best possible team, including one or more likely successors.

Managers who have come up from the creative side offer important skills and perspectives that are generally absent or thinly represented among other managers. First and foremost, we come at the role with new perspectives and the energy and enthusiasm to make a difference. Second, we are not afraid of change; we are likely to question why the business operates as it does, and at the risk of embarrassing those who have been sitting too long in one place, we challenge the company to improve. And then, we provide a clear path (here's where the concept-to-completion training becomes a huge advantage). We can show the way. And we can inspire employees to follow and put their hearts into their work. A solid creative leader can shift the dynamics of departmental or company management.

From the individual creative professional's point of view, there's more control and input with regard to company activities, a higher salary and better overall compensation, and the opportunity to serve as a role model and mentor for the next generation of managers.

From both the company's and the individual manager's perspective, there's a higher than average level of risk. If you don't handle the situation well, you could be perceived as a creative person wearing a business mask. Other managers might not take you seriously. This can become a tough situation: You're no longer a creative, not quite the manager you thought you could be. You might not be very good at this type of job, after all. (Sigh.) It's easy to underestimate the number of weeks, months, years required to truly feel comfortable in this role, or to evaluate the amount of time spent dealing with politics.

The company might put you on a short leash, limiting your responsibilities and/or decision-making power until it's sure that you're not going to really screw things up. Truthfully, if you've made it into the job, you'll probably do fine. But there's another possible pitfall: You might do a very good job, but your way of working (challenging assumptions, encouraging improvement, emphasizing the importance of the best people) could threaten others.

With two chapters down, it's up to you to define your package and how it fits into the marketplace. A variation on the Balanced Scorecard[17], used by MBAs and executives to define a company's strategy, is a good way to do this. The following exercise should help to consolidate your thinking about the first quarter of this book.

DEFINING YOUR PACKAGE

This chart should be easy enough to complete, but I suggest you begin by working off the chart, on four sheets of paper or large index cards.
Label each sheet and simply make a list. Then, try to prioritize each item before you write them into the chart below.
(You'll find a useful prioritization tool on page 313. It can be applied here as well.)

STRENGTHS: MY CURRENT ASSETS	WEAKNESSES: WEAK POINTS THAT CAN BE FIXED
1.	1.
2.	2.
3.	3.
4.	4.
5.	5.
OPPORTUNITIES: ASSETS WORTH DEVELOPING	THREATS: ISSUES LIKELY TO REMAIN ISSUES
1.	1.
2.	2.
3.	3.
4.	4.
5.	5.

---

[17] For more information, see Robert S. Kaplan and David P. Norton, *The Balanced Scorecard*, HBS Press, 1996.

You might use this tool to analyze your current situation within a particular job or company—do you have any opportunity for advancement? Or, you might use it to analyze a new job offer.

You might also use the chart to look at yourself as an employee vs. a freelancer. Should you start your own company or continue to work as a solo act? You'll be impressed by the tool's usefulness and flexibility.

CHAPTER 3 - Managing Resources

This chapter covers three areas: time, space, and the tools used to do creative work.

Managing Time

Ben Franklin said, "If you love life, then do not squander time, for that is the stuff that life is made of."

I schedule my time, but I can lose hours deep in my work. Like many people, I know precisely what must be accomplished each day, week, or month, but when I head into a new project, I lose track of time. Perhaps this behavior is familiar to you, too.

Flow

According to the altogether brilliant author, Mihaly Csikszentmihalyi, "flow" is a quality of a deeply involving experience, an activity that "stretches the person's capacity and involves an element of novelty and discovery." Csikszentmihalyi identifies nine aspects of flow:[1]

---

[1] SOURCE: Mihaly Csikszentmihalyi, *Creativity: Flow and the Psychology of Discovery and Invention*, (Harper Collins, 1996).

- Clear goals every step of the way
- Immediate feedback
- Balance between challenge and skill
- A merger of action and awareness
- An exclusion of distractions
- No worry of failure
- No self-consciousness
- The activity as an end in itself
- A distorted sense of time

When I'm deep in a creative work, all of the above are true.

What's interesting is that after extensive research, Csikszentmihalyi found these traits common among athletes, artists, religious mystics, scientists, and ordinary people who described their most rewarding experiences with remarkably similar words.

Flow is not a place that most creative professionals visit for more than a few hours per day because of that vast field of muck between you and your good work.

Basics of Time Management
Start by clearing away some interpersonal clutter.

If you're working in a company where meetings are scheduled throughout the day, you won't find yourself with a solid hour for quiet desk work. Those responsible for creative deadlines must speak up: "If you want the design by Friday, I can't be stuck in meetings all day Wednesday and Thursday."

If people nearby are noisy and distracting, quiet them down or move to a physical space where you can get work done. Combine polite reminders with visual reinforcement: a hotel door's hang-tag works: "Do Not Disturb." (And if you're messy, try flipping the tag when the day's work is done: "Please Clean Room." Maybe someone will.)

At home, time-clutter from loved ones must be managed; kids need to understand when it's okay to disturb their work-at-home mom or dad.

I figure, if a four-year-old can understand the idea, there's hope for a forty-year-old boss in the office.

Next, clear your mind so that you can settle down and work. Or is it?: "I'll start working just as soon as the *Brady Bunch* is over." "Why can't I find the latest version of the creative brief?" "I wonder whether there are any more sandwiches in the conference room?" "Maybe if I go to the gym this afternoon and do the comic strip tonight?" "There's no way I should be doing this much work for so little money!" "Maybe a nap first?" "What I really should do is research. If I do the research first, the writing will go faster." "This deadline is ridiculous. I'm going to have to stay up all night to get this work done. And if I have to stay up all night, I'm going to need some food, and I'm not going to want to get interrupted later, so it makes sense for me not to start working now, but to get some food now, and while I'm out, I can also pick up some supplies, and maybe catch the DaVinci exhibit at the museum when it's not too crowded like it will be on Saturday."

And, when you're ready to work—you discover you're out of pencils; the printer cartridge is out of toner; the file is missing; or your computer trashes your e-mail. All of this is just muck—separating you from productive work.

Preliminary preparation and research are parts of the process. When a designer scours the Web for useful images, she is teaching herself what the project ought to, and ought not to, look like. When you're making thumbnails or first drafts and tossing most of them, you're in the useful process of focusing. Your mind is learning how to think about the specific project, training itself while you're doing the mundane chores associated with starting something new.

Advertising executive Jack Keil, whose voice you know from the "Take a bite out of crime" public service announcements, recalled:[2] "While I concentrated on the basic problems of the moment (phone

[2] SOURCE: John Keil, *The Creative Mystique*, New York: John Wiley & Sons, 1985, pp. 17-18.

calls... decisions and so forth) for one hour, the subconscious mind kept probing and dissecting various solutions to the big problem. So when the morning ended, I had a solution. The simmering on the back burner had helped. But to simmer, something's got to be in the pot. And knowing what that something is—and when to let it simmer—is a creative instinct born of experience."

Tod Machover, who studies and applies his ideas about the future of music at Massachusetts Institute of Technology's Media Lab, "speaks of the benefits in having numerous projects on different time tracks to completion: 'I think it's interesting to simultaneously set up problems that have different time scales...This may sound familiar—short-term/long-term investment balance. But time frame also affects the way people see, think, and behave with respect to innovation. We all think differently about a one-year project than we do about a ten-year project.'"[3]

Billable Time

Lawyers often bill by the hour in five-minute segments. After each meeting or phone call, the attorney notes the client's name and the time spent. At the end of each month, software calculates and bills the attorney's time by client.

How can anybody account for every minute of every day? Here's an hour from my life as a senior executive of a public company.

11:00 - 11:05 A.M.	Hunt for a chocolate chip cookie
11:05 - 11:10 A.M.	Approve a new logo and color palette
11:10 - 11:15 A.M.	Hallway discussion about a new hire
11:15 - 11:25 A.M.	Walk around and make sure the staff is okay
11:25 - 11:35 A.M.	Schmooze boss, gently suggest need for management meeting
11:35 - 11:45 A.M.	Poke around Web, hoping to solve a client's problem with a brilliant idea

[3] SOURCE: Shira White, *New Ideas About New Ideas*, pp. 159-160.

| 11:45 - 11:50 A.M. | Outline the idea, interrupted by three brief phone calls |
| 11:58 - 11:59 A.M. | Start again on the outline, interrupted this time for a vitally important emergency lunch meeting |

On the one hand, it's sad that part of my adult life continues to rely upon a search for cookies. On the other, I accomplished a lot in an hour. Note that I set aside at least ten minutes out of every hour for informal conversations with co-workers. Creative work requires more than a few minutes between phone calls; on this particular day, the work was done over take-out sushi after everyone else had gone home.

Can this activity be billed hourly? Advertising agencies do it, but most other creative concerns bill by the project, not the billable hour.

In fact, I play both sides: executive in the office, author in my home/office. Here's what happens to that same hour at home:

11:00 - 11:01 A.M.	Get chocolate chip cookie from the jar downstairs
11:01 - 11:02 A.M.	Select and play appropriate CD
11:03 - 11:06 A.M.	Clear the latest e-mails
11:07 - 11:59 A.M.	Write, without interruption

With fewer interruptions, I get more done when working at home. I could bill most of an hour to a client. However, as people who work at home know, most hours aren't nearly as efficient. How do you account for an hour taking a walk? You could make a case for thinking while walking, but it's hardly billable time.

Your Clock vs. the World's Clock

If it's okay to dedicate an entire book to someone, I suppose it's okay to dedicate a section of book as well. This section is dedicated to my friend, the author Stewart Wolpin.

I met Stewart when he was an R&D manager at John Wiley & Sons, a book publisher. Stewart hired me to develop and produce the company's first line of books on audiotape (our first title was Jack Keil's *The Creative Mystique*). Stewart came up through the editorial ranks, but he really wanted to be a full-time writer.

Fast-forward a decade or so. It's 9:30 A.M. and the telephone rings. Stewart wakes, startled and a bit annoyed that a new publicist has called to pitch him a story so early in the morning; most publicists know to call him after eleven. It's time for a shower, a bite of lunch (or breakfast, or whatever), then a call with an editor and a telephone interview for research, then a mid-afternoon movie. When Stewart returns around four, he turns on The History Channel (his background music) and goes to work. Taking his customary break for David Letterman, he finishes at 3 A.M. He relaxes an hour, then gets his seven hours of sleep. In fact, Stewart worked nine or ten hours. He just re-jiggered his schedule to write at night, when he can work without interruption, and catch a movie by day, when Manhattan's theaters aren't crowded. Stewart designed a practical solution to the workaday world, one that's custom-tailored to him. He's also remarkably efficient: "The idea is that I go to bed when I'm really tired, so I fall to sleep immediately instead of forcing myself to sleep; this allows me to spend less time in the sack," he explains with perfect logic.

Recently, Stewart and I worked together on a television series. He wrote it, I executive produced. One of my responsibilities was approving his written material. We developed a system that worked for both of us. He wrote on his usual schedule. When I started my day at 9:30 A.M., I checked my e-mail and spent the morning editing the material that he'd submitted around 3 A.M. By the time Stewart was up and running at noon, my comments were waiting in his mailbox, and he was ready to rewrite. Each day, Stewart wrote late into the night. Sometimes, we'd chat by e-mail around midnight; I was shutting down for the night, while he was in his midday. (The same might apply to someone in another time zone, but this was more like a collaboration between New York and Fiji.) The system worked beautifully because Stewart managed his time so well.

Stewart can serve as a model for another attribute of creative people with regard to time: adaptability. I've seen Stewart work twenty-four hours in a row, without sleep, and out-produce any three other writers, often with superior material. Why? Because Stewart is a trained creative professional—the sort of person who would, in some parallel universe, carry an advanced-level license to do creative work.

I've seen my father do the same thing while producing a variety show. Once, in L.A., he pulled an all-night video editing session, not unusual for producers. When I arrived to pick him up in the morning, the room smelled of hours-old Chinese food. Three members of his production staff had been sleeping since midnight. Dad had been editing for over twenty-four hours, and was still making sharp decisions. The videotape editor had gone home to sleep; another had come and gone after a twelve-hour shift; and the original one had returned. My father never stopped; he needed to get the show done. My dad ought to be a licensed professional. Those with inferior skills, attitudes, or without clarity of vision need not apply.

The Price You Pay

There's a price to behaving this way. For my father, there were a few crazy days, and then he went home, slept it off, and returned to the normal daytime working world. Stewart has fashioned his own home life so that he's sufficiently in-sync with others to enjoy a social life and find time to catch his movies, along with a remarkable number of Mets and Yankees games. Not everyone is so skillful, careful, practiced, talented, or as good with time.

Long-term, though, it's no fun to work while everyone else is sleeping, or to sleep until everyone else is having lunch. You feel weird, and people treat you like you're from another planet. For a creative person who lives so much of his life through imagination, it's terribly important to remain a part of real life. A project might be compelling, but real life ought to be more interesting than the stuff that came out of your head.

Stephen Sondheim wrote a song for his Broadway musical *Sunday in the Park With George* that expresses the sentiment of the artist, the problem he creates for himself, and the ultimate sadness in completing the project but losing a part of life along the way. Called "Finishing the Hat," the song is one of several from that show that expresses the inner struggles of creative people.

Efficient Use of Time

If you're working on an interesting project, it's easy to forget or ignore the amount of money you're receiving in exchange for your time. You might spend more time, and consider the time an investment in personal development or potential future projects. Still, you should be mindful of the time a project requires and the additional time you devote to the project, for love or perfection. Or because of inefficiencies that can sink you: lousy planning; poor use of time by others; limited resources; an inability to get started because of client or inter-departmental delays; a lack of understanding of the project's real requirements prior to accepting the job; or a deadline that forces a "just work hard and do the best you can" approach. To some extent, you can plan for these little nightmares. Ultimately, they are a cost of doing business.

How to become more efficient? Try logging your time by the quarter hour, like a lawyer. Rather than assigning time by client, log it using these categories:

- Planning the assignment
- Gathering supplies
- Gathering research and resources
- Studying the research
- Developing the project design
- Spending time on the phone or in meetings with the client
- Spending time on the phone or in meetings with co-workers
- Putting together a draft or prototype
- Getting input

- Revising
- Completing
- Packaging for delivery

Add the number of hours spent on each categorized activity on your list. Patterns will emerge. Maybe you're spending half your time in meetings. Maybe you spend a little time planning and a lot of time revising.

Log for four weeks. Then, analyze the results, perhaps with the help of a market researcher or a financial analyst. Once you understand your working patterns—the real ones you've logged, not the ones you vaguely perceive—you can develop a plan to work more efficiently. Then, each month for the next six months, log a typical work week, work through the analysis, and set some new goals for yourself. Over time, you will notice some changes in the way you spend your work hours.

Why bother? You'll work under less pressure. You will earn more money per hour of effort. Your output might improve, and your work habits will become more fluid (it's better to plan than revise, for example). Also, you learn not only how to delegate, but also what to delegate, and what to hold onto for yourself.

Some people become fans of this logging-and-analysis process. It's a helpful regimen for career development and estimating future jobs. If you begin each new project with a written estimate (which you keep on file for yourself, not necessarily for a client or employer), then track actual time expenditure and analyze the results, you'll develop a keen sense of how you spend your time and how you earn your money. This can be very valuable knowledge.

Budgeting Against Unknowns

Most projects move smoothly. A revision here, a change order there, but overall, the project planned is the project delivered.

Some projects are bumpy: A key person leaves; the client changes his mind; the individual client is replaced by someone else with different opinions; the timetable is compressed; the money doesn't show up on time; and so on. With skill and experience, you can usually manage through these problems.

The Project from Hell

And then, along comes a project from hell. Sometimes there are clues, but in the early stages, clues masquerade as a client or employer's peculiar way of working. The client might seem bright, passionate, well-intentioned, and experienced. The initial project specification might be slightly vague or dubious. These are not uncommon early stage characteristics; in fact, a creative professional's job often involves sorting out the early stage clutter. So, you dutifully gather the available information, meet the people, take plenty of notes, and then you go away to make sense of what you've learned. You return with assorted preliminary ideas. The first tell-tale clue emerges: a lengthy discussion about a tangential topic. Is the client distracted? Does he not understand the important matters that must be resolved at this meeting in order to stay on schedule? Is he trying to send you some sort of message? You try to focus the conversation. The feedback is not everything you hoped for, so you can't quite move from point A to point B—yet. You allow a few days to sort it out and set up a next meeting as soon as possible.

The next meeting is somewhat uncomfortable. You find yourself pushing for answers and suggesting possible strategies to keep the train moving on the right track. The client is not focusing, or he is again pursuing what you believe to be a tangent, or he is revisiting the initial creative concept, or referring to important people who are mysteriously unavailable.

You are in trouble. At this point, there is no way to accurately plan your time, stick to a schedule, or estimate the cash that might be sacrificed during this wayward journey.

What to do? First, resist thinking of yourself as a hero or a victim. Nothing here says that the show must go on, or that you must stay with it. If the project isn't personally or professionally important, you might politely suggest alternate vendors. If the project is important, you can dig in and try to wrestle control. You might find that you can manage certain aspects of the project (which might be enough to get the job done), and with luck, you might turn it into a win. Often, these situations end with good results, even though they cost more time and money than planned. More often, if the project is flawed from the start, it never recovers. The problem project might be delayed, or canceled; the creative leader or team might be fired. In the worst situation, lawyers become involved, attempting to affix liability, or to recoup monies lost. What's more, the project might flop (then again, even a well-focused, perfectly managed project might flop).

Prepare for the worst. Hope for the best.

Budgeting Time for Projects of Varying Size

One of the key differentiators between creative professionals and other types of workers is our adaptability to divergent projects. A stage director, for example, finds that no two productions are alike—each requires its own plan. Writing an article about Sunday markets in France is not the same as writing an article about Thailand's floating markets. Painting a mural is not much like painting a magazine illustration.

When I start work on a book, the number of words in the manuscript is prescribed in the contract. I use this figure and the ultimate delivery date as a basis for planning the entire project; you are reading about 100,000 words in this book. I don't think in terms of words, I think in terms of manuscript pages. I know that each manuscript page contains, on average, 250 words. Dividing 100,000 by 250 gets a 400-page manuscript of eight chapters, each fifty pages long. One week per chapter, eight weeks of writing, plus two more at the end for rewrites, adding missing facts and stories, and polishing. Best not to do this all in one session, but instead to spread it over six months, as the contract allows.

A TV series schedule is more complex because it coordinates multiple work groups. Scripts require the longest lead time; besides, most departments cannot work without completed scripts. For twenty episodes, I might allow three weeks for each individual script to be written, rewritten, and polished. That's sixty weeks—too long because the delivery date is six months away. Two writers can do the work in thirty weeks; four writers can do it in fifteen weeks. (I'd add another three weeks for rewrites due to multiple voices; each series must have a consistent voice.) Two months in, there will be enough scripts complete to start the production staff on casting, scenic design and construction, costumes, music, and so on. The work of each department relies upon several others; the result is an interlocking schedule that ultimately assures the whole project's timely completion.

The Importance of Planning

When things don't go well in the theater, it's often because the underlying script was not adequately developed, or because the director did not think through every move. This lack of proper planning is often the root cause of difficulties in motion pictures and television series as well. This quip sums it up:

"If it ain't on the page, it ain't on the stage."

Those who manage film and television productions encourage the creative team to make decisions early—and to stay with those decisions. Changes are costly, more so as production progresses. A writer's change in an early draft costs only a few hours or days. The same change in a later draft burns time for the writer, director, and perhaps several performers who began to memorize their lines or walk through the parts. When the director makes the change during rehearsals, everyone must wait for the rewrite, and then scenic plans or construction must be stopped (and, perhaps, some materials discarded), actors must unlearn, logistics must be undone. The same change during a late-stage rehearsal might involve throwing away finished scenery, props, and costumes, and late night stress as a replacement scene is written, rehearsed, and staged. If the project is a film, an editor might spend hours reworking other elements in order to cover for the last-minute decision. Which means:

"A dollar spent in development is worth ten dollars in pre-production, one hundred dollars in production, and one thousand dollars in post-production." (This is so often said, it's tough to know who said it first.)

Advertising, architecture, Web, and design clients sometimes hurry. With no time to think through a strategy, adequate work is done quickly. Often, rushing causes problems. As a result of a speedy timetable, more money is spent, often for lesser results. Another popular saying:

"Pay me now to design it properly, or pay me more later to fix it."

Delivery and the Final 2 Percent

One of the peculiar aspects of creative work is the amount of time and effort required to close a project and deliver all of its components. You work for weeks or months on a project, and everything falls into place. Here and there, a clearance or a photo is missing, or a bit of research. Something is too long and will eventually need to be edited. Pieces are moved around, so the entire project must be reviewed for continuity. There are a million small details, and it's nearly impossible to accurately forecast the amount of time required to complete each one.

The best way to minimize the impact of that final 2 percent of work is to deal with every detail as it comes along. Don't allow the to-do list to become too long. If this is impossible, then multiply your estimate of the closing by 300, 400, even 500 percent.

When you do deliver, be sure you make copies of every single deliverable. Assume that the client will lose, break, or otherwise mishandle anything and everything. When you package the project, be sure to label every piece: You will not remember specifics in a year or two. Also, be sure to provide all backup documentation, and keep copies of this material on file, too.

The next time you begin a big project and you're budgeting time, be sure to re-read this little section. It's so easy to underestimate the time required to close.

Managing Space

Until the 1970s, most elementary school classrooms looked the same: desks arranged in rows, students placed in alphabetical order by last name, teacher in the front, blackboard behind her. No frills, nothing in the room besides a blackboard, students, a teacher, a noisy radiator, maybe some posters or a cursive writing chart, a clock, perhaps a hamster cage. Fast forward to the present day. Desks are clustered in workgroups, set asymmetrically to optimize the space. The room has no front, back or sides; the teacher selects his position based on the activity. The hamster is part of a small zoo. There are computers, a TV, VCR, DVD, CD player, a library of useful books, a quiet corner, a sink, and perhaps a bathroom. The room is carpeted and probably air-conditioned, a far more pleasant year-round learning environment.

The old arrangement spoke of discipline—students faced the authority figure ceremonially positioned at the front of the room. The newer arrangement speaks to collaboration. Here, the teacher is a guide, not a disciplinarian.

Offices have changed, too. Private offices are less common, except among senior managers and executives. Cubicles simulate offices, but because they lack doors and windows, they encourage social interaction. The dot-com companies pushed collaborative design further with workspaces that resembled open-plan newsrooms. Space previously connoting respect and authority has been replaced by communal work areas. MBWA ("Management by Walking Around") has changed the way bosses and employees work together; meetings might be brief and informal.

Open environments can be problematic for people who need quiet in order to get work done. Open space can also be confounding for the writer, artist or other creative professional who works best while listening to music (and, often, it must be just the right music to match the specific work project, or the time, day, weather, or mood). Working under headphones all day is a lousy solution. Ditto a work environment where each individual discreetly plays barely audible music through cheap PC speakers.

On the other hand, for people who are energized by others, the open environment is a dream come true. Instant meetings tend to be brief, unstructured, and often decisive. Under the right circumstances, there's a wonderful upbeat team spirit that feeds on itself.

Working at home, or in a very small office, you get the privacy, but you sacrifice human interaction. That's good for some people, but lonely and possibly depressing for others.

Before you accept your next job, explore the space where you will actually work. Do you really need your own office? Why? Would you benefit from more human interaction every day? Does the place look right, feel right? Is it too noisy or too quiet? As you answer those questions, don't think only in terms of your past work habits. Think about the positive changes in your life that could be promoted by a change in work space.

The Effect of Environment on Creative Work

When I was in college, I often took the overnight bus from Rochester to New York. There was a three-hour layover in Scranton, from 2 A.M. to 5 A.M. I never felt safe sleeping in the skanky bus terminal, so I sometimes wrote a script for a college radio drama series to pass the time. Ancient vending machines provided the only food; the few other humans were homeless and sometimes, deranged. At the time, I was writing crime drama; maybe the environment helped my work.

Today, I'm writing in a cushioned leather chair, with a jazz saxophone playing a ballad on a wonderful stereo system. The space is clean, well-lit and comfortable. To be honest, my writing process has little to do with the physical environment; it happens mainly in my head. I wrote most of a book about blues performers while holed up in plain vanilla Marriott hotel rooms around the country. Now that I'm taking drawing classes, I regularly see stunning sketches of human forms done by students drawing while crunched up against their locker doors.

Of course, I'd prefer writing in my home office to Scranton's bus station. In fact, I've devoted a whole lot of time and attention (and money) making my workspace great. Most likely, you've done the same, or you will in the future.

Light

Painters in the northern hemisphere's most populous regions often prefer a large window with northern light. Windows facing east or west flood the room with harsh sunlight; in the northern hemisphere, for much of the year, the sun's arc is in the southern sky, so a southern exposure also provides harsh light. On the other hand, northern light is consistent, never harsh and less subject to the bluish haze of morning light and the orange haze of sunset. Painters also appreciate natural light with its wide color spectrum; incandescent light is yellow-orange and fluorescent light tends toward a yucky alien blue-green. Direct artificial illumination can be harsh. Ambient, reflected light is always preferable.

An artist who mainly works in Adobe Photoshop might be invigorated by natural light but has no greater need for a big window than any other office worker. If you argue about how the artist's soul hungers for invigoration through contact with nature, your co-workers will tell you to shut up and take a walk. Go outside instead. At least once a week, combine a one-on-one meeting with a stroll. Schedule group meetings in a nearby park, under a tree. The excellent professor who took his class outside on nice days had the right idea—it's your job as a creative thinker to change the way your department or company works. I regularly abduct meetings to outdoor locations; I suggest you do the same.

Color

Color expert Shigenobu Kobayashi[5] associates colors with feelings and moods, and also with regions of the world. For example, northern climates are more likely to use the deeper, darker reds that we tend to associate with the outside of a British pub or a streetcar or a Chinese restaurant.

---

[5] SOURCE: *Colorist: A Practical Handbook for Personal and Professional Use* (Kodansha, 1998).

You'll find powdery blues and greens in areas associated with the sea or seaports. Golden yellows and pale yellows are more often abundant in areas with warmer climates. In city centers, browns, tans, ochres and grays predominate. The next time you travel, notice the coloration of the place.

The same book demonstrates connections between colors and time of year. It also recommends particular color combinations to communicate specific styles and ideas: the strength, power, and intellectual intensity of browns and earthy greens; the casual fun of primary and secondary colors; the stark modern attitude of darker blues and grays; the warmer tonality of colors used at home; the crisper businesslike attitude of the grayed shades at work.

Studies of color in the workplace tend to produce varied results. Still, if you have the opportunity, it's worth experimenting. Just be sure to consider the feelings and sensitivity of everyone who works in the space—and the impression the color might make on clients.

Feng Shui

Pronounced "fong-shway," this ancient Chinese design discipline combines spirituality with a regimen for the arrangement of physical space. It's a way of seeing and organizing the world where you live and work, a complex system that requires years to truly understand. In order to achieve the most advantageous flow of energy ("*chi*"), a *Feng Shui* expert combines natural and symbolic elements with the arrangement of physical spaces.

It is certainly possible to employ certain *Feng Shui* techniques in the design of one's creative workspace, but without a thorough understanding of the underlying principles and their basic belief system, these techniques are unlikely to have much impact. For example, some people decorate with crystals or wind chimes. They might look or sound pretty, but unless they are very carefully placed to adjust the direction and vitality of the *chi* as it moves through the space, neither crystals nor chimes are likely to relieve the unwanted pressure that these devices were intended to counteract.

Still, the best way to approach *Feng Shui* is not by reading a book, but by experiencing several facilities designed by talented, experienced *Feng Shui* practitioners. In the exterior, for example, you are likely to see strategically placed trees. Very leafy trees provide a kind of spiritual protection to the dwelling. Trees that block a path to the world are trimmed so that the path widens as one moves away from the building. Neither limbs nor leaves block windows, or touch the outside walls. Inside, the color and position of the entry door is very important—it is the way that life enters your space. When the "big door" (as it is called in Chinese) is opened, the view should be expansive and balanced. If the front door is in perfect alignment with the back door, then *chi* will flow directly through the home or work site without visiting any of the rooms within it.

The study of *Feng Shui* also encompasses the use of specific symbols, numbers, materials, and colors. A sailing ship pointed toward the workspace signifies incoming rewards and prosperity (yes, some of this seemssimilar to superstition). A pair of goldfish brings abundant success. Six coins in the northwest portion of the home or a room stimulates luck for a father and encourages success in business relationships. The relationship of water and mountains (or skyscrapers, considered the modern equivalent) to the home or workspace might be auspicious or negative, depending on compass points, the shape or path of these objects, or other factors related to physical positions and other nearby objects. Red is associated with good luck and wealth (you've probably seen small, red, shiny envelopes associated with the Chinese New Year, often accumulated in a "wealth bowl" for good fortune). Nine dragons on the east side of your office will energize good fortune. A small waterfall is also recommended.

For a larger-scale introduction to *Feng Shui*, visit any good bookstore, new age shop, or public library for colorful, interesting books on the subject.[6] And, for those who understand *Feng Shui* to be a part of a far more

---

[6] Try these books: Steven Post, *The Modern Look of Feng Shui: Vitality and Harmony for the Home and Office.* New York: Dell Publishing, 1998. Lillian Too, *The Illustrated Encyclopedia of Feng Shui.* Boston: Element Books, Inc., 1999. Derek Walters, *Feng Shui: The Chinese Art of Designing a Harmonious Environment.* New York: Simon & Schuster, Fireside Books, 1988.

complex, integrated system of living and learning, it's best to find a local teacher to provide a higher level of guidance than any book can muster.

Putting It Together

Light, color, *Feng Shui* and other factors all come together in a disciplined "environmental design," which is not about any one thing, but instead the whole thing. The functional, aesthetic and mystical design all contribute to a workspace's value and utility.

Design of space for creative professionals should begin with a series of questions: What does each individual person do? Does it make more sense to organize people in project groups or in groups of people who do similar work? Publishers of multiple magazines face this issue often. Does it make more sense to house the entire staff of each magazine together because they're all working on one project, or is it more sensible to place all editorial people in one area, the designers in another, and the sales force in another? People who do similar work are likely to share ideas and learn from each other—but what is "similar work"? As a designer, do I have more in common with other designers or with other people who work on my magazine? Most of the time, companies organize by job function, not by project. I prefer work groups clustered together, but mine is a minority opinion.

Abundant desk and counter space are essential; so is storage space, but this can be a short walk away. Cubicles aren't brilliant; neither are old flat doors balanced on shaky file cabinets. If you're clever, you can develop your own solutions. If budget allows, you could select solutions from innovative manufacturers like Steelcase and Herman Miller (explore their catalogs and Web sites for ideas). Extra chairs encourage interaction and double as extra shelf space when arranging larger projects. Local light must augment environmental light. Varied light energizes. Do everything possible to control ambient sound; a noisy workplace can be a challenging place to work, but silence is uninspiring, even funereal. The place should have life, but without too many distractions.

High ceilings are preferable, and so are public areas with window views. Matthew Ryesky, who worked in the facilities department at CDNOW, was always trying to promote the idea of hanging an ever-changing series of works from local Philadelphia artists on the company's walls. Looking back, Matt had a great idea; I wish we had implemented it.

The space should be designed to encourage walking around. With e-mail and instant messaging, it's easy to communicate quickly and efficiently, but human interaction yields better results than communication exclusively via screens and keyboards. A public message and idea posting area, plus public areas for chatting and relaxing, encourage people to communicate and ideas to flow.

A more formal meeting place is essential: a space where groups can comfortably and productively work together. This should be more than a conference table and chairs. A large whiteboard, perhaps several, always well-stocked with a multitude of colored markers, plus a TV set, a VCR, a DVD player, at least one computer with an Internet connection connected to a video projector with a proper screen—these are small additions that almost any employee can bring about. In an ideal world, there would also be a coffeemaker, water cooler, small refrigerator, and popcorn popper. The walls should either be soft and cork-like for use as a bulletin board, or hard and slick enough to accept adhesive tape or enormous Post-It sheets. (Maintain a complete inventory of supplies in the room, so you won't lose time searching for new white board markers.) The meeting place should be well-ventilated, well-lit with dimmer controls to vary the lighting (helpful during long sessions), with a reliable telephone with multiple lines and a full-duplex speakerphone (so you don't have to wait for the other party to finish before you can interrupt). The space need not resemble a corporate board room with a mega-sized conference table. It just needs to be a space where everyone can work, see, and speak with one another. This is not blue-sky stuff; it's essential equipment for any creative professional group work environment.

Certainly, it's helpful if you are personally in control over the environment. In most companies, a facilities manager works with a senior executive to design and approve workspace design. Get involved. You can make a difference.

Music and Sound Design

Terrifying Science Experiment of the Past #422: Play the music faster and the mice run the maze faster! Play faster music in the factory and the workers will pack more boxes per hour!

I would love to say that listening to the second movement of Beethoven's Fourth Symphony will help you to get your work done 62 percent faster, or that listening to Miles Davis's early recordings will improve your output, but I won't because they don't. Background music might block out distracting sound and put you in the mood to work. For me, music seems to complete the experience of doing creative work, filling in some empty spaces in my consciousness.

Your Physical and Virtual Workspace

Regardless of where you settle down, you need a proper desk. A truly great desk is an under-appreciated contributor to the creative process. If you don't believe me, track down a euphoric song by Harry Nilsson about his love affair with the perfect desk, called appropriately, "Good Old Desk."

I have two desks. I use one for my computer and the other for writing, organizing, drawing, and other work that doesn't involve computing. The computer desk was our dining room table. Hang on a second— I'll measure it for you. It's three-and-one-half feet deep and seven feet long, enormous by desk standards, but never large enough for the latest project. The second desk is three feet by four feet; and it gets cleared for each day's work. I work with eleven feet (yikes!) of desk space, and wish I had twice that amount.

I don't bother with desk drawers. The dining room table desk is topped with Levenger's Project Boxes—sixteen horizontal compartments, each with space for a bunch of files and a loose-leaf notebook. One office wall is covered with a wall unit: twenty-four one-cubic-foot-plus cubby holes. Each cubby is large enough for two dozen books or a set of three drawers, several inches deep. All sorts of interesting stuff ends up in the cubbies: magazines, baseballs I've caught at minor and major league games; a century-old watercolor box from Winsor & Newton I found on eBay, a lovely antique camera given to me as a birthday gift by a good friend; a world band radio so I can listen to the BBC or languages I've never heard before; a nine-inch TV set with a built-in VCR; some fancy kaleidoscopes and the good-luck *daruma* (little laughing Buddha) that brought me good luck on *Carmen Sandiego*. Some stuff is functional, but it's all important.

You need a proper bookcase, too. Several, if you have the space. You'll lose the better part of one shelf to computer manuals and another to your growing library of CD-ROMs and other digital storage.

You also need a world-class desk chair. I'm addicted to my deep, comfortable, ergonomic black leather desk chair. Another contemporary symbol of a successful worker is an Aeron chair—sleek, black plastic netting on an endlessly adjustable frame. Invest in a chair that will keep you fresh and comfortable, one designed to minimize potential back and leg problems.

If you're dealing with words, a collection of reference books is essential. Here's my list:

• A dictionary too heavy to lift. *Random House Unabridged Dictionary*, with 2,256 pages and over 300,000 entries, is the best under-$50 investment you'll make this year. Better still is *Webster's Third New International Dictionary Unabridged*, which costs twice as much, but carries 50 percent more entries and a stronger scholarly reputation.

• A high-quality thesaurus from any of the top dictionary publishers (the Roget's imprimatur is fine, but Merriam-Webster, Random House, and other comparable works are as good).

• *The Synonym Finder* by J.I. Rodale, which is handier than any thesaurus and more often comes up with the right word.

A few foreign-language dictionaries: certainly Spanish and French. These are not expensive and they're easy to find used. No reason not to have German, Italian, Portuguese, Japanese, and Russian around for the few times you need them.

• A rhyming dictionary. Even if you're not a poet or lyricist, you'll doubtless rhyme from time to time.

• A great atlas, preferably one from National Geographic, if for no reason than to feel the connection with their tradition.

The Computer Area

The computer has become a communications center and a primary creative tool. The object of this computer game is to maintain productivity; an outdated computer can and will sap your time, energy, and cash.

Keep your computer up to date; a three-year-old computer is old. Soon after your first issues with software that's too new for your machine, or age-related problems with hardware or operating system incompatibilities, move on. A new machine is almost always worth the investment. You will save time and you will be more productive with a new computer.

Apple's computers are elegantly designed and they're easier to set up, maintain, use, and network with. If you're working solo, stick with or switch to Apple. If you're in a company environment where Windows is the norm, choose your battles. You probably won't win a campaign to change the company, and you probably won't get an Apple for your desk or briefcase. Software designed for Apple and Windows computers is similar, but not always identical. Be a grown-up; you can get over the differences.

My primary office machine is an Apple, but my portable is Fujitsu LifeBook[7] running Windows XP. For the few tasks that an Apple cannot do, it's helpful to have a Windows machine. Rather than wasting time with networking issues in my small office, I inject a tiny USB Flash Drive into these machines to quickly transfer files. Avoid the temptation to perfect the technology; just choose the path of least resistance and go on with your work.

Portable or desktop? Both, if you can afford them, a portable if you cannot. After years of desktop-only work, I've (belatedly) discovered that I can keep myself fresh by working in the living room (deeply comfortable leather club chairs); outside on the deck; and in the car on long trips, day or night (my wife drives). I prefer my desktop machine for projects that require many open files, work with Photoshop, and Web design (both benefit from the larger screen).

Around the Computer

Sit up straight in your ergonomically correct chair. The top of the computer screen should line up with the tip of your nose. If you extend your arm, your fingertip should just touch the top of the screen. Your feet should be flat on the floor. The space behind the screen should be uncluttered so you can concentrate. No direct light or window reflections should fall on the screen. If you spend hours computing, this stuff matters.

I use a Wacom pen tablet in place of a mouse. It's more precise for graphic work and, with practice, easier to use than a mouse or trackball. Experiment with several input devices; for some, the changeover makes a big difference. What's more, pen tablets last for years.

---

[7] Fujitsu's computers are not generally available in retail stores in the USA. They are durable, reliable, and reasonably priced. They're also lightweight, a primary consideration for any portable in my mind. The S-series machines weigh less than four pounds; others in their line weigh less than three pounds. See www.fujitsupc. com.

CD-ROMs and DVDs are the preferred storage media. Daily or weekly backups of all documents on your hard drive—including your e-mail—are essential. Remove old projects from your hard drive and archive them on disks filled with clearly marked project folders. Smaller, incomplete projects should be stored not by project but by year. Be sure to label every disk clearly, on the spine of the jewel box, the paper sleeve (which should list all file contents, by date), and on the disk itself (date burned, plus general list of contents).

Organizing Your Output

Digital files take up almost no physical space. But what about the files, finished goods, research, and all of the other paper, boxes, posters, and ephemera? Yikes. Keep or toss?

Here's what to keep:
- The final versions of every project you do.
- The creative brief or other description of the project's starting place.
- Several key documents or interim steps you took to develop all but the least important projects.
- A contact list for every project, to remember people's names and find them again.
- Any reference materials that were especially helpful in putting the project together.
- The contract, invoice, final budget, any signed forms, and all the legal and financial documentation.

Here's what to toss:
- All incremental changes, unless there's a great idea in there somewhere.
- The basic operational memos, e-mails, revisions in meeting times, corporate blather (unless you may need to cover yourself later).
- Any expense reports that have been paid (keep these for a few months after the project closes, just in case).

• The inevitable "thought you might find this helpful" documents that didn't prove especially helpful after all.

Maintain a personal library of every completed piece of work, and at least three finished copies, preferably in different locations (one at home, one at the office, and one somewhere else). In all cases, storage should be secure, free from the potentially damaging effects of direct sunlight, water, very hot or cold air, humidity, and critters (including your own young children). Also keep a dozen or so additional copies that you can submit as part of a pitch for other jobs. *Always* ask for these materials back, unless they're digital; they are not replaceable and you will eventually run out of samples.

Put together some sort of scrapbook or digital demo file so that excerpts from the material can be freely distributed via disks, color copies (on paper), or via the Web. Keep this resumé file up to date, or once a year spend a day updating the digital versions.

What about projects that didn't complete, didn't get sold, or morphed into other projects?

• If you're absolutely positive that the project is completely dead and will not rise from the grave, keep everything a few months anyway because you might be wrong.
• After the project disappears from memory, follow the "Here's What to Keep" and "Here's What to Toss" rules above.

Where do you keep all of this stuff? Although most documents are stored digitally, I have learned to keep paper copies of anything important. A disk that is no longer readable, for whatever reasons, leaves you without samples of projects that you worked hard to produce, and might need for future marketing.

And what if you're short on storage space? If it's an office situation, you can almost always find a closet or other company space where a few cartons can be stored. There's also professional-grade business storage. As a rule, it's also wise to keep personal copies of your work at home. If your home is crowded, arrange for safe storage elsewhere. Be selective, but keep the essentials.

The history of my professional life can be found in loose-leaf notebooks (for larger projects) and in file folders. Whenever I start anything new, I grab an empty file folder and label it with both the name of the project and its component part—"New Century Television – Market Research," for example. Anything related to that topic gets stored in the appropriate folder. When a folder approaches an inch thick, I break it down into smaller folders. Right now, I'm staring at around a hundred active folders on projects ranging from choosing a new camera to interesting restaurants to the codes and instructions on hosting a Web site. I used to store (and forget) folders in a drawer, but I now prefer my Levenger Project Boxes. Right now, for example, one cubby is devoted to this book. Another is devoted to my next book. Three are devoted to a new company that I'm starting (and, to stay organized, one stores active work, one is an archive and one stores odd-sized items).

What happens when the project boxes get full, or more space is needed? Well, the material is already well-organized, so it's easy to transfer the folders into clusters, and file them away for future reference.

Why bother? I sometimes think I waste time staying well organized, but then, when I need a document for a meeting, or I want some reference art for a new drawing, I know precisely where it can be found. Certainly there are alternatives to my systems, but these work for me, and I suspect you need something similar.

When you archive, be sure to (a) do it every month, so the chore doesn't become overwhelming; and (b) thin out the folders as you go, so that you're not storing tons of paper that you'll never need again.

What about awkward-shaped stuff that doesn't fit into file folders?

If you pile it up in a corner, it will get dirty, damaged, or you will forget it exists. Pick up a stack of plastic boxes of various shapes and sizes at any home improvement store. The Light Impressions catalog[8] sells a very wide range of boxes, plastic bags, and other storage systems suitable for most of our needs. To avoid damage by light, heat, humidity, water, etc., store your materials in a controlled environment. Make an inventory map, so you know what's inside each box, and update it regularly so the passage of years won't cloud your memory.

Supplies

The digitalization of the tools used in many creative professions has eliminated the need for stores specializing in, for example, art supplies or photographic materials. If you need blank media, or a new monitor or scanner, you can almost always order them via the Internet for next-day delivery. What's more, a Staples or OfficeMax store is probably a short drive from your home or office.

Supplies that are very specific or hard to find should be kept on hand. Otherwise, use valuable office space for purposes other than materials storage.

The Importance of Excellent Tools

Robert Dodge, who teaches art techniques at my community college, sometimes chides students who draw on newsprint paper. Certainly, newsprint paper costs about 75 percent less than other paper but it's junk, suitable for warm-up exercises only. A good drawing is better when it's made with proper materials. What's more, better materials encourage superior work. The legacy of creative professionals past can be felt in the selection of particular musical instruments, cameras, and other tools and materials.

Buy the Best Tools You Can Afford

In the digital world, one software product often dominates a field. Most digital artists use Adobe Photoshop; most writers use Microsoft Word; most videographers use either Adobe Premiere Pro (for Windows) or Apple Final Cut Pro (Mac). The only real choice is Windows vs. Apple,

---

[8] The web site: http://www.lightimpressionsdirect.com.

and the computer's power and storage capacity.

In the analog world, where many creative professionals enjoy a craftsman's love for tools, there are more choices.

Digital photography is changing rapidly, with one camera replacing another every year or two. In the analog world, photographers cherish vintage and new lenses from Leica, Nikon, and Hasselblad. The vintage material costs less and carries a patina, a legacy, a sense of responsibility to the past. The newer lenses are technically superb, better than any that have come before. Several photographer friends now regularly use large-format cameras because their 4" x 5" negatives produce excellent results. At the same time, they are learning to combine this older technology with newer digital work, in part because of the image control that digital media provides. A used lens, perhaps two dozen years old, is fine, but only the very latest digital equipment is acceptable.

In nearly every creative domain, there is some version of the push and pull of old versus new. I love painting watercolors from an antique Winsor & Newton metal case. The control that I get from the same company's very best sable paintbrushes makes me feel as though I'm doing good work; for me, the extra investment (and the obsessive comparisons between competitive brushes) has been part of learning about watercolor tools. When I write longhand, I spend time seeking out just the right paper and the right pen.

The bottom line about tools: Buy the best you can afford. Don't buy beginner's products. Instead, invest in gently used versions of the best. You are carrying on a legacy of excellent work.

The Value in Legacy

Several years ago, my wife's father passed away. He was an excellent artist and illustrator. Cleaning his old workspace, we found two tins of watercolor tubes, well-used but viable. I had never attempted watercolors before. When I tried his paint and brushes, he inspired me. I now love watercolor painting, and I thank his memory for the unintended gift.

Legacy matters. Creative people value mentors, teachers, people who elevated the art form. An artist's tool can be a powerful talisman. Often, it's an old work table or some equipment from a teacher or a friend or a relative. A viola once played by a master. A beat-up old banjo case. An antique paperweight. A vintage fountain pen. A fifty-year-old Leica camera. It's not unusual to find some antiques in the most modern creative professional's kit.

Technology has improved so many creative tools, but along the way, we've lost craftsmanship. Sometimes, we're faced with the choice of a newer model with superior features or an older one that's beautifully built. This situation is commonplace in photography and in the choice of musical instruments. Newer isn't always better. More features don't always mean an improved product.

Occasionally, I'm impressed by the quality of work output from a creative professional working with inferior tools. The artist makes claims about the lack of need for expensive or overpriced tools or materials. And I can't help but wonder how much better the professional's fine work would be if better tools or materials were in her hands.

You Have My Permission...

Quality matters. Quality in the work you do. Quality in the way you spend your time. An investment in quality is always a good idea. Sometimes, the investment will do nothing more than make you feel more positive about your work. Sometimes, you'll buy tools or materials beyond your skill level; that's okay—most likely, you'll rise to the occasion.

If you need someone to give you permission to spend the money on a better computer so you can edit digital video faster or more effectively, or superior woodworking tools for greater flexibility or precision, use me. You have my permission to spend the money. And if you need to convince a spouse, partner, parent, or a co-worker that you ought to spend the money, feel free to hand a copy of this paragraph to them. (This offer is automatically rescinded if you: (a) need the money for food, clothing, shelter, or your children's education; (b) have already used this paragraph within the past twelve months; or (c) have a habit of buying expensive stuff that you never actually use.

Maintenance and Repair

Even the highest-quality tool requires periodic maintenance. You can do some cleaning and polishing on your own, removing dirt and tarnish, but a professional shop can get inside and do the job completely. Every few years—or more frequently, if necessary—bring your most-used gear to the best repair shop you can find and spend the money necessary to keep your equipment operating properly. An undetected problem can worsen over time, perhaps causing failure when you need your tool to perform at its best. Lack of proper maintenance could slowly destroy the tool you love. Be sure to select the repair and maintenance shop with the utmost care.

Shopping—and Shopping for Discounts

Nearly every creative profession that involves tools, materials, or supplies is now served by a specialty discount retailer. These retailers are accessible via the Web; many also send out catalogs. Some operate one or more retail stores as well. Should you buy from them?

In our frenzy to save money, we Americans have put most local specialty stores out of business. On the drive back from Best Buy, we wonder what happened to the record store on Main Street.

Several moments of reflection. Please indulge me.

The place is Kyoto, Japan. A tiny shop sells handmade Japanese watercolors, brushes, and paper. The shop has been in the same location for over 150 years. Local artists congregate on the store's one small bench. A woman sits on a raised *tatami* mat in reach of every pan of paint in the store. She speaks only Japanese, but she patiently caters to the many foreign visitors attracted by the shop. Each customer leaves the store with a tightly wrapped package of exquisite paints and handmade brushes. Local artists relaxing on the bench provide customers with encouragement and point to their own work hanging on the store's weathered wooden walls.

In Washington state, there's a catalog and Web operation that specializes in pastels: www.dakotapastels.com. They stock every brand on the market, plus more types of papers and other pastel supplies than any other company in the world. They've answered my every question about choosing pastels, often in considerable detail.

Clearly, I prefer smaller stores staffed by personnel who care about their product line. I also worry about these stores, particularly in an era when every Web site can access any warehouse and computerized inventory list. Will these specialty stores all disappear? (Most are already gone, an endangered species with no law to protect them.)

Even when money is tight, I've tended toward smaller stores. I suspect I've saved money because I've listened to the knowledgeable store personnel's informed advice and I've bought the right stuff—and not too much of it, either.

Still, the argument is imperfect. Cheap Joe's Art Stuff (www. cheapjoes.com) is a customer-centric mail order discounter in the art supply field. Prices are low, inventory is wide and deep, the staff is friendly and knowledgeable, they run workshops at their North Carolina headquarters, they run a wonderful charity program for disadvantaged kids, and they have an old-fashioned storekeeper's sensibility—even a sense of humor. The exception makes the rule, I guess.

The Importance of Research and Reference Materials

The creative process benefits from abundant stimuli. At SBK Pictures, a producer of television commercials, a large bathroom wall is filled with cut-out images from magazines—crazy stuff, soft and cuddly pictures, random words set with odd type treatments, an intentional barrage of visual stimulation in an unexpected place.

Some creative professionals decorate their workspaces with eclectic toys, travel souvenirs, photos and props from past projects, pictures of heroes (Ché Guevera, Albert Einstein, John Belushi). Others surround themselves with a library, from college filmmaking text books to old trade show guides. Or maybe a bulletin board filled with a random assortment of travel snapshots, or production stills. A bulletin board filled with anything even vaguely relevant to a current project makes a wonderful mess. I think a huge bulletin board is the best center point for a group project, especially in its early stages—a place where everyone can help define a concept by placing objects, images, words, or ideas on a big open wall space for everyone else to explore.

I don't care how great the Web turns out to be—it's still essential to surround yourself with books. Production Design Group (PDG), one of New York City's top scenic design firms, has an office lined with books about all sorts of art and design. On one project, when we wanted to explore the boldly geometric posters associated with Russian propaganda, there was no pause in the discussion—we just grabbed several relevant volumes off the wall and got to work.

Let's close this chapter with wisdom from Eric Nisenson's *Ascension*, about jazz master John Coltrane: "Books, however, continued to be the main source of Coltrane's intellectual and spiritual search. He read everything from biographies of other artists to books on esoteric philosophy and religion."[9]

---

[9] SOURCE: Eric Nisenson, *Ascension*, p. 167.

CHAPTER 4 – Doing the Work

Andrew McDermott won the grand prize in *Pastel Journal*'s annual Pastel 100 contest. In his winner's interview, he said: "It is better to paint for one minute a day than to think about it twenty-four hours a day. You learn more in that one minute of painting than you do in thinking about it for twenty-four hours." [1]

McDermott also said, "When I'm walking, I'm always looking around and thinking, 'I should be painting that light!' It really becomes a lifestyle, being an artist. I become obsessed with it."

Oh, to be a pure artist, one who simply creates and then sells his work to an eager marketplace. Most of us never even visit that planet.

A Look Inside the Creative Process

Much has been written about the creative process, and we'll get to that in a moment. Right now, I think it's best to widen the view, so that the creative process is set in a proper context.

Creative work begins in one of two ways: You come up with an idea, sell it and produce it; or somebody comes to you with an idea and you produce it.

---

[1] SOURCE: Both quotes from *Pastel Journal* interview with Andrew McDermott, grand prize winner, Pastel 100, March/April 2003.

Selling Your Ideas

Even in the best of times, selling creative ideas is very, very difficult. I've sold dozens of projects, perhaps even a hundred projects over several decades. For every project I sell, there are ten more that never sold, and in most cases, never even made it to a pitch meeting.

If you've gotten this far into the book, it's probably fair to assume that you know how to develop and produce projects. In just a few pages, we'll take a closer look at that part of the process. None of that matters at all without a clear understanding of the marketplace and a knack for selling projects.

For me, the process of selling a project usually begins with an idea that wants to be developed. I come up with some ideas on my own, but more often the idea will come about as a result of a formal or informal collaboration. I immediately filter the idea in terms of what I know about the marketplace: who the potential buyers might be, what their recent buying history has been, the relative cost of the new idea and how it compares with current spending by key buyers, my personal relationships with potential buyers, and an analysis of similar, comparable, and competitive products. All of this analysis takes a day or two—it's a preliminary assessment, nothing more.

The next step is to develop the idea, to flesh out the details, to make it real. Of course, at this stage, nothing is real, it's just a bunch of ideas on paper or floating in my brain and perhaps in the mind of a co-conspirator. We do not develop the entire concept. Instead, we develop just enough of the concept to show it to potential buyers. This step might require considerable discussion and development, but it might also be kept at a conceptual level. The potential buyer will not lavish more than a few minutes on the new idea; she is inevitably busy filtering dozens of other ideas every day. So, we look for a generally positive response, and then we develop the idea further (most often on our own nickel).

Weeks or months might pass, as the project is shaped based upon the potential buyer's feedback and upon the increasing amount of information we now possess about the marketplace. Then we do the pitch.

The pitch itself is likely to run about a half-hour, or, if it's in print, between ten and twenty pages. It's likely to be vivid and graphic; the objective now is to convince the buyer to understand the vision as we see it, and to demonstrate sufficient creative competency to be trusted with the project. At this stage, it's important to have assembled a team of people with appropriate credentials. The story is ultimately told by one or two people with some passion but also with a degree of cool. The buyer does not want to be overwhelmed by the passion of the creator. This is a business, and a degree of detachment and humor is always appreciated.

And then, there's the yes or no decision. Or, more often, there's the noncommittal answer. Do more work? Let it sit for a while? Call the potential buyer the next day or a week later? What exactly did he say during the meeting? This is the shaky part of the process: Most of the time, you have no clear understanding if you're going to make a sale.

Whether you force the issue or the buyer volunteers the feedback, you finally hear that (a) there's more work to do; (b) the timing's not right; (c) the project's not right; (d) it's a good idea, but you're not the one to do it; or (e) go ahead. Sadly, (e) doesn't happen more than 10 percent of the time. So, you keep the project alive, and start the process with another buyer, or you rework the project and pitch it again, or you move on to another project.

PITCHING, SELLING AND CLOSING THE DEAL: A PRIMER

Although many of us are not fond of the process, creative professionals spend a lot of time selling themselves and their ideas.

At the extreme end of the spectrum is the performer's audition. Imagine spending a hundred days a year hustling for the opportunity to audition, only to be turned down for parts after a five-minute reading. On the other is the focused sell: You work hard for months and then present every detail to a potential client in a meeting that lasts several hours and is followed by several more.

Different as they are, some similarities are worth noting:

Mostly, the buyer is responding to your personal presentation: the way you look, speak, and smile; your eye contact; intelligence; and understanding of the project and the role. These factors mean as much as performance, be it in an audition or in a corporate pitch.

- You must choose your words carefully. Your intention is to attract some attention and to be memorable, but you must not cross the line and frighten the buyer away.
- Be prepared. The old Boy Scout motto rings true.
- Pay attention. You must care as much as the buyer.
- You must make the most of your experience, but you must tell the truth.
- You must be aware of time. If you prepare the pitch for a half-hour, you must smoothly respond to the "we only have 15 minutes" surprise.
- You must read the room and adjust your pitch accordingly.
- Never second-guess yourself in the meeting. Be flexible, but demonstrate clear thinking.
- Never let them see you sweat.

As for closing the deal, it's worth reading your choice of how-to books about consultative selling. Moving a potential customer along from like to love to buy is an art. Many projects linger on the wings of good wishes and hope, then drop out of sight because the deal was never completed.

Making a deal is always about more than money alone. In our business, a deal is always more likely to close if it solves a specific problem for the employer or the client. Timing matters; problems are always related to current market conditions, and these change quickly. Timing of deliverables also matters; if you can deliver the project within the client's ideal timetable, the odds of closing a deal, and doing it soon, are improved. Reputation and trust matter. Those are the foundation points of many deals.

Then, there are business, financial, and ego issues. In show business, dealmakers are sometimes in the game to win. If there's no win, or no perceived win, there's no deal. Also in show business, the possibility of a deal with client A will cause client B to react and to try to close the deal if for no reason except to tweak client A. Generally, "money controls the deal"; that is, the financing and distribution company typically sets the basic terms. A book publisher, for example, generally works within specific guidelines for the advance, royalty, and control over rights; authors have limited flexibility, unless some other factors come into play (the client A, client B strategy is one that sometimes works, for example; being a celebrity author is another).

Every deal has its own momentum. Deals that take a long time to negotiate often lose momentum and do not close. Deals with troublesome players are likely to fall apart. Deals that come together too quickly are also risky; as quickly as the deal gets made, it can get unmade with a perfunctory "never mind."

And remember: it's not a deal until both parties sign the contract. And even with those signatures, deals sometimes fall apart.

Somebody Comes to You with an Idea

I've been more successful with this approach than in selling my own projects. A production company owns the rights to a project and needs someone who knows what they're doing to develop and produce it. A marketing company has just been given an assignment, and they need more experienced hands.

In these situations, you have more control. The process typically begins with a telephone conversation outlining the key points of the project. This is followed by an e-mail filled with some sketchy (or not so sketchy) information that you are to read before the first in-person meeting. At that meeting, the client or employer is looking at you with the sincere hope that you can deliver. Your resume matters, but your personal style and your grasp of the real issues associated with the project matter more. Your confidence matters, and so does your willingness to collaborate.

From here, assuming you get the job (the batting average here is likely to be .500 or better), it's a matter of negotiating and learning as many of the potential pitfalls as possible before making the commitment.

Mapping the Creative Process

With the project now sold, the creative process kicks in. Even so, the vast majority of ideas that will be processed will never make it out the other side.

The mapping process, looks something like this:

- Identification
- Saturation
- Doing the Work
- Verification
- Revision
- Acceptance/Rejection

It's important to remember that we haven't understood the creative process for more than a century or so. As the story goes (as told by Morton Hunt in *The Universe Within*): When nineteenth-century German physiologist and physicist Hermann Helmholtz described his own scientific process in stages, he was among the first to do so. "The first stage," according to Helmholtz, "was saturation; it consisted of the initial investigation, carried on until he could make no further progress with the problem. Next was incubation—a period of rest and recovery during which, without conscious awareness of it, the materials in his mind were moved about and reorganized. Third was illumination—the appearance of a sudden and unexpected solution. In 1908, the French mathematician Henri Poincaré described the creative process in much the same way, but added a fourth step, verification."

I'd add a step before Helmholtz's saturation: identification. The first step in the creative professional's process is to specify the question or problem. Also, I'm not wild about Helmholtz's "sudden and unexpected solution." Eureka! moments happen, but we more often create without saying or thinking that we've stumbled into some glorious discovery.

My work is more like Michelangelo's (gee, I'm glad I wrote that...): "In every block of marble I see a statue as plain as though it stood before me, shaped and perfect in attitude and action. I have only to hew away the rough walls that imprison the lovely apparition to reveal it to the other eyes as mine see it." You see what needs to be done, and you work away until what needs to be done is done.

Identification

The identification statement can be as simple as "let's write a song" or as complex as "find a better way to fund public television." A clear, one-sentence description of the issue is usually enough for me, but I also prefer to read some background so that I understand why the question or problem is posed in the first place. Sometimes, the identification is closely linked to an early problem-solving step called *ideation*.

Ideation begins when somebody poses a problem or an open-ended question. Logical, tried-and-true answers are the first responses; then, the game begins: Yes, George Washington is widely known as the first U.S. president, but the U.S. became a nation in 1783 and GW didn't become president until 1789. So who was running the place before George? (Here's where ideation always begins—by questioning the norm.)

Saturation

Science fiction novelist Ray Bradbury explained saturation perfectly: "If you stuff yourself full of poems, essays, plays, stories, novels, films, comic strips, magazines, music, you automatically explode every morning like Old Faithful. I never had a dry spell in my life, mainly because I feed myself well, to the point of bursting. I wake early and hear my morning voices leaping around in my head like jumping beans. I get out of bed to trap them before they escape."[2]

How to become saturated (or, marinated, which seems more precise)? Talk to everybody who understands the question, but spend most of your time with the target audience or customer. These people know more about the problem than anybody else. (If you are writing a children's book, spend a lot of time with children!) Read the best material on the subject, but do not submerge yourself in written research. Immerse yourself in the authentic experience, not in what select people have decided to write about it. Then, think for yourself.

As a college student, I taught myself to get an early start on major assignments. Just as soon as class let out, I headed for the college library. I was always the first to get the reserve books, and often the first to explore the research. After I was familiar with the material, I did what every college student does: I waited until the last minute to complete the assignment. Was I incubating, or just procrastinating?

These days, when I am first assigned a project, I immerse myself, talk about it endlessly, and develop an increasingly clear image of the completed project. I compare notes and ideas with peers and with the intended audience. Is this incubation? To me, incubation is a back-burner activity; what I'm doing feels more active. And while I'd like to use a fancy label, I call this step "thinking about the project." (Sorry to be so boring).

Sometimes, saturation is linked to confirmation. The way to tease out an idea's worth is to gather information. I just did a Web search on "First

---

[2] SOURCE: SARK, *Creative Companion*, p. 57.

U.S. President." Within seconds, I found my confirmation: John Hanson took office in 1781, while the Revolution was still being fought. He was chosen by Congress, and his term ran one year. Hanson was followed by six more one-year presidents before the U.S. Constitution was ratified and George reset the counter.

Doing the Work

At this stage, I don't illuminate, I just do the work. I sit down at the computer, or with the project team, and we knock tasks off a master list. Sure, the process is sometimes illuminating in that it's interesting and informative, but mostly, it's just the kind of work that creative people adore: making things.

Let's illuminate with George Washington. Factually, we've got the story down. But does the story have value? Or is this an idea that should be dumped? Illumination comes from the marketplace. If you were working for The History Channel, you might construct a proposal for a series, "Before George: America's First Presidents." If you were working at a children's magazine, you might pitch an article. As a teacher, you might structure a unit on early America based upon unexpected facts, and try that out on the kids. As an author, you might outline a historical novel and show it to an agent or editor. Most often, the idea is briefly illuminated and then gets shoved into a dark catacomb. This fate awaits Mr. Hanson....

Verification

In the form of a question, verification is asking: "Did I get it right?" That's the most illuminating step of all—when you present the concept, in all its glory, to people who control resources. If they like it, verification is an apt term. If they don't, then clarification is probably better.

So you practice. You pitch the idea to friends, associates, then to clients. Gradually, you learn to explain the idea; you memorize bullet points and stories that bring the idea to life. Maybe you open with the expected

"Who was our country's first president?" and wait for the expected wrong answer, then go into your dance. You might also confound people with the events' timing: "When did the American Revolution end? When did George Washington become president? Who was in charge in between?" Or, you could take a biographical approach: "Let me tell you about John Hanson. He was a president before Washington and before our Constitution. And he was the guy who prevented the overthrow of the young government by its own troops. He also prevented George Washington from becoming our king. He caused all foreign troops to leave our land and all foreign flags to be removed (for the first time since 1492!). He also established Thanksgiving." Too much information? Does the pitch center on the surprise and the subsequent unrolling of the facts, or vice versa? Or, do you quickly move from Hanson to your own unique treatment of this story? Is the pitch about the content itself, or what you will do with that content?

You learn by talking briefly, then listening expansively. You read the room, study the body language, and you watch their eyes to see whether you're making a connection.

Revision

In the real world, the creative process rarely ends with the pitch. Instead, the pitch is where the process really begins. After the pitch comes revision, which might lead you back to the start of the whole process. You revise the pitch based upon market reaction. Then you revise it again. Time after time, the Shannon-Weaver model (see chapter one) comes to mind.

Acceptance/Rejection

Eventually, you get one of these answers:
   - "Yes"
   - "Yes, but" (a qualified yes, which could be turned into a "yes")
   - "No"

- "No, but" (a qualified no, tough to turn into a "yes" but worth a try)
- No answer at all (matures into a "no" over time)

Only "yes" allows the project to proceed. A "yes" quickly becomes a stack of paper or a bunch of files: schedules, budgets, contact sheets, telephone calls to make, e-mails to send. The project is under way.

Ways to Generate Ideas

Chris Van Allsburg, whose illustrations you've seen in his wonderful books, *Jumanji* and *The Polar Express*, said, "I've been asked often, 'Where do your ideas come from?' I've given a variety of answers to this question, such as 'I steal them from neighborhood kids,' or 'They are beamed to me from outer space.' It's not really my intention to be rude or smart-alecky. The fact is, I don't know where my ideas come from. Each story I've written starts out as a vague idea that seems to be going nowhere, then suddenly materializes as a completed concept. It almost seems like a discovery, as if the story were always there. The few elements I start out with are actually clues. If I can figure out what they mean, I can discover the story that's waiting."[3]

Most creativity books focus on idea generation. When I hire the right group of people, idea generation is rarely a problem, so I've always dismissed the books. Besides, idea generation is not a single step, it's inherent in the entire process. Still, I liked what Doug Hall [4] said about ways to think. Below are some of my favorites from his far longer list of "Mind Dump Stimuli-Gathering Prompts."

• Think Perceptions—what do people believe about you/it, what are you best at, what are you weakest at.
• Think Overt Benefits—what do you give your customers.
• Think Irrational First Instinct—devious and funny thoughts,

[3] SOURCE: *Publishers Weekly*, July 17, 1995.
[4] SOURCE: Doug Hall, *Jump Start Your Business Brain*, pp. 201+.

unrelated thoughts, sarcastic.
- Think Sensory—sights, smells associated, textures and tastes.
- Think Real Reason to Believe—emotional benefit, rational benefit
- Think Absurdly—what if unlimited funds, what if unlimited time, what would make the competition laugh.
- Think Historically—what has been key to your success, what has scared you most, your biggest mistake.
- Think Aggressively—how could you most annoy the competition, could you double quality, cut price in half.

...and so on. For Hall's complete list, see his book, *Jump Start Your Brain*.

I also find the *Six Thinking Hats*[5] exercise useful. It forces everyone in the room to consider a problem from other people's perspectives:

- White Hat—White is neutral and objective, concerned with facts and figures.
- Red Hat—Suggests anger (seeing red), rage and emotions. Gives the emotional view.
- Black Hat—Somber, serious, cautious, careful, points out idea's weaknesses (black hat is not the bad guy).
- Yellow Hat—Sunny, positive, optimistic, covers hope and positive thinking.
- Green Hat—Grass, vegetation, abundant, fertile growth, indicates creativity and new ideas.
- Blue Hat—Cool, color of sky (which is above everything). Concerned with control, organization of thinking process and the way other hats are used.

From the same author,[6] two more unconventional, provocative activities:

---

[5] SOURCE: Edward DeBono, *Six Thinking Hats*, p. 14.
[6] SOURCE: Edward DeBono, *Serious Creativity*, pp. 164+.

- Escape—Start with what you assume or take for granted, then remove a key element so that the generally accepted conception is no longer true.
- Stepping stones—Reverse the logical direction (of a process that occurs over time, for example); exaggerate one aspect of the flow; distort the relative size or importance of one aspect.

Brainstorming

Brainstorming is well known, but most organizations get only part of the process right. Here's the proper way to brainstorm, based mostly on Alex Osborne's original work,[7] comments from Jack Keil[8] and my own experience. If you brainstorm right, you will generate better results, attending to the formal steps.

Several weeks before the brainstorming session, select a group leader. She will clearly and concisely frame the problem, select an appropriate group of brainstormers, and distribute background information to each of them prior to the meeting. This leader should be an experienced manager, not a creative type.

Ideally, eight to twelve people (plus the leader) should participate in the session; six will do in a pinch. Half of the participants should be affiliated with the company, the others should be unaffiliated. Several company participants should not be working on the current problem. Everyone should be bright, open, non-judgmental, articulate, and creative—and prepared because they've read their packets (not on the day of the session). Everyone is asked to come with three ideas.

A conference room allows everyone to see one another. Each participant gets a water bottle (keep it small, so you get through the meeting without a break); some doodling pads and colored pens or pencils; and a copy of the information packet (just in case they

---

[7] Credit for this process goes to Alex Osborne, an advertising executive who led the agency BBDO (he was the "O").

[8] SOURCE: Jack Keil, *How to Zig in a Zagging World*, Wiley, book on audiotape, draft script.

forgot it). Supply light munchies and avoid foods that are very salty or sugary.

The best meeting times are 10 A.M. (by that time, everyone ought to be awake and nobody should be stuck commuting), or 3 P.M. (lunch has been digested, so people aren't sloggy). The meeting should run for two hours (gets people out at noon, in time for lunch, or 5 P.M. in time to go home or catch up on end-of-day work). The group leader should manage the time.

Immediately afterward, two people from the project team (one who attended the meeting, one who did not) categorize the cards, noting the best ideas in each category. The information on the cards is then summarized and distributed both to the project team and to the people who participated in the session. The people who participated also receive thank-you notes and perhaps a small gift. The ideas are then reviewed, evaluated, and acted upon by the project team.

Mind Maps

Creative thinking often associates one idea with another. Various authors and experts lay claim to the design of visual thinking now commonly known as a mind map.

You can do mind mapping by yourself, but it's more fun and often more productive to do it with one other person. A third person makes an already sloppy process unmanageable. However, you can do a mind map as a larger group exercise, on a large whiteboard, even if this slows down the process and causes some ideas to be forgotten.

A mind map begins with one central idea. The idea then branches off into other ideas, which then lead to several more. Before you know it, the mind map contains dozens or even hundreds of connected words, ideas, and images. Here's a sample:

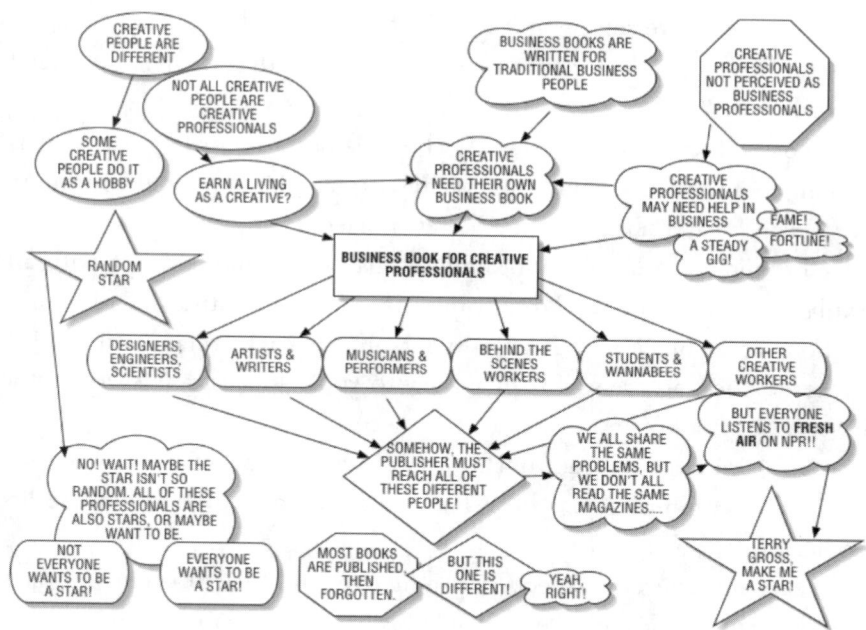

Up and Down the Abstraction Scale

While learning about corporate America, I was taught to think about employees at various levels by envisioning what they could see. The CEO sees a very broad view, but almost no details. The project coordinator sees only details because he is so close to the ground. The VP of marketing might see a broad view, but only of his part of the world. This metaphor is useful for every employee's understanding of the workplace. As it happens, it's also useful for the ideation side of any project.

Early in my career, I was involved in the development of the books on audiotape business. We often struggled with the best way to explain our product to retailers and consumers.

The product could be explained in a very specific way: "We sell audiocassette recordings that feature actors reading abridged versions of books."

That explanation is accurate, but boring. Better to move up one level of abstraction: "We sell recordings of actors reading books."

Better, but do we really need to mention the actors? "We sell recordings of books."

More difficult to understand. A book is not a recording, so what is this all about? Still, for purposes of this explanation, we could continue with even greater abstraction: "We tell stories."

Too general, but also appealing. Perhaps combine concept with an explanatory sales pitch: "You commute an hour in the morning and an hour at night. Why not enjoy yourself. Sit back, relax, and one of America's best actors will read a story to you. Not just any story, but a best-selling book."

Or: "Too busy to read, but love books? Why not let us read to you while you commute, jog, or relax. Listen to one of our new audio books…"

I find this exercise especially productive, and I use it often. Edward DeBono suggests a similar exercise in his book *Serious Creativity*.

Ways to Get the Work Done

In an ideal world, every project would be fully planned and then executed according to plan. In the real world, most creative endeavors are improvisations based on a foundation plan. Still, it's useful to have a plan underneath it all, and a way to manage that plan.

The Miracles of Planning and Project Management

In an instant, many creative people can envision a concept and a completed work. That Eureka! moment isn't worth much if you can't pull the pieces of the dream together. The project might be clear in your mind, but you must take the time and do the work necessary to engage others who are essential to the project's success. A solid plan goes a long way toward inspiring confidence in you and in your project. The plan should include (a) a description of the project and the reason(s) why it's worth pursuing; (b) a rundown on similar projects and how they have fared; (c) a detailed description of the resources required; (d) a budget; (e) a schedule; (f) a marketing plan that explains the path from concept to market; (g) financial or other projections that describe the project's value in terms that the specific marketplace will understand.

The first person you must sell is yourself. You can talk all you like about your personal confidence and capabilities, but you must also define areas where you will need help. For example, I know that I'm strong in conceptualization and early planning and in market analysis. As the project gets under way, I'm good at guiding the team, shaping the ideas, shoving the concept in new directions, tying concepts to strategy, and keeping everyone focused. I also pay attention to budget and schedule, but only at a high level. I know that I *always* need someone to manage the project and deal with the details. I can do it, but other people do it better.

Project management is the control of resources to assure the successful delivery of a completed project. These resources typically include budgeted dollars, people's time, overall project time, equipment, facilities, and processes. A project manager plans both the budget and the schedule to operate in synchronization; it's all about dependent variables. (Huh?)

Let's say you were making a pastel painting. The first step is to sketch several thumbnails; the second is to make basic color choices and to choose the ground (drawing surface); the third is to either underpaint the ground with broad areas of color or to sketch the basic design; the fourth is to paint with pastels... and so on. For the most part, these steps are completed in order.

For the sake of example, let's say each of these steps is now assigned to a separate person. The sketcher, who is responsible for the first step, estimates four hours of work. The color chooser, who does the second, cannot easily estimate the amount of time required—her work depends upon the sketch, and besides, it's a matter of trying different combinations until the answer becomes clear. (A vague answer to "How long will it take?" is the project manager's worst nightmare.) The underpainter, who handles the third step, can't begin until the color chooser has finished. That could take hours, even days. What's more, the color chooser is busy on other jobs and has child care issues, so she works only three hours a day and never on Tuesdays. By making reasonable, thoughtful assumptions, and by allowing for flexibility in the right places on the schedule, the project manager does the impossible: She comes up with a viable plan that makes sense to everyone on the team. Now, she's got to manage it: to make sure that the schedule flows, and that the money that has been budgeted for each step is both sufficient and not overspent.

For even a modest project, the plan is put together either on a spreadsheet (which most people know how to use), or on a big white-board (equally common) or with project management software (which allows tracking of each dependent variable and the project manager to see the big picture). Individuals are interested only in their part of the whole. The project manager makes certain that incremental deadlines are met, that client or managerial reviews and approvals are timely, and that there are few unforeseen delays.

The term "project manager" can be replaced by any number of other job titles, including but not limited to: managing editor, production editor, production manager, associate producer, and art director.

Hiring the Best Possible Team

Most creative work is not the result of one person's effort. Instead, the work is done by a team. The better the team, the better the end product An experienced team will more often than not produce better work than a group of people who have never produced a similar project.

In the real world, there's always a mix of people on a creative team—and that's a good thing. Typically, there's one person who is the senior creative leader, who possesses specific experience that's relevant to the client needs or to the employer's specific goals. That person might manage the entire project or handle only the creative aspects. More often than not, a creative project requires both conceptual and production expertise. A senior level producer or project manager handles the logistics and might serve as the day-to-day manager of the entire project. On some teams, the pure creatives (the writers on a prime-time television series, for example) keep to themselves so that they can provide the best quality material within a limited time. The production group works with their output and puts together the rest of the project.

By design, there is a degree of conflict every time. One step relies on the successful completion of the one before. Every team member must understand these interdependencies and take them seriously. So when hiring, one of the most important questions that a potential employee must answer is whether they understand how to work as part of a team, and whether they have any issues with meeting deadlines. My next one would try to tease out the candidate's temperament with regard to changes. What I really want to know is how the person works. Will she spend lots of time up front so that few changes are required later? Will she hand in a rough draft so that the production staff can get started and fix the issues later? Is she a prima donna who always considers her first work to be final?

I also want to hear that the person really enjoys the work, that he is taking the job because he does it well. I'm not especially interested in providing new opportunities, not during the hiring process. Once the person is part of the team, however, I will provide every opportunity for the person to grow and to move beyond their current level of responsibilities. I believe that every hiring manager should work this way, and that we have a duty to help the next generation grow. But this discussion is not part of the interview process.

Then there's the chemistry. I always assume that a new creative venture will require long hours and plenty of time together. If I hire the right people, nobody will object to the extra time. If the people don't get along, nobody will want to be in the office at any time. As a rule, I try to hire people who are pleasant, fun, easy-going, and capable. I'm not wild about hiring high-maintenance staff, regardless of how talented they may be, or how much the client might want them to be a part of the project. I also discourage the hiring of people who show signs of being abusive, too serious, too flighty, too loud, or otherwise objectionable. Again, I'm hiring the entire package, not just the talent to produce output. I also look for people who enjoy working as part of a team, who get into the whole feeling of joint purpose and singular mission.

I look for excellent people who are willing to make the same commitment that I am willing to make myself. I want people who are skilled, talented, capable, fun, and either experienced or capable of learning fast. We're all in the project together. And we will all learn from one another.

Poor or Wrong-Headed Plans

It happens more often than anybody would like to admit. Things get messed up. For whatever reasons, bad decisions are made, and the project becomes ordinary (at best) or a nightmare (at worst).

Sometimes, the idea itself turns out to be ordinary, or even lousy. Early on, it might have seemed like a great idea. In the light of day, with a creative staff working around the clock, there are whispers: "Why are we doing this?" When that happens, consider your options: (a) Try to make the project better; (b) just get it over with; or (c) leave. For your own sanity, your reputation, and because you have some responsibility to client, boss, staff, and audience, it's best to strive for as much of (a) as possible. Unfortunately, available time, money, and enthusiasm more often point to (b). Certainly, you can always leave. Just don't make a habit of (c) or you won't have the opportunity in the future.

Sometimes, the process itself becomes mucky, uncomfortable, political, a power struggle, or unhappy for other reasons. On most projects, whose cycles are measured in weeks or months, your options are most likely going to be (b) and (c). Most people roll with it for a while, then devise an exit strategy. If the project is longer, you can try to make it better.

Sometimes, the creative execution is wrong. Broadway producers try to protect themselves against this problem with out-of-town tryouts. The show is rehearsed and presented months before it reaches Broadway. Creative issues were resolved in Chicago, Broadway audiences knew nothing about them, and *The Producers* won a tubful of Tony Awards as a result. The out-of-town route doesn't prevent every flop, but it's a sensible hedge. Television networks follow a similar strategy by producing pilot episodes and testing them with target audiences and advertisers before committing to a series. Web designers don't produce the entire Web site in one step. They first develop and distribute a "wire frame" and show sample graphics to the client prior to production.

If the situation still doesn't improve, the powers-that-be might add a co-leader to the mix. It's not easy working side-by-side with the person who might replace you if things don't work out; motivations become confused, and energies that ought to focus on the project are instead spent arguing and scheming. In order for this job cohabitation to work, roles and responsibilities must be clearly delineated (if necessary, codified on paper). When this system works, it can really change things for the better. Unfortunately, it's not easy and more often than not, somebody exits.

Always remember:

Often, The Creative Process is Sloppy, Improvisational, and Resistant to Planning.

When I first submitted the proposal for this book, I included a one-page summary of each chapter. When I signed the contract, I turned each summary into a detailed three-page outline, then wrote the first draft according to this plan. Then, with most of the words in place, I reworked as necessary.

Neil Simon[9], who is more productive and talented than I will ever be, writes without a plan. He begins each play with a basic conception of characters and then just starts to write. Characters lead Simon through the story. After two or three dozen manuscript pages, he knows whether

---

[9] SOURCE: *The 60 Minute Interviews: Neil Simon,* CBS News and TVLand.

the play is going to work. If it works, he continues, then he rewrites until every line is perfect. If the first pages don't work, he stores them for later reference (in a now-legendary trunk in his home). Simon also writes longhand, a difficult habit to change after decades of success.

Film director Tim Burton, whose imaginative use of special effects often requires considerable planning, wrote, "A lot of people in the movie (*Pee-Wee's Big Adventure*) were from improv groups like The Groundlings and I really started to get into it, because when people are good at improv it's really fun and it's kind of liberating. And I started to feel that I was going to storyboard less because it's more fun to build up to a spot and let it happen on the stage. You have to plan enough of an idea to know what you're doing, but as much as you plan, there's something about the reality of being on the set with the actors, costumes, lights, and the rest of the environment that changes things."[10]

Artist Robert Rauschenberg expressed similar sentiments: "For me art shouldn't be a fixed idea that I have before I start making it. I want it to include all the fragility and doubt that I go through the day with. Sometimes I'll take a walk just to forget whatever good idea I had that day because I like to go into the studio not having any ideas. I want the insecurity of not knowing, like performers feel before a performance."[11]

When writing a novel or play, a "figure it out when we get there" might be the appropriate, organic route to the best possible result. When money is on the line and actors are on the set, this strategy is pretty risky. In television, and in most other creative endeavors, too much overlap between development and production phases will cause a mess. The script should be written and completely revised before the play is cast. The client must approve the entire architectural plan before the materials are purchased. Regardless of what kind of project you do, you really ought to figure everything out before anybody else shows up.

---

[10] SOURCE: *Burton on Burton*, p. 47.
[11] SOURCE: quoted by Michael Kimmelman in an article about Rauschenburg, *New York Times*, Arts & Leisure section 2, August 27, 2000, p. 26.

Replanning

The "back to square one" approach to creative management doesn't earn many friends. When things aren't working out, time, enthusiasm, energy, money, and patience wane. This happens on movie sets from time to time; the dailies are lousy and it's obvious that the film is heading for turkey town. By this stage, the creative group has become a family and everybody wants a successful outcome, so they start making suggestions. Problems are the stuff of gossip, and soon people who are tangentially involved show up with suggestions. This help might be well-intentioned but not often relevant. It's not easy to ask for help—it feels as though you've stupidly managed to swim into deep water without a way to get back to shore, with the entire team watching you splash around. Once again, you could leave. You won't learn much if you do.

Instead, you want to take control. You do this by assembling a small group of trusted team members, plus one or more people who know the business but aren't involved in the project (similar to brainstorming). You get away from the eye of the hurricane for several hours, perhaps a full day. You work with a large whiteboard, and you list every problem and potential problem that might be sinking the ship.

You then identify the five most critical problems, and you work together to develop scenarios that reduce those problems to a manageable size. These solutions could involve (a) changing the project; (b) changing the people; (c) resetting expectations among the team, the audience, or the boss; (d) not doing something, or doing it on a much smaller scale. Work through the basic details, but don't get caught up in intricate implementation issues (the staff will take care of those later). You then look at all the other problems on the board, and you cluster them into (a) issues that will be minimized when the five critical changes are made; (b) problems that can be solved later; and (c) problems that cannot be solved.

When the meeting ends, get right to work. Make changes. Pull the staff together and explain what you think has gone wrong and how you are correcting the situation. If your solutions are perceived as honest goodwill, not as patronizing or as cover-ups for the real problem, you will gain ground. People will extend themselves and help.

With this approach, you get one big chance to make things work. Before and afterward, you can make small improvements, but any second "big change" will deflate confidence. Wait for the right pitch, but resist the temptation to hit the ball out of the park. Instead, get a few runners on base and score some runs. The team will take care of the rest.

Getting Lost in the Details

Spend enough intense time with the details of any project, and you will lose the big picture. Components will become somewhat indistinguishable from one another. You'll begin to lose track of some details, while obsessing about others. At this point, it's helpful to: (a) get away for a few days; (b) get away for a few hours; (c) review everything you've done so that you regain the big picture; (d) act out your frustration by being silly, angry, frustrated, accusatory, or distracted and exhausted; and (e) just keep moving so that you get the job done. All of these and none of these work very well.

The Value of Rehearsal

Tenor saxophone player Cannonball Adderley on his years with Miles Davis, said: "As for rehearsals, we had maybe five in two years I was there, two of them when I first joined the band. And the rehearsals were quite direct, like, "Coltrane, show Cannonball how you do this. All right, now let's do it."[12]

Film director Jim Jarmusch said, "We do a lot of improvisation in the rehearsal process: In fact, we rehearse a lot of scenes that are not in the film but are the characters in character. They are scenes I play around with, and out of that I get a lot of new ideas. Then while we're shooting,

[12] SOURCE: Joe Goldberg, *Jazz Masters of the Fifties*, p. 79.

how much improvising we do depends on the actors. Obviously, I prefer to improvise in rehearsals because you're not burning money."[13]

Rehearsing is always a good idea. Start with a plan. Be loose, but focused. Get it right. Then practice, practice, practice.

The Usefulness of Skill

Bear in mind what Michelangelo said some 500 years ago: "A man paints with his brains and not with his hands."

Early on, most creative people migrate toward a set of foundation skills. Learning how to write an effective trade ad. Understanding and then practicing how to use split filters to improve texture and contrast on a black-and-white print. Controlling your body's breathing apparatus to blow clean, clear notes from your trumpet or trombone. Developing a solid work ethic. Knowing how and when to work hard and when to let it rest.

Then, we build on those skills and expand our capabilities. In the darkroom, it's no longer about cropping, f/stops, or controlling time in the developer; these come naturally. Now, it's about bleaching, selenium toning, and other advanced techniques. And then, it's back out into the world to shoot better images. We learn how to do the job better. We learn how to capture more of the imagination of more and different audiences, clients, employers. Our job is to understand human emotions and to know how to press the necessary buttons. That's the essence of this book: to help you press those buttons so that your new play is successful, so that your new commercials sell cars or soap, so that your political campaign gets the candidate elected.

In time, every creative professional possesses all of the requisite skills to do the job. So why does one creative person succeed while another struggles? Some reasons favoring success:

• A keen understanding of the marketplace

---

[13] SOURCE: *Jim Jarmusch Interviews*, edited by Ludvig Hertzberg; Peter Keogh, 1992, *Sight and Sound*, Vol. 2, No. 2, August 1992, p.8-9.

- Abundant self-knowledge
- Your ability to engage others in your creative work
- The right combination of integrity and cooperation
- Willingness of others to work with you (based on track record, industry reputation, personality, quality of the opportunity)
- Your ability to raise necessary resources and/or support

To put this another way, the creative process does not exist in a vacuum. Instead, you are part of a community. The way you behave as a member of that community will affect your success more profoundly than your ability to dance, juggle, sculpt, arrange the horn section, or any other skill-based endeavor.

The Value of Superior Technique

"Steve Lacy, the young soprano saxophonist who worked with Thelonius Monk in the summer of 1960, says, 'If a technique in jazz is the art of making sense, then (Monk's) got more technique than anybody. Or if technique is not wasting any notes, then he's got more technique than anybody. And he certainly can play the piano. He can get more varied colors, sounds, rhythms, and shapes out of the piano than anybody I know. He plays the whole instrument. He gets more out of one note than any other piano player, perhaps with the exception of Duke or Cecil Taylor. He's got fabulous technique…'"[14]

Some creative professionals are called "an artist's artist" or "an actor's actor." This confusing terminology refers to the professional's superior technique. A professional with the finest possible technique doesn't fake it. He is the real thing, the standard that measures the rest of us. Sadly, the best possible technique doesn't necessarily equate with commercial success.

---

[14] SOURCE: Joe Goldberg, *Jazz Masters of the Fifties*, p. 27.

PRACTICE!

Author and Harvard clinical psychology professor John J. Ratey, M.D., tells two stories that apply directly to the value of practice in any creative endeavor.

The first story is about Temple Grandin, now a 50-plus doctor of animal sciences and a leading expert in animal handling. Dr. Grandin, at the time of Ratey's story, was training herself to deal with certain aspects of her autism. She would spend hours approaching the automatic doors at a local Safeway food market, each time teaching herself to relax. She put together this training program in order to stop a bad habit: approaching people who interested her with such energy that she physically knocked them down. Grandin taught her brain about the connection between approaching doors and approaching people. The brain understood the connection, and in time, Grandin's body did the right thing.

How that lesson was learned is also explained by Ratey, this time through a group of squirrel monkeys whose brains were implanted with electrodes. Scientist Michael Merzenich, of the University of California at San Francisco, mapped the neurons that fired as the monkeys learned to remove banana-flavored pills from a progressively smaller series of cups. With each of the four cups, the area in the brain associated with this behavior became progressively larger (that is, the number of neurons in the cortex associated with this task increased). And then, with the fifth cup, "the area shrank again; as the skill became automatic, it was delegated to other parts of the brain lower down in the chain of command. The expanded portion of the executive part of the brain, the cerebral cortex, was no longer needed to carry out the skill and guide the hand."

Want to become a better writer? Then spend your time writing. Frustrated because your illustrations don't include the best possible pictures of people? Take a drawing/anatomy course and do the homework. In time, sketching a foreshortened arm or a body in motion will become second nature. With the practice, the activity becomes second nature. Without the practice, you'll be learning all the time, but never mastering, all the while struggling to achieve the next level.

How Much Will You Be Paid?

As a rule, the marketplace will determine your general level of compensation. In some situations, these rates are formal, as in the case of American Federation of Television and Radio Artists (AFTRA), Screen Actors Guild (SAG), and other entertainment industry unions. Magazine publishers hire freelance writers at various rates; one publisher might pay ten times as much as another for a given article. You will find your way into the appropriate pay scale for the work you do. Freelancers are beholden to marketplace conditions. With the Internet, it's easy to compare notes and to make sure that you're not being exploited.

If you freelance, you will most likely earn several hundred dollars per day. If you work for a salary, you will generally earn somewhere in the $35,000-$75,000 range per year, for work as an artist, writer, editor, producer, marketing manager and so on. If you work for a larger firm, or in a large city, or you're both a creative contributor and manager, you will earn more, perhaps twice as much. Naturally, each creative professional's goal is to break through the rate structure, to become a highly paid contributor, perhaps setting some comfortable work rules in addition to the cash compensation. In fact, the only way to do this is to work for yourself—to own a percentage of a product that sells very well. You are less likely to break through as either a freelancer or an employee (unless you get lucky with an acquisition or stock whose shares dramatically increase in value).

Employee compensation is typically established through a combination of company policy and marketplace research. When a human resources department is working properly, a compensation expert will research similar jobs in comparable markets and then arrive at a salary range for your position. You will be paid a salary in the lower end or the middle of that range, allowing room for raises later on. In some cases, you might supply some salary research to help out (some compensation experts welcome the help, others find this intrusive). The salary range for your position will then be compared with other, somewhat comparable roles within the company, and the offer will be made by the company to you, a potential new employee.

At this stage, you can try to negotiate for special considerations. In most cases, this will be a waste of time and energy, and, perhaps a sign that you are not a team player. In all but the smallest companies, management will insist on consistency in the number of hours worked per week, the start and end of each work day, limitations on outside work, and special office or workspace arrangements. In general, creative employees are treated just like other employees. However, there are a number of special situations in which a selective request list should be a part of negotiations. Key discussion points should be:

Bonuses. Creative people generate value (think in terms of patents, copyrights and new products). The company benefits, but the individual creative genius behind the new idea should be specially compensated for successes. This is not likely to be an easy discussion, and it is likely to be escalated beyond the HR department. If you are in a strong negotiating position, you could pursue this direction. Most companies will be dismissive; it is in their best interest to behave this way.

Compensatory Time. Creative people often work long hours on specific projects. Compensatory ("comp") time should be available—both coming in later in the morning and taking days off to compensate for weekends worked, etc. The objective here is not to establish a separate class of employees, but instead to be sure that company policy is fair to all employees, including those who put in considerable amounts of extra time. Most often, this is not handled as a condition of employment, but is instead handled in an informal manner by the manager in charge.

Contract. Companies tend not to sign contracts with employees. If you are reasonably senior, and you are bringing a very specialized skill set to a company that really needs you, then you might be able to convince the company to put you under contract. This binds them to certain terms and conditions. Of course, you will also be bound to the terms of the agreement.

Title. You can also negotiate for a particular title. This is always worth a discussion, as every company seems to have its own peculiar policies and traditions regarding job titles.

In general, if you are working for an established company, your long-term success with that company increases if you behave like a regular employee, not as a special case. Put your ego aside—you will receive the same benefits as the people who you work with every day.

Chapter 5 - Overcoming Obstacles

You'll find no shortage of obstacles. Fortunately, you can manage your way through many of them. Some present opportunities. Others, you can learn to live with....

Our Love-Hate Relationships with Obstacles (and Boundaries)

Imagine yourself in total control. The boss or client adores you. Complete creative freedom is yours to enjoy. Assume you are an architect specializing in office buildings. You can choose any piece of property, build with any materials, and spend whatever time or money you need. Imagine! Complete creative freedom!

If you were a second-grader, you'd get out your crayons and draw your dream building. But for better or for worse, you're a grown-up. So what's the first thing you do? You challenge yourself to live inside the building, to occupy the finished space. Immediately, you make decisions: The place needs entry, egress; it must be safe and functional; it must...

Say *sayonara* to complete freedom. Instinctively, you set up rules, boundaries, obstacles. Whether form follows function or the other way around, most creative professionals can't get anything done without some rules.

In some ways, creative work never stops being a homework assignment.

Art teacher Robert Dodge asks students to "answer a question" every week by creating a new drawing. Not just any drawing—this week it's an assignment that demonstrates your understanding of the human knee. Draw in whatever medium and size you want. Parameters. Boundaries. Obstacles.

In fact, the knee is not easy to draw: It's a rounded bony object surrounded by thick muscle. Many students find the knee especially challenging because of perspective or foreshortening (a necessary visual distortion to make a drawn or painted body part look "right" in the finished work). Another obstacle: homework during a busy week with limited available time. Curse the deadline, but the agony won't last more than a week because that's when the assignment is due.

It's common for the creative team at an advertising agency to start work with a one-pager called a "creative brief," complete with project summary, target audience, project tone, messaging highlights, competition's approaches and three key words to describe the brand. Web development shops employ a similar brief. Are these rules, boundaries, or obstacles? If the project's target is women in their thirties, then anyone not of that demographic lies beyond the boundary. A creative concept inconsistent with the desired tone exists beyond the fenced-in area, and so it's unacceptable. And so on.

Let's look at the obstacles you're most likely to face.

Working to Deadline

There is joy in battle. Troops are focused on the goal, single-minded in their quest for success. The team becomes one; adrenaline junkies have their day; the excitement of overcoming the impossible becomes the only thing in the life of the team.

And then, the project ends. Everyone collapses. No real work gets done for the next week as people check out and recharge.

Next deadline, next battle. There is some dissension among the troops, but the mission is accomplished on time and on budget.

Third time out, nobody's too enthusiastic. It's no longer a race to the deadline; instead, it's unlovingly called another "fire drill." People go through the motions, but don't give their time or heart so freely. They want more money, payback for the past's impossible hours and for the time they've sacrificed.

Now and then, a deadline rush is probably a good thing. It's one way of getting a team to gel quickly. It's also a way to meet the occasional deadline and to encourage rapid bonding between team members (the technique works especially well with new teams). Everyone learns what they are capable of doing—how much work they really can turn out in a short period. As a manager, I sometimes use the deadline rush technique when a project doesn't seem to be getting off the ground; one good night, with sufficient Chinese food and a clear agenda, can focus everyone. It's best if that agenda includes a specific deliverable, so the entire team takes part in putting together the proposal, sample materials, etc.

Apart from the occasional sprints, there is little value in pressing against deadlines. Stress levels rise, and by and large the quality of work is bound to be better if it's done over time, with proper reviews, critiques, and revisions. There is a myth among creative people who claim they work best when a deadline is imminent. I think this is utter nonsense. I believe that the thoughtful, focused time immediately prior to delivery can make a huge difference in polishing a project—but only if the bulk of the work has been done over an extended schedule. (In fact, I am in that position now. This book has taken months to write, but in this final draft, I find myself resolving many organizational problems and filling gaps that somehow never got filled. I'm focused; I want to hand in a good manuscript that the editor will like—in part because I don't want the manuscript back in my hands with more editorial comments. I simply want the project to be over, so I'm doing my best to make it perfect.

Difficult People and Their Afflictions

Most people don't understand what a creative professional does for a living. How do you explain why a walk in the woods can be so productive when designing a new math curriculum? Or why you can't just write a funny joke without first reading a newspaper? Or why you must immerse yourself and then emerge from the darkness of self-loathing before you can even hope to audition for a romantic lead role in a musical comedy? Or why your work involves so much laughter and loud conversation? The fact is, the creative process rarely proceeds from A to Z. Instead, it's more like A; B; X; Q; antelope; gnu; nothing, what's new with you; General Tsao's Chicken; I need a haircut; Z. Working with us is no picnic.

THINKING DIFFERENTLY

A few years back, Apple Computer ran a popular advertising campaign featuring posters filled with the faces of Alfred Hitchcock, Albert Einstein, Thomas Edison, Pablo Picasso, Amelia Earhart, Joan Baez, Ted Turner, Lucille Ball and Desi Arnaz, Ansel Adams, Jim Henson, Bob Dylan, Miles Davis, Martha Graham, Maria Callas, Gandhi, and others. The message was clear: just like these great innovators, people who use Apple computers are innovators, too.

If you were to assemble these extraordinary people in an Apple conference room and asked them to discuss Apple's latest innovative device, there would be little consensus. For example, Ted Turner might point toward unexploited business opportunities. Edison might be fascinated by the technology, and interested in further improvements and implementations. Gandhi and Baez might see the potential for social good. And it would be fascinating to see whether Lucy or Einstein would be the first to say something funny. Smart, creative people can be very engaging, but in order to get anything done, you'll need some shepherding skills.

Despite the frustration that various afflictions can cause, angry responses rarely accomplish anything at all, and yet, that's the way many creative people respond to difficult personalities. Confrontation and aggressive behavior are always bad ideas. To paraphrase Tolstoy, every difficult person is difficult in their own way. Understanding the most common patterns can go a long way toward overcoming obstacles related to difficult people.

No Concept

Definition: Complete lack of understanding the project, context, requirements.

Symptoms: Inability to explain the concept, or to allow others to explain what the project is about and what is required to make it happen. Repeated pattern of discounting the project's importance, difficulty, and key contributors.

Key Statement: "Yes, I completely understand what's involved. It's no big thing."

Short-Term Cures: Work around the clueless person, even if he is the leader. Keep the person posted through e-mails, invitations to meetings, and other briefings. Give the person appropriate credit to avoid a mess.

Long-Term Cures: It's difficult to educate someone who is clearly wrong for the job. Deal with the person as a figurehead, and if he doesn't get in the way, keep moving. If the person becomes a problem that won't go away, consider leaving.

Lack of Clarity of Project or Mission

Definition: A bold but extremely general vision of the future, with not much understanding of the work involved in bringing that future to life.

Symptoms: Initial discussions are confusing and hard to follow. Varying degrees of impatience with people who ask specific questions. Resumé is dodgy, with unexplained gaps. Could be accompanied by personal insecurities, unexplained work absences, quirky habits, work time spent discussing politics. Lack of preparedness for meetings. Large numbers of complicated charts and graphs prepared by small personal team whose work is not easily understood by others. Might be accompanied by mud-slinging and by a leader turning against team members. Might blame others.

Key Statements: "There's more in my head than I'm telling you right now." "Don't worry, the details will become clear to you over time." "There are reasons why I cannot tell you everything right now."

Short-Term Cures: Ideally, stay out of her way. Resist your desire to become part of this person's inner circle; she will crash and burn and you don't want to get hurt. Try to keep this person away from team members, lest they sense sketchy leadership and either checkout or leave. A no-win situation.

Long-Term Cures: The person needs to be removed from a position of responsibility. A subleader might be able to fill the gap for the rest of the project. Since these people sometimes get high-visibility jobs, your stint could become a useful resumé item.

Can't Envision Concept to Completion

Definition: A small-picture thinker, capable of understanding and implementing parts of a project, but incapable of putting the pieces together into a coherent whole.

Symptoms: Attempts to simplify the current project beyond any reasonable or productive degree; long conversations about irrelevant or tangential topics in which the individual can exert a higher degree of control; reliance on line managers to gain deeper understanding of the entire project.

Key Statement: "The big picture will take care of itself; let's focus on what we can accomplish right now."

Short-Term Cures: Provide information and project flow in smaller pieces that can be absorbed by the individual. Avoid conceptual conversations. Demonstrate reliable attention to detail. Be very specific when requesting feedback.

Long-Term Cures: Generously prepare the individual for every longer-range conversation so meetings are not sidelined. Identify other leaders in the organization who can provide big-picture leadership and support or work around this individual (preferably the former unless the situation becomes dire).

Inability to Communicate

Definition: An individual who hasn't thought through a project and cannot communicate its details, or one who might have it all in his head but can't articulate thoughts or messages productively.

Symptoms: Tends not to write to communicate. Speaks in vague terms or talks a lot without saying much of anything. Might rely on catch-phrases that lack clarity or meaning. Might be well-intentioned, but a poor communicator. Might be incapable of envisioning the result or the path to the result.

Key Statement: "At our next group meeting, maybe you could explain it. You do that better than I do."

Short-Term Cures: It is possible to ask a series of increasingly directed questions to cause a decision to be uttered. Do not interrogate; instead, build from a friendly relationship. Don't allow the person to appear foolish. Handle with care.

Long-Term Cure: Some individuals can be trained to improve their verbal and/or writing skills. Of course, the behavior change is dependent upon the individual's willingness to change.

Does Not Share Information
Definition: Individual collects information related to the project, but does not distribute the information, or distributes it in a limited manner.

Symptoms: Evidence of a desire or need to control as an aspect of personal power; insecurity in other areas; willingness to share only certain information with certain people; warnings against sharing with others on the team; evasive answers; documents promised but not delivered.

Key Statements: "I'll tell you what you need to know." "Don't worry. As long as I know everything, we're fine."

Short-Term Cure: In this case, a gentle confrontation is probably appropriate. The goal of confrontation is a degree of behavioral change: respect for the person's authority along with an earnest plea for sharing as a means of managing a more successful team.

Long-Term Cure: The root of the problem could run deep. Serious retraining is needed to change the behavior. Best to design information flow systems that are flat, not hierarchical, so no single person controls flow.

Minimizes Importance of Third-Party Buy-in
Definition: Individual sees herself as the center of the project and considers other parties to be tangential.

Symptoms: Secretive; resists interaction with peers or superiors with regard to project; delays meetings; limits e-mail interaction. Discounts the importance of keeping others informed or getting approvals on key milestones.

Key Statements: "If I say it's okay, that's good enough." "Let's keep this within our group. When the time is right, we'll involve others."

Short-Term Cure: Investigate to find out whether other departments are required for help, for buy-in, etc. If so, discreetly build some bridges.

Long-Term Cure: Devise a more complex series of mandatory interactions between stakeholders.

Underestimates Level of Complexity

Definition: Individual sees the big picture, but fails to recognize the complexity associated with the details.

Symptoms: Unable to read or understand a complicated schedule of interdependent events; surprised by the number steps or people required; doubtful about pulling together so many resources; evades in-depth discussions; becomes easily bored when conversation turns to details of implementation.

Key Statement: "You guys work that stuff out. Just let me know when you need me."

Short-Term Cure: If the individual is willing to leave the details to the professionals, no cure is required. However, if he has undersold the project and resources are constrained as a result, the individual must be trained to acquire additional resources and to involve others in planning future projects.

Long-Term Cure: Discourage the individual from pitching or closing on projects without team interaction and approval of general and specific plan.

Doesn't Understand How and Why Schedules or Budgets Work

Definition: Individual can inspect a schedule or a budget but doesn't absorb the information. Or, operates in constant state of denial.

Symptoms: Spending money or causing delays without attention to available and/or budgeted resources. Assumes the budget or schedule will morph into a shape that embraces the aberrations.

Key Statement: "Let me worry about the big decisions. I'm sure you can work your magic and keep us on track."

Short-Term Cure: Hide some time and some money to protect the perpetrator from himself. (You can try to discourage the behavior, and you might win a few battles while losing the war.)

Long-Term Cure: Continue to hide time and money until you are able to find another job.

Doesn't Play Well With Others

Definition: May or may not realize that she does not work effectively in group or team situations.

Symptoms: Might be non-communicative, intentionally or unintentionally negative; might ask multiple people to do the same task; might delegate poorly or fitfully; might cause people to rush through important steps or to waste time on less important ones. Might be a negative influence, and may not inspire trust or good work.

Key Statements: "Just do it my way." "Why do you always ask so many questions?" "This is your problem, not mine."

Short-Term Cure: Work around the person as much as possible. Involve her as needed, but get the project done with the people who do work together. You might need to sacrifice some credit to the problem individual; it's worth the trade. You are not going to train this person about the fine art of creative work; just move on.

Long-Term Cure: Either wait for the person to be de-positioned, help make that happen, or find another job. Some individuals can be retrained, but this is a non-trivial task and you probably have better ways to spend your time.

Poor Listener

Definition: No matter how many times you deliver a message and how many ways you communicate your ideas, the message is sent but not received.

Symptoms: Denial that the conversation ever occurred; forgetfulness; "nobody's home" when you're having a conversation; individual looks at other things or other people when you are talking; nonresponsive to questions; lousy body language; talks over you.

Key Statements: "You never said that." "I know what I heard, and I did not hear that from you."

Short-Term Cures: Try communicating in multiple ways: Say it, write it on a whiteboard, send in an e-mail, recap in a memo, have other people repeat the key points. When you say something, begin by explaining what you are going to say, then say it, and then repeat what you've said. Ask the individual to repeat the key points of what you just said. Handle with care; these individuals can get rattled when challenged.

Long-Term Cure: Most likely, the lousy listener experiences other problems (at home, etc.). Better habits can be taught to those who are willing to learn (there are experts who teach listening skills). If the relationship is worth the time and trouble, hang around, and you might become a better listener, too.

Disorganized

Definition: Loses things. Often.

Symptoms: Maintains a general idea of what's happening, but never manages to have the correct information at the right moment. Office is a mess. Often runs behind on meeting schedule, returned phone calls, etc.

Key Statement: "Hang on, I'll find it in a minute." "Are you sure that you gave it to me?"

Short-Term Cure: Actually, there are consultants who can help. Also, a good assistant or other staff support can work wonders. Big if: the individual must be willing to be helped.

Long-Term Cure: Stay organized yourself, so that you always have the necessary information on hand. Also, learn the person's peculiar mental pathways to help him maintain focus.

Changes Direction without Warning

Definition: Doesn't signal before turning.

Symptoms: Attends meetings and makes decisions that affect the group without consulting the group. Might make decisions based on personal good, not project good. Might not understand that she is making changes or the severity or complexities associated with the changes; might be well-intentioned while leaving chaos in her wake.

Key Statements: "What? I didn't change anything. Oh that, well, that's no big deal. I can tell you exactly how to get the job done quickly."

Short-Term Cure: Sit the person down and explain the situation. She will deny it, or suggest improvements. Teach her to recognize the behavior and its consequences. Be patient; over time, her behavior can be unlearned.[1] Find ways to attach accountability to these actions, if possible.

Long-Term Cure: Encourage the staff to work together to help her see the error of her ways and to suggest planning and approval systems to minimize future trouble. If that doesn't work, then either put up with the behavior or find another job.

Just Plain Nasty

Definition: Someone you would not invite to your home or to a public gathering.

Symptoms: Curses freely. Often on the edge of abusive language or behavior. Frequently very negative. Says bad things about coworkers. Highly critical. Operates within own limited band of reality.

Key Statements: Inappropriate for print!

Short-Term Cure: Keep him reasonably happy by paying appropriate political attention, but then move on. You are not going to change this behavior.

Long-Term Cure: Choose to work with somebody else.

Not Competent, or Marginally Competent

Definition: Might seem to work like a normal person, but doesn't actually accomplish tasks in a reasonable way. (A job title, even if it is senior, or a seemingly accomplished resume, does not necessarily equate with competence.)

---

[1] I know, because this was me, and I did unlearn it.

Symptoms: Makes indefinite or wrong-headed decisions. Causes delays without concept of the consequences. Speaks negatively about others doing a bad job, whether they are or not. Might suggest a broad-based plan to keep everyone engaged, but the plan might have holes. Chooses one or several scapegoats, but rotates the privilege so many are hurt. Might cover up. Might not communicate details. High-handed manner. Especially poisonous among senior executives, whose careers and lives could be destroyed. Often, a good politician. Might surround herself with MBAs to demonstrate departmental competence, but show up at the office only when convenient.

Key Statement: "I know what I'm doing." "Don't tell me how to do things. I've been doing this since (before you were born)."

Short-Term Cure: Steer clear. Involve yourself only as absolutely necessary, regardless of the person's corporate or political power.

Long-Term Cure: Choose to work with somebody else.

Lack of Smarts
Definition: Significantly less intelligent or street smart than you are.

Symptoms: Slow on the uptake. Does not contribute to important conversations. Fearful of asking questions, so silence or occasional comment might be perceived as a form of restrained wisdom. Fails to understand the marketplace or the value of products created.

Key Statement: "No, no, I do understand. I understand completely."

Short-Term Cure: Be nice. Include him in all relevant activities, but avoid a path in which he must be gatekeeper or final decision maker. If he is well-intentioned but a bit slow, you can help focus the person and help him succeed.

Long-Term Cure: Depends upon the person and the situation. A smart co-worker is certainly a worthwhile asset, but not everybody needs to be a smarty pants in order to succeed or to add value. Learn to relax. Leave if you must, or if your learning or career path is hampered.

Sheer Ego

Definition: Self-confidence the size of our forty-ninth state.

Symptoms: Makes statements and decisions based on personal power and advancement. Does not consider the group, except as an extension of herself. Takes credit for other people's work. Sometimes makes others small in order to become larger.

Key Statements: "This is all about me." "Enough about me. Let's talk about you. What do think of me?"

Short-Term Cure: Roll with it. If she can help you learn or to do projects that you want to do, ego is not the toughest problem in the world. (Show-business people have coped with this issue for centuries.) Laugh about it, too. Chances are, the egotistical individual will recognize her own behavior and laugh with you—but she will not change behavior that has brought her this far.

Long-Term Cure: Depending upon your own personality, you could either eventually tire of the game or decide your role is okay.

Working with Difficult Situations

Apart from the people, difficult situations are typically caused by not enough time, not enough money, and/or some other resource constraint.

Not Enough Money

At the risk of oversimplification, a project leader faced with insufficient funds faces just a few possible solutions:

Do Less

The most sensible resolution is to do less. That is, refine the project's specifications and requirements for cash so that you accomplish everything you possibly can with the money available. In fact, just about every creative endeavor takes this approach. In most cases, a budget is approved when a project is approved; if not, then rough budgetary guidelines are likely to accompany the go-ahead. If the project was budgeted properly, there ought to be enough money to do everything that is necessary. Unless, of course, the project changes midstream, or unless work needs to be done more than once.

Scenic design for television provides a helpful case study. At the start of a major project, the producer, director, and designer discuss the theoretical look and feel of the show. A budget is discussed. The designer returns with conceptual set sketches, walks them through each element, and explains that the budget will not buy everything in the sketch. The producer and director are disappointed (this happens all the time). At this stage, the designer is working conceptually; the design must be estimated by one or more construction shops. Every idea on the sketch gets a price tag. While maintaining the design's integrity, materials and sources are evaluated. If the etched glass panels could be replaced by plastic ones with an appliqué...; if drapes were rented rather than made...; the floor could be painted, not built from custom tiles; elements on the sidelines, not often seen on camera, can be simplified. Compromises are made; the set gets built. The smart producer sets aside some money for inevitable last minute changes—modifications after the set is built and delivered.

Find More Money

Another sensible (if challenging) solution to the "not enough money" problem is to find more money. In many situations, this simply isn't possible: The project is on a fixed budget. Some project leaders have a knack for pulling money or other resources out of the sky. The need for money becomes the impetus for making a phone call that you've put off, and suddenly you find a new market for the current project or an opportunity for a new one. Good advice can be summed up in just two words: "Always ask." The worst someone can say is "no," which leaves you in no worse shape than before. The best they can say is "yes," which could go a long way toward solving the current problem. *Always ask.*

Find Some Friends

There are always other solutions, some unconventional. One trick involves enlisting talented hands without paying for them. When I produced a low-budget game show pilot for Lifetime, we were short on staff and needed somebody to keep score. So we hired (at no cost) one of the company's bookkeepers, who was thrilled to leave his desk for the day. The occasional use of interns, friends and lovers, or the boss's teenaged children can ease the load without spending valuable budget dollars. These are tricks; use them too often and they'll lose their effectiveness.

Remember: the average person rarely gets the opportunity to become involved in creative endeavors. The next time you need four women to wear traffic cones on their heads for a giant billboard that will sit beside an interstate highway, just go into a beauty parlor and ask. More than likely, you'll have more than four volunteers. (Yes, this really happened.)

Also, consider your existing staff. When I was the editor-in-chief of a national magazine, we used to hire top illustrators to do the cover designs. One illustrator handed in an illustration we could not use, but his contract required us to pay him anyway. So, we had a magazine to put out, but no money to pay for the cover art. One of the staff artists had been showing off her illustrations of animals—they were exquisite—and when the opportunity to show her work on the cover of the magazine presented itself, she was more than willing to help out. She created the new cover in a few days, kept us on schedule, and added a significant credential to her resumé.

Seek Out Efficiencies

This old corporate management trick works for creative endeavors as well. Throughout the first year of *Where in the World Is Carmen Sandiego?*, each episode's comedy and musical numbers were staged live. The bits placed a large rehearsal burden on the daily schedule and required performers to hang around several hours for their turn to rehearse. A budget crunch forced us to rethink our shooting schedule. I forcefully argued against prerecording bits. My arguments came from the heart, but *I was wrong* (I always learn more by being wrong than being right). We saved tens of thousands of dollars by rehearsing and recording the season's musical numbers and comedy bits in one session. This approach allowed for concentrated planning of these segments, focused the writing, made rehearsals more productive, and reduced "waiting around time" for performers. And we learned to produce the series for less money, with fewer people, less overtime, and fewer headaches than we ever dreamed.[2] Not only did I learn a lesson, I became an evangelist for this type of efficient project management.

Not Enough Time

Clearly, some money-saving solutions also save time. To save me time writing and you time reading, I've bulleted the time-savers:

- Do less: Refine the project requirements so you can finish faster.
- Find someone who knows how to design and manage efficient systems, then let the person(s) do their work.
- Negotiate for more time. Sometimes, this is easier than negotiating for more money. Extend the deadline; move the delivery date, the

---

[2] Credit to producer Jonathan Meath for making this work.

publication or air date; or complete only portions of the project before deadline and complete the remainder later on. (There may be some costs attached, but they might not be substantial.)

Efficient Work Groups

In general, an individual can work faster than a small team, and a small team can work faster than a larger one. This sensible approach to management is too often forgotten.

An individual requires little supervision and wastes no time in meetings. With staff comes complexity, varied opinions, coordination to maintain consistency, plus meetings to keep the project on track, and review and approval processes.

A duo can be equally efficient, especially when the task list is divided between them. My new company works this way. My co-founder and I review task lists daily, then each of us gets to work. We live about a mile from each other, but we see one another only a few times a week, mostly for client meetings. I spend my days selling, writing plans and proposals, designing graphics, and developing marketing programs. He spends his days working out budgets and financials, producing and editing video, setting up sales calls, and managing production and technology. Together, we are a formidable small company. Over time, we plan to build a larger team, but we know that we will sacrifice a high percentage of our time to managing it. For the present, clients are surprised by the amount of work that two experienced people can do in a week. We work long hours, stay very organized, and don't waste time in meetings or on unimportant projects.

One more reason our little company works: We are not managed from above. There is no senior manager resetting our priorities. There are no company politics. However skillful or well-intentioned, a senior manager affects the way the team spends its time. When the system works properly, the senior manager sets direction and provides a clear path for approvals at key intervals. The senior manager should not get involved in the details—that is not his job.

These days, many teams are geographically separated. E-mails with attachments are one way to move information, but an ftp site, where everybody can access every file any time is a better way to organize and distribute information. Regularly scheduled group meetings or conference calls are essential and should be arranged daily (for short-term projects) or weekly (for longer ones). Meetings are most effective when they reliably happen as planned, begin and end on time, and work to an agenda distributed beforehand. The purpose of each meeting should be clear: information-sharing, group brainstorming to solve a particular problem, a decision. Meetings also encourage interaction between busy people; the resulting human connections can be more powerful than the agenda itself. Reliability and consistency are essential, particularly when the group is large and the project is complex; do not move or reschedule meeting times.

Not Enough Resources

"In the Japanese martial arts, there is a saying: Zen seven, ken three. Ken refers to the sword. The meaning of the saying is that success in swordsmanship is seven parts Zen, or inner approach, and three parts ken, or technical ability."[3]

A project's most valuable resource is not the money or the tool, but the people who do the work.

Nowhere is this better illustrated than in the project made outside the mainstream, without the customary network of resources: a theatrical production staged in a natural location, not a traditional theater; a storytelling festival held in a stark concrete convention center; a musical performance in a gymnasium. It's an imperfect world; all we do what we have to do to get the job done. Often the job involves resources or constraints that are unique and therefore challenging.

---

[3] SOURCE: Laurence G. Boldt, *Zen and the Art of Making a Living*, p. 293.

Hire Experienced Professionals

If you are working in a difficult situation, surround yourself with an experienced team. Producing a movie in the middle of nowhere is tough enough; doing this with someone who has never directed a movie before is a bad idea. The more difficult the situation, the greater the need for professionals. Training newcomers is fine; just avoid on-the-job learning on difficult projects.

Why? Experience brings a greater inventory of possible solutions, more resources, people to call for answers—years of "been there, done that." A professional might not have experience with a specific problem, but after years of doing more or less the same sort of job, the experienced professional will possess a good sense of what not to do and may have previously done something useful to get out of today's jam. The ability to sense the situation and quickly adapt comes with the professional package; amateurs stumble, professionals make it work.

Make the Most of Your Co-Workers

Few creative endeavors are provided with sufficient resources. When resources and some aspects of management are lacking, the team members must deliver despite the difficulties. This is most efficiently accomplished in several practical ways. First, establish clear roles and responsibilities. Every team member should understand where his job begins and ends. Second, establish peer reviews, so that the entire team shares information about interdependencies and learns how to cope without sufficient resources or management. Third, be clear on the aspects of a project that are lacking and be smart in expressing these needs to management or other powers-that-be. Complaining and random negative comments are not the way to get what's needed. Instead, when a trusted creative professional approaches management with a clear, well-considered list of problems and potential solutions, the likelihood of getting what's needed is increased.

Be More Practical (or Figure Out How to Make Less Practical Work)

In an ideal world, every photographer would be able to extend the hour before sunset for golden light. In the real world, when a photographer is hired for a location shoot, it's by the day, so there are only one or two opportunities to shoot during golden hour—even when golden hour lasts only twenty minutes. To some extent, a photographer can fake golden hour with lights, gels, filters, and, later, in Adobe Photoshop. Often, the game is about alternative solutions—finding some way to accomplish the task without sacrificing the project's integrity.

How does one become more practical? Experience is one way; flexibility is another. Listen to other people--you might not have the right idea, but you might be smart enough to recognize the right idea when someone else suggests it. A complete understanding of available tools is also essential: A director who understands not only performance but writing and lighting is going to have more available options than one whose experience is mainly with the actors. If you lead with your ego, you're not going to get much help. If you operate as a team member, group smarts and experience kick in.

Don't Overcompensate

A music video is not a feature-length motion picture. A short story is not a novel. Don't try to make a modest project larger than it needs to be. From the start, set expectations for yourself, your co-workers, and the audience.

Every project is different, and to some extent, *you* must be different for every project.

The moment I tell a Web designer, "Well, when I worked in television, we did it this way," I am off base. Web design is not television design; Web design involves fewer resources and more direct hands-on work. I try to adapt my thinking and my style to each situation.

When the movie *Hollywood Ending* begins, Woody Allen plays a movie director stuck shooting a hemorrhoid commercial instead of a feature film. He's a neurotic mess, partly because he wants the commercial to be a feature film instead. It's only a hemorrhoid commercial—a paycheck, nothing more. We all shoot hemorrhoid commercials from time to time—not our favorite way to employ our God-given talent, but sometimes necessary. It's not your role to make everybody miserable because you're not playing the game you want to play. It's your job to make the best of it (or not to do it at all). Just do the job and move on to the next one.

Listening, People Skills

There has been a considerable amount of academic research and thought related to listening strategies and skills. Professor John Drakeford wrote: "*Hearing* is a word that describes the physiological sensory processes by which auditory sensations are received by the ears and transmitted to the brain. *Listening*, on the other hand, refers to a more complex psychological procedure involving interpreting and understanding the significance of the sensory experience."[4]

According to Robert Bolton,[5] listening is an activity that apparently occupies 70 percent of our waking hours, yet requires largely undeveloped skills. He evangelizes the value of paraphrasing, which assures the speaker that her message is being understood; reflecting feelings, which provides the speaker with a sense that the message context and impact are also understood; and summary reflections, which demonstrate the depth of the listener's comprehension of the speaker's world. All these skills are lacking in most people who do creative work for a living. Even an incremental improvement can make an enormous difference.

Much of a creative professional's success is dependent on clear sensory input: listening to the client's requirements and feedback, for example. If you have the opportunity to take a course in listening skills, take it. Few training courses prove so valuable.

---

[4] SOURCE: John Drakeford, *The Awesome Power of Listening* (Waco, Texas: Word, 1967, p. 17) (italics within paragraph are mine).
[5] SOURCE: Robert Bolton, Ph.D., *People Skills*. These are based, in turn, upon the work of Thomas Gordon, who wrote *Parent Effectiveness Training*.

Critics and Criticism

An art student's moment of truth is known as "the crit." Every student posts his work on a large bulletin board, then listens to comparison, review, and criticism by the teacher and the class. If the crit goes well, the student is elated; talent has been confirmed by peers and a mentor. If the crit goes poorly, the student is depressed for a week and wonders why she is bothering at all.

Our work is constantly reviewed and criticized. Only the performance of politicians is more closely scrutinized. Ambrose Bierce, a commentator, writer, and journalist, once defined painting as "the art of protecting flat surfaces from the weather and exposing them to the critic."

Ideally, a critic should be well-versed in the history of the art form and genre, technique, and literature of the medium. Glenn Kenny, *Premiere* magazine's movie critic, possesses a passion for film and literature, an extensive understanding of the filmmaker's craft, and an encyclopedic knowledge of film history. When Glenn writes a critique, I value his words more than, for example, the work of a local newspaper's reviewer.

Most people don't discriminate. Magazines like *Entertainment Weekly* present a somewhat more balanced view by providing a thumbs-up or thumbs-down chart showing major critics' reactions to the week's most talked-about films. Imagine working hard on a project for months, then seeing your work reduced to a cartoon drawing of a down-turned thumb? Why bother?

Some critics are worth reading. Seek them out; their observations and comments can help you to achieve better work. Ignore the others. Ignore the person who doesn't understand what you do. No amount of explaining, worrying, or campaigning will change that. Ignore the ignorant writer who hasn't taken the time or trouble to write with understanding. Also, ignore excerpts; they are without context and are meaningless.

Of course, most creative professionals don't deal with criticism from newspapers or magazines. Instead, they hear from the boss or the client.

The Boss or Client as Critic

In a fit of frustration, I wrote the following paragraph for a book on audiotape[6] about creativity. I still like it. I hope you do, too. It bluntly addresses the way that a boss or a client should work with a creative professional for the best possible results.

"Here's a quick rundown on the best ways to criticize someone who's trying to zig—without causing the zigger to become a zagger: Start with a compliment. Recognize the amount of effort, the amount of caring work that has been done, and find something positive to say. But don't fake it—if you sound like you're stroking, I'll check out on you. Then, don't pussyfoot around. Tell me what you think and tell me *why* you think that way. Give me reasons. The more specific, the better. And make sure your arguments are defensible—because mine sure will be. Don't try to solve the problem for me; that's why you asked me to come around in the first place. If you hire me to zig, and then you decide to start in on my territory, I'll become very frustrated or I'll become resentful. Either way, you won't get my best work. And don't get emotional. I'm looking to you for sanity. You're looking to me for great ideas. And if those great ideas come with a little craziness, that's my prerogative. Your prerogative is to treat me as a professional, or not to work with me again. If there's a middle ground, *guide* me to it. Don't push me. Because I'll either push back, or I'll stop pushing entirely, and give you what I *think* you want. I'm not a prima donna. I'm just a working stiff at heart, trying to please my boss. But I'm not connected the same way zaggers are put together, so you've got to give me some space as you're criticizing my work. Got it?"

"When Alexander the Great visited Diogenes and asked whether he could do anything for the famed teacher, Diogenes replied: 'Only stand out of my light.' Perhaps some day we shall know how to heighten creativity. Until then, one of the best things we can do for creative men and women is to stand out of their light."[7]

---

[6] SOURCE: John Keil, *How to Zig in a Zagging World*, book on audiotape, draft script, Wiley.
[7] SOURCE: John W. Gardner, as quoted in *A Writer's Life* by Kenneth Atchity.

Colleagues as Critics

When a colleague is a critic, one must consider his relationship and motivation. If the colleague is a mentor, or a fellow worker with no political agenda, and if the colleague is one you respect, then the criticism should be taken as friendly, constructive advice. There's nothing better than working with other talented people who share their ideas, their candid assessments, and their techniques for the good of the whole department. There's a wonderful sense of teamwork; everybody plays a role.

Unfortunately, the process can also become confounding. Quickly you learn that certain types of questions should be asked only of certain people. Are you choosing to solicit advice only from those who will provide positive feedback? (And is that valuable at all?) Or should you seek out the one person who will see only the problems in your work? (You'll learn more from that person, but your ego might be bruised.) Humans, particularly insecure creative humans, are more likely to seek out reward than punishment. All this points toward group criticism, where everyone's work is periodically reviewed by the entire group. This is not always practical, but it does tend to sort out individual agendas, negativity, and other bad behavior. It's also helpful to seek out friendly advice and criticism from qualified peers who work in other organizations—this reality check allows you to better understand your value in the marketplace, not just in your office.

Criticizing Your Own Work

You are not an objective observer of your own work. *(Read that sentence again; it is worth remembering)*. Yes, we all self-edit, but at the end of the project, you are not the one who can say whether the work is good, meaningful, or significant.

Okay, I'll take back what I just said. You are the only one who has any right to criticize your work. You are a skilled professional. Your judgment about your work will, almost by definition, be superior to any external critic, regardless of their skill, education, or background.

"The greater knowledge we have in any field, the subtler the degree of difference we can perceive."[8]

Gender and Race Issues

I surprised myself by including this section. The issue came to light when I discussed "this book's" Denzel Washington biography with my son. Michael knows movies, so I asked him to name black actors who were strong enough to carry a movie at the box office but who were not action heroes, comedians, musicians, or sports stars. He named plenty of white actors, but no African Americans (except Danny Glover, who hasn't made a movie in a while)—and no Asians, no Middle Easterners, no Native Americans, and only a few Latinos. We discussed authors and came up with a number of well- known, reasonably successful people. Our list of musicians was more limited. Much has been written about the lack of anyone except white actors on most TV series—except those specifically intended to appeal to black audiences.

Though we'd like to deny it, race is a factor. Of course, it's easier to cope with the race issue if you "play to type," accepting the marketplace reality that most African American and Latino male actors can only get jobs playing either bad guys or cops. I can't believe it's 2005 and I am writing this! Hopefully, by the time you read it, this section will be stupidly out of date. (Behind the scenes, the situation is no better. In the U.S., creative professionals are overwhelmingly white.)

Our discussion shifted to gender. That's when I realized that the vast majority of examples in my current draft involved only men! (Yes, I felt out-of-date and ignorant.) Apart from writers and artists, and some photographers, there weren't many creative professionals until women joined the work force in large numbers. I added more women to the next draft so that you'd never know the real story.

There's not enough space in this book to describe the many perceived

---

[8] SOURCE: Laurence G. Boldt, *Zen and the Art of Making a Living* , p. 465.

differences between male and female creative professionals, nor have I seen much research on the subject. For now, let's consider this fundamental difference between girls and boys.

"When girls play together, they do so in small intimate groups with an emphasis on minimizing hostility and maximizing cooperation, while boys' games are in larger groups, emphasizing competition. One key difference can be seen when games boys or girls are playing are disrupted by someone getting hurt. If a boy who is hurt gets upset, he is expected to get out of the way and stop crying so the game can go on. If the same happens when a group of girls is playing, the game stops while everyone gathers around to help the girl who is crying."[9]

The Challenges *You* Impose

Walt Kelly, the artist and writer behind *Pogo*, said it best on a 1970 Earth Day poster: "We have met the enemy, and he is us."

Internal and Emotional Obstacles

If you know who you are, and you can clearly explain why you are doing a project, you will be happier. You will exert a positive influence.

Or, as the *Bhagavad-Gita*[10] explains:

"For one who has conquered the mind,
The mind is the best of friends,
But for one who has failed to do so,
His very mind will be the greatest enemy."

---

[9] SOURCE: Daniel Goleman, *Emotional Intelligence*, p. 131.
[10] SOURCE: *Bhagavad Gita* (Swami Prabhavananda and Christopher Isherwood), translated, *The Song of God: Bhagavad-Gita* (NY: Mentor Books, 1951).

WHAT'S MOTIVATING YOU?

Every project you do, you do for a reason. In the rush of a busy life, it's easy to lose track of the reasons why you decided to become involved, and it's easy to confuse yourself regarding your own motivations. This small worksheet can help. When you accept a role in a new project, take five minutes to fill out the worksheet and keep a copy of it on file. With each new project, add a worksheet to the file. Every year or so, spend a half-hour and review the worksheets to analyze the patterns.

Start by placing these motivators in order, from 10 (most important) down to 1 (least important). Here and there, feel free to reword the motivator, but it's best to mostly stick with the printed list.

MOTIVATOR	RANKING (10 is best, down to 1)
Money	
Opportunity to work with specific people	
Opportunity to work with specific company	
Publicity value —high-visibility project	
Personal ego gratification	
Proving myself to myself	
Proving myself to others	
Satisfying a specific personal goal	
General career advancement	
Personal growth	

Keep these sheets in a binder and make a new one for every project you do. Then, every year or so, track the trends. If you're only in it for the money, it's nice to know that. And if you've spent three years mainly proving yourself to others, you ought to know that, too.

Emotional Trouble Spots

How can I say this politely? Hmmm...maybe the problem isn't other people after all. Maybe the problem is *you*!

(Sometimes, you just gotta be direct.)

Many creative people are a little crazy, and some of us are a lot crazy. People who are crazy but also competent, friendly, influential, or funny can get away with a lot. People who aren't, don't. Either way, you've got to learn how your behavior affects others. You can decide to change, or improve, and you can be surprisingly successful with personal changes over time. Or, you can decide that you are who you are and deal with the consequences.

So what do I mean by "crazy"? I'm talking about emotional ice slicks, places where the slightest provocation could cause you to skid and possibly hurt yourself or others.

This list of abnormal behaviors is based upon (where else?) a list published on *Family Fun's* Web site, which in turn comes from *The Disney Encyclopedia of Children's Health*.

- Avoidance
- Aggression
- Attention Deficit Hyperactivity Disorder
- Compulsive behavior
- Depression
- Imaginary friends
- Jealousy
- Night terrors
- Profanity
- Regression
- Schizophrenia
- Shyness
- Substance abuse

Honesty time: I can't recall a week when I haven't exhibited at least half of these behaviors. If you think you're better off, you're lying to yourself.

I also know that I am a reasonably normal person who tends to avoid uncomfortable conversations; routinely pretends and makes up silly stories for my own and other people's amusement; likes to engage total strangers in conversation to make them laugh; uses profanity when I'm simultaneously surprised, frustrated, and angry; wakes up in the middle of the night and magnifies the importance of something so that I can't easily fall asleep again. I also eat too much, and when I read a book about ADD, I wonder how the author knew so much about me.

Everyone exhibits these kinds of behaviors from time to time. It's only when a behavior becomes frequent, intense and/or difficult to control that professional medical care is required.[11]

Years of living and working with myself and others have taught me how to manage myself. So for me, and for most creative professionals, it's not whether we are a little crazy. It's how deeply, frequently, and negatively our crazy behaviors affect others. If you can manage this on your own, through friendly conversations and feedback from coworkers, excellent. If you need professional help, don't hesitate. If you're under control, you will enjoy your work, and others will enjoy working with you.

Triggers

You begin a new job or project with every intention of enjoying yourself, giving everyone their fair share of time to talk and to find their own way. Then, without warning, you find yourself in another shouting match. Or, you listen to the other crazy people arguing and you just shut down and check out of the conversation.

Every behavior on the list of emotional slick spots has its triggers. There

---

[11] Thank you to psychologist Stephen Britchkow, who recently confirmed both my relative normalcy and also the trio of out-of-control issues that should cause concern.

is *always* a specific reason why your behavior changes. Learn to identify and to manage those triggers and you'll be happier, and, perhaps, more successful.

One trigger is situational: Whenever you find yourself in a particular scenario, you behave in a certain way. There are essentially three possible solutions: (a) avoid the situation entirely; (b) learn to change your approach and behavior within the situation; or (c) make a conscious effort to change, but do so with a coach and log your incremental progress.

Some people just make other people nuts. Doesn't matter what they say or do. These two people should not be working together. When they do, conflict resolution tools can help.

Conflict and Other "Creative Disorders"

Back to Robert Bolton of *People Skills*: "I hate conflict. I wish I could find a healthy way to avert it or transcend it. But there is no such path. I detest conflict because it is at best disruptive, and at its worst it is destructive. Destructive controversy has a tendency to expand. Often, it becomes detached from its initial causes and may continue even after these causes have become irrelevant, or have long been forgotten. Conflict frequently escalates until it consumes all things and all people it touches."[12]

Philosopher John Dewey offers a contrary opinion. "Conflict is the gadfly of thought. It stirs us to observation and memory. It instigates to invention. It shocks us out of our sheep-like passivity, and sets us noting and contriving. Conflict is the *sine qua non* of reflection and ingenuity."

Bolton details a strategy for conflict resolution. Assuming that emotions can be brought under control, and that the problem behind the conflict is clear, and that there are no hidden agendas, the following approach ought to work pretty well:

First, state the problem not in terms of possible solutions, but instead in terms of what each person needs, and why. Be detailed.

Second, jointly develop a list of ideas that satisfy the needs. The process must be entirely non-judgmental; every idea is valid. Both parties

---

[12] SOURCE: Robert Bolton, *People Skills*, p. 206.

brainstorm in favor of themselves and the other.

Third, match needs to the best solutions from the brainstorm. The basic thinking: Both parties' needs are valid and deserve reasonable solutions.

Fourth, develop and implement a very specific plan of action. Assign names and timetables to each task. Follow up as you would with any project.

Fifth, evaluate the results on a regular basis. Promise to meet again to evaluate progress and to discuss further improvements.

Temper

Some creative people really are out of control, but nobody did it better than the great classical conductor, Arturo Toscanini. "He worked like a demon and expected everybody else to do the same. If things did not go his way, he went into a tantrum, one of his famous tantrums. His rages were legendary. 'It was among the most horrifying sounds I have ever heard ... and seemed to come from his entrails. He would almost double up, his mouth open wide, his face red, as if on the verge of an apoplectic fit. Then a raucous blast of unbelievable volume would blare forth....' Unknown to Toscanini, the Victor engineers kept an open microphone on many of his rehearsals ... on some of these discs Toscanini can be heard in a full eruption and the sounds are positively Vesuvian."[13]

How to temper a bad temper? You can try to tame it yourself—but those who tend toward violent outbursts aren't typically introspective— or (better), you can get the help of a therapist. (I'm guessing the maestro had some other issues.)

When faced with vocal thunder and the inevitable abuse that comes with it, I usually just watch the theatrics and keep an eye on the door just in case vocal violence becomes physical. The person with the tantrum is usually frustrated, tuned way too tightly, and dealing with frustrations well beyond the bounds of the current conversation. Just keep your mouth shut (resist the temptation to argue back), protect yourself physically, and wait for the storm to pass.

---

[13] SOURCE: Harold C. Schonberg, *The Great Conductors*, p. 262.

Fear

According to John J. Ratey, M.D., "Fear is a universal emotion that includes everything from the decision to fight or flee to the insidious mounting of stress. It can also cause us to 'freeze.'"[14] Ratey explains that the fear response bypasses much of the brain's circuitry and sets up the body for an immediate animal reaction to danger.

Is stage fright similar to fear of a nearby komodo dragon?[15] Is the insecurity that says "I'm not funny enough"; or "I can't really sing"; or "There's no way that I can design that building" related to instincts developed as a cave dweller? "Yes" is the correct answer, but it's also an outrageous simplification of neuroscience (see chapter six). A little fear is normal. A dose of stage fright pumps up the body, and before a speech or a stage performance, that's a good thing. A dose of insecurity encourages the body and the brain to focus, also a good thing. However, when fear prevents you from performing or leaving your home, a professional can help you get straight.

"Never let them see you sweat" is a slogan that most team leaders take seriously—the creative team will perceive nervousness and insecurity as signs of weakness and will quickly lose faith in both the leader and the project. Team members must also learn to keep their own insecurities and fears to themselves—except through the (entirely acceptable) release of the dark humor related to the project itself. That is: it's okay to crack devastating jokes about the situation and the project as a whole or in its parts, but it's never okay to admit how scared you really are, except to the mirror. We're all a little frightened. Creative work is about doing things people have never done before. And "novel" situations—to use Dr. Ratey's word—are a primary cause of fear.

Boredom

Boredom is the other devil. You've done it before, you don't want to do it

---

[14] SOURCE: John J. Ratey, M.D., *A User's Guide to the Brain.*
[15] A komodo dragon can eat a goat in minutes.

again. This project seems like every other project you've done for the past decade. It's tough to stay focused, to stay awake, to go through the motions just because you're being paid to work. You know the way to get the job done, but everyone else needs to cycle through the steps in order to gain the necessary experience to make their own smart decisions.

Many creative professionals avoid repetition. Once they've mastered a project, no matter how major, they move on to a new domain. Jerry Seinfeld was a good example. After his hit sitcom, and despite an open offer from every network to do another, Seinfeld returned to the basic act of performing standup comedy. The documentary *Comedian* shows the performer starting over as a standup comic in mid-career.

The counter-argument: After years of developing your skills, processes, and contacts, why would you throw that away? In fact, you don't throw anything away. Instead, you build on the experience, and if things go well, your opportunities become more interesting over time. Sometimes, though, we all get stuck in a rut, or find ourselves without options, or simply need money to pay the bills. Don't confuse a short-term solution with a career move.

Ego (and Power)

Almost by definition, most creative jobs are short-term gigs. They might last months, they might even last several years. But they rarely last forever. Child actors have overexposed this problem on syndicated talk shows, demonstrating challenges associated with disintegrated fame. Not every job pays as well as your best job. The value of a professional's services is whatever the market will pay at any particular time. The fluctuation makes the stock market seem calm and reliable.

Money and power feed ego. If you earn tons of money, you may get away with the big shot act; when the money goes away, act and ego quickly deflate. The power trip is more problematic. It's difficult for an architect to transition into a role as a construction worker; he will not easily accept the role and coworkers will not be any more comfortable.

Ditto for the composer who takes a job as a musician in the orchestra, or the marketing VP who takes a job in market research to keep the dollars coming in. Few people can succeed in any job at any level; most people operate best within a narrower range of responsibilities.

Power comes in at least two flavor:

There's *power over people*—control over resources, people's jobs, roles, and promotions. When you're in a power position, people will respond to you in that role. When the role disappears, so does your power. The most enlightened among us are able to find other ways to express this power, sometimes within volunteer setups, for example. More often, the previously powerful person finds himself wondering why he no longer feels important. Often the result is self-image problems.

The most satisfying type of power—the power to accomplish—tends to stay with the person, regardless of the situation, and it does not require other people's acceptance. In short, you are in control, not reliant upon the confirmation of others. This is where you want to be. Your ego is satisfied, but under control.

The famous stripper, Gypsy Rose Lee, said, roughly, "Just keep working." Deep down, we all acknowledge that she's right: The idea is to remain productive. You know Gypsy's story: an overbearing mother who told her she wasn't talented; a show business family that struggled up the vaudeville ladder only to find the business gone when they reached the top; a realization that burlesque and stripping paid better than vaudeville and offered more long-term opportunity; a biography that became a classic Broadway musical; her later life as an author and TV personality. How did she do it? How do we all do it? We just keep moving. Along the way, humility provides some welcome seasoning.

HE'S A GENIUS

He's a Genius;
Give him whatever he wants.

He's a Genius;
Give him whatever help he needs.

He's a Genius;
Help him to stay on course.

He's a Genius,
But he's beginning to drive me crazy.

He's a Genius,
But he needs some support in some areas.

He's a Genius,
But we need to help him get through this.

He's a Genius;
Let's find an appropriate role for his talents.

He's a Genius,
But he needs supervision.

He's a Genius,
But he needs professional help.

He's a Genius;
Let's remember not to hire him again.

Rationalizing

Or, making excuses to yourself. This is a popular variation on self-talk, particularly among creative professionals in search of a reason not to work or not to do the best possible work.

According to Steven Pressfield, "Rationalization is Resistance's spin doctor....Instead of showing us our fear (which might shame us and impel us to do our work), Resistance presents us with a series of plausible, rational justifications for why we shouldn't do our work.

What's particularly insidious about the rationalizations … is that a lot of them are true. They're legitimate. Our wife really is in her eighth month of pregnancy; she really does need us at home.…What Resistance leaves out, of course, is that they all mean diddly. Tolstoy had eleven kids and wrote *War and Peace*. Lance Armstrong had cancer and won the Tour de France three times and counting."[16]

Family, Friends and Personal Expectations

Living, working or maintaining a friendship with a creative professional can be a tough challenge. Our priorities are often out of sync with the rest of the world. We work late. We cancel dinner at the last minute. We set up all-important meetings for Sunday mornings, and what was to last two hours runs through the night. One day, we have plenty of cash, and the next we're wondering whether we can afford to go on vacation after all. Some of us hang around with famous people, then tell friends we can't ask for autographs or other favors. For those on the sidelines, friendship with us can become tiresome.

With family members, set realistic financial expectations. Money may be steady for a long while, but it's not going to be steady forever. Saving is an absolute must; there will be dry periods when savings and related investments are necessary for financial survival. This can be tough for an eight-year-old to understand: Yes, I appear on TV every night, but no, you can't buy a new video game system. The situation can be tough for the spouse, too, despite the most earnest, logical, reasonable attempts to set up and follow a family budget. The current paycheck is just too appealing, and besides, everybody else in your position is going to *those* restaurants, buying *those* cars, living in *those* houses. You can kid yourself, too. Do set the expectation from the start: You are in this for the long term and you must make certain that you can survive. (At some point, you might find lifelong financial security. See chapter seven.)

---

[16] SOURCE: Steven Pressfield, *The War of Art*, p. 52.

Setting expectations with regard to time is no less challenging. What you want to avoid is a sense that every project is more important than your life at home or with friends. The occasional indiscretion is okay—friends understand that creative professionals experience time and deadlines differently—but they will be quick to judge patterns. If you cancel dinner once, that's acceptable. Twice, you might get away with it. Three times, and you'll either lose a friend or you'll have a lot of rebuilding work to do. Time commitments with regard to your own children are probably most important. Given the choice of a school play or a meeting with a producer to direct your own play, you really do need to attend the one at school. Your lack of appropriate prioritizing is going to leave a scar—and not just on the kid. When I close my eyes and try to remember small details of my kids at certain ages, I can't because I wasn't around. I was busy finishing the hat, or producing the show, or having the meeting with someone whose name I don't now recall.

Your own expectations for yourself are also a big factor in the obstacles that you lay down with every project. If you have specific goals, how does this project fit into those goals? Are you living up to your potential? Do you have a sense of how great you really could be? When's the last time you sat yourself down for a good daydream?

Now would be a good time to do just that, in the form of another exercise.

But first, a thought from Henry David Thoreau: "If you have built castles in the air, your work need not be lost. That is where they should be. Now put foundations under them."

DAYDREAM A LITTLE DREAM

Congratulations! You have won the ultimate creative prize! As a result of your consistently excellent work, you are now in complete control of the next two years of your life. Money is no object, neither is time nor resources nor the availability of people. This is a limited time offer; if you do not complete this little daydream in the next 20 minutes, it will float away.

1. Where are you going to spend your time? (More than one place is okay, just be specific with your answers.)

2. How will you spend your time? Fill in a typical week. (It's okay to fill in the same answer over multiple blocks.)

	SUN	MON	TUE	WED	THU	FRI	SAT
Early Morning							
Morning							
Early Afternoon							
Late Afternoon							
Evening							
Late Evening							
Overnight							

3. Most of the time, are you working or playing? Why?

4. Who are you working and playing with? Make a list of the people (or critters), and explain why they are present, and how you are spending your time with them. (This can be nobody, just one person, or a whole lot of people.)

Person	Why	What You're Doing Together

5. At the end of two years, what have you accomplished? (If anything at all. The answer can be a "deliverable" or it can be more personal, or philosophical, or whatever. Just be specific in your answer or, if you like, your top three answers. Or more, because you own this book and can actually do whatever you like with this exercise.)

Habits

Stanford professor James Adams stated the inherent conflict rather succinctly, "Habits are also not always consistent with creativity. Creativity implies deviance from past procedure and therefore is at odds with habit....Habits can cloud our decision-making capability, decrease our ability to communicate successfully, and get in the way of education."[17]

One difference between an amateur and a creative professional is the consistency. We know what we're doing because we've done it plenty of times before. Yet, anything that has been done repeatedly before can fairly be considered a habit.

There are good habits and bad habits. I'm a planner; that's good. I tend to read documents carefully, and I suspect that's a good habit, too. When I review or edit someone else's document, the length of my comments might exceed the length of the original work. That's a bad habit that has gotten me in trouble.

The best way to deal with habits is to first acknowledge that they exist. Then, take the time to ask people about the good and the bad. I've been told that my "zillions of footnotes" are tiresome, but I've also been complimented for the helpful comments I've provided. I suppose most habits have good and bad sides.

Some habits are just annoying. Habits that don't exhibit themselves in the workplace are not relevant to this book, but some habits come to life regardless of when or where you are. One of my all-time favorites: a boss who mindlessly opened his penknife and probed the inside of his outer

---

[17] SOURCE: James Adams, *The Care and Feeding of Ideas*, p. 61.

ear. He didn't know he was doing it, but the habit drove everyone else nuts. And yes, you have at least one habit that's probably worse.

HABITS

As they come to mind, make a list of your ten most common habits (you might need a friend to help you). And remember, the objective here is self-improvement: Don't become angry with a friend who is only trying to help you...

Why others think it's a good habit	Why I think it's a good habit	HABIT	Why I think it's a bad habit	Why others think it's a bad habit
		1.		
		2.		
		3.		
		4.		
		5.		
		6.		
		7.		
		8.		
		9.		
		10.		

What you will not change, and why (these are the valuable habits that are part of your good work):

What you will keep:	Why:

Finally, a list of what you ought to change, and how you might go about changing:

What you will change:	How you will change:

Slumps & Blocks

In *A Writer's Time*, Kenneth Atchity wrote, "Slumps are different from general depression. I used to think slumps were natural phenomena, a reaction to the highs of productivity, and that the progress of a productive life was a cycle of ups and downs. I thought the slumps were the price you paid for the triumphs. I no longer believe that. Instead, I think you can work without the slumps if you have enough willpower (discipline) and introspection (which allows you to trick the mind into behavior that your dreams demand."[18]

Yes, it is possible to minimize the number of blocks and their severity. You can fill your head with stimulating ideas. You can spend time with interesting, provocative, nurturing people. You can do everything right and, for whatever reasons, the good stuff doesn't come. Or, the good

[18] SOURCE: Kenneth Atchity, *A Writer's Time*, p. 9.

stuff comes, but nobody wants to buy it.

Advertising executive Jack Kiel taught, "One of the best ways to 'beat the block' is to keep it from consolidating into a position of power. It's easier to beat when it's small."[19]

Asked about being inspired in order to write, author Somerset Maugham answered, "I write only when inspiration strikes." "Fortunately, it strikes every morning at nine sharp."[20]

We all experience slumps. Most slumps and blocks can be chased away by leaving the work for a while. Taking a walk is one good antidote, eating a wonderful meal, or getting lost in a book or a movie, is another. Physical exercise works, and a regular regimen of walking, running, aerobics, or time in the gym will improve your outlook. A longer slump might be bearing down, doing more research, interacting with others. If that doesn't work, leave for a few days, maybe a week. Do something else for a while. Get your mind to focus elsewhere. When you return, try changing location, your way of working, or some other major component. If that doesn't work, you'll need to dig deeper for the root of the problem.

Being Underpaid

Everybody has a price. And most people will work for less than their price. At a certain point, however, you begin to think less about the money that you are making on a job, and more about the money that you're not.

If you feel underpaid, you might build an obstacle. To avoid this is to first figure out what you ought to be paid, and then, if necessary, negotiate for adjustments. If that's not possible, learn a lesson for next time.

HOW MUCH IS YOUR TIME WORTH?

This tool is not going to result in a finite answer but will instead provide a range into which your daily fee or salary ought to fit.

---

[19] SOURCE: *How to Zig in a Zagging World*, book on audiotape, draft script, New York: Wiley.
[20] SOURCE: Steven Pressman, *The War of Art*, p. 67.

Part 1: Your Personal History

Gather up your Federal 1040 tax forms from the past five years. Go to the section labeled "Income" and write down the number on the first line: Wages, Salaries, Tips, etc. (this is the information reported by employers on W-2 forms).

Year	W-2 Income
20__	
20__	
20__	
20__	
20__	
TOTAL	
Div. by 5	
AVERAGE	
Div. by 240	
DAILY VALUE	

To transform the annual average to a daily average, divide by the number of working weekdays in the year: 240 is a fair divisor, allowing for holidays and vacations. If you did this exercise correctly, a sample formula might be: (($50,000 + $60,000 + $70,000 + $80,000 + $90,000)/5)/240 = $291.67).

If you worked every day of the year, as an employee would, then you would be fairly paid if you earned about $240 to $325 per day, plus benefits and the employer's contribution to taxes. If you worked instead as a contractor, you would have paid your own taxes and benefits, and for your own workspace. These add up to about 25% of the total fee. If your numbers resulted in a $300 day, then your time is actually worth 75% of that figure, or $225. Admittedly, this is a somewhat dubious argument, but it always results in the same place: an employee earning $300 plus taxes and benefits who works in someone else's office is doing better than a contractor earning the same daily fee.

Part 2: Marketplace Trends

Gathering salary information is an unreliable science, but it's important to learn all you can about people doing similar jobs. The web is a good source, and so are trade magazines. Agents, lawyers, and managers who negotiate fees and contracts are helpful, at least within the entertainment sector. The best source is, of course, the person who is doing a job like yours, in a more or less similar company, in a similar geographic region.

Take on the task of identifying ten sources per year, and try to fill in the chart below annually. This will not provide perfect data, but it will be useful in combination with the first and third parts of this exercise. If you're filling in a contractor's information, discount the annual salary by 25%.

	Job Title & Company	Annual Salary	Divide by 240 for day rate
1.			
2.			
3.			
4.			
5.			
6.			
7.			
8.			
9.			
10.			
	AVERAGE		

Part 3: Employer Information

If you work for a large company, you can feel very comfortable visiting the compensation manager's office and simply asking about the salary range for your job. Most likely, the answer will be expressed within a range of annual salaries. This range is typically used by department managers when hiring, promoting, budgeting, and arranging for raises.

If you work for a smaller company, the very act of requesting this information might be suspect. If you're comfortable doing so, and you're not violating company policy, you could simply share salary information with coworkers. You can also find out how much contractors are paid for similar work.

	Job Title	Annual Salary (or range)	Divide by 240 for day rate
1.			
2.			
3.			
4.			
5.			
	AVERAGE		

Summary and Results

To determine a fair rate for your services, complete the chart below with the information you've gathered through this exercise.

	Average Day Rate
Personal History	
Marketplace Average	
Employer Average	
BLENDED AVERAGE	

If you are earning within 25% of the blended average number (up or down), you are being fairly paid.

Optional Exercise to Drive Yourself Crazy

Okay, you've gone this far. Why not have some obsessive fun with the numbers? Just follow the formulas on the chart below:

Blended Average Day Rate	$	$
Average Hourly Rate	(divide above by 8)	$
Average Per-Minute Rate	(divide above by 60)	
Average Per-Second Rate	(divide above by 60)	

Just in case you were wondering, someone who earns $300 per day earns $37.50 per hour; 62.5 cents per minute, and just over a penny each second.

Dealing with Rejection

I know a writer who wallpapered his bathroom with rejection letters from book publishers. An artist made a papier-mâché sculpture with her rejection letters. My favorite rejection story comes from New York University professor and author Neil Postman, who was writing about Columbia University's admissions process:

"The student applied to Columbia University for admission and was rejected. In response, he sent the following letter to the admissions officer:

'Dear Sir:

I am in receipt of your rejection of my application. As much as I would like to accommodate you, I find I cannot. I have already received four rejections from other colleges, which is, in fact, my limit. Your rejection puts me over this limit. Therefore, I must reject your rejection, and as much as this might inconvenience you, I expect to appear for classes on September 18...'"[21]

University of Pennsylvania researcher Martin Seligman "defines optimism in terms of how people explain to themselves their successes and failures. People who are optimistic see failure as something that can be changed so that they can succeed next time around, while pessimists take the blame for the failure, ascribing to it some lasting characteristic that they are helpless to change."[22]

[21] SOURCE: Neil Postman, *Conscientious Objections*, pp. 24-25.
[22] SOURCE: Daniel Goleman, *Emotional Intelligence*, p. 88.

"I always compare any idea to a golden wire," says Looney Tunes animator Chuck Jones.[23] "It's really gorgeous, a lovely thing, but also a bit fragile. You come trotting in with this idea, and it's a YES ... and yes means contribute, help me—I need help to get the strength to survive. And then when we come up with what a No looks like, it's a monolithic, ugly thing. It's made of cement. But some people have made their entire reputation—become presidents of motion picture companies—by saying No! It's one of the most horrible words in the English language. This No can destroy an idea, because you have this fragile little yes trying to survive. Anybody can drop that monstrous No on the yes before it has a chance for life."

How to cope? You could lean on some quotable quotes.

John Kennedy said, "There are costs and risks to a program of action, but they are far less than the long-range costs and risks of comfortable inaction."

Thomas Jefferson said, "I'm a great believer in luck, and I find that the harder I work, the more I have of it."

Or avant-garde experimental composer John Cage, who didn't much mind what anybody thought: "I can't understand why people are frightened of new ideas. I'm frightened of the old ones."[24]

Or the *Tao Te Ching*, an ancient Chinese manuscript by Lao Tzu, "Care about people's approval and you will be their prisoner."[25]

Finally, Confucius said, "Our greatest glory is not in never failing, but in rising every time we fail."

You will be rejected. You will be rejected often. Your best ideas will be rejected. Sometimes, the rejection will be personal. Even the most successful creative professionals hear more no's than yes's. To improve your ratio, you must look into yourself, for the solution is there, not in the marketplace, and not in the unsold presentations. Then, figure out the marketplace and build a killer presentation.

---

[23] SOURCE: Daniel Goleman, Paul Kaufman, Michael Ray, *The Creative Spirit*, p.131.
[24] SOURCE: Shira P. White with G. Patton Wright, *New Ideas about New Ideas*, p.44.
[25] SOURCE: *New Ideas about New Ideas*, p. 4.

Managing Through Tough Times

Creative people tend to invest their soul in their work. When the work does not go well, or is poorly received, the soul can be damaged. It's not unusual to find a creative professional—even the most stable among us—dealing with some challenging internal struggles.

When an excellent project ends, or your role is suddenly minimized, you will feel sad. You have experienced a loss. Melancholy is a common, appropriate response. "Sadness due to a loss closes down our interest in diversions, fixes our attention on what has been lost, saps energy for new endeavors," Daniel Goleman explains.[26]

Anger is also common, but it's more complex than its visible manifestations. There's anger with yourself because you could have, should have done a better job. There's anger with yourself because your role does not match your self-image. You might be angry with others because they are not meeting your expectations, or because they are exhibiting what you consider destructive behavior. Anger might also run deep—it's not unusual to find issues with parents as the root causes of anger.

The Frustrations of Lay-offs and Free Falls

Several weeks ago, I watched the James Cagney film, *Yankee Doodle Dandy*. It's a grand old show-business story about Broadway legend, George M. Cohan and his family. In one scene, his family (mother, father, sister) is in a boarding house, unable to pay its rent. The reason: Nobody will hire the family act because young George is such a troublemaker.

In any case, I got to thinking about show business layoffs. When a vaudeville act wasn't working, it was said to be laying off for a while. They hoped for another booking; sometimes it came and sometimes it didn't.

Contemporary show-business folks, and creative professionals in general, haven't much improved the situation. One gig ends and there is no guarantee the next one will materialize. The cycle is always the same: The first few days or weeks are a flurry of activity, meetings, proposals,

---

[26] SOURCE: Daniel Goleman, *Emotional Intelligence*, p. 69.

interviews, phone calls, e-mails, promises. Then the activity slows down. People stop calling you, or calling as often, so you try to keep the activity going by being proactive. After a month or two or three, if nothing is happening, there is reason for concern. First, there's the issue of money coming in. Second, there's the darker issue, the potential obstacle, the deeper questions. Can you continue to sell what you have been selling? Has the market changed? Did you do or say something that has damaged your reputation? You begin to question your own abilities, and some degree of frustration, or depression, sets in.

You pick yourself up, dust yourself off, and develop some new projects. No money, but at least new projects will get you out into the world, preferably with a collaborator to keep you pumped, to encourage you as you encourage her. At this stage, something good often happens. You might not sell the project that you had hoped to sell, but the exposure and the willingness to try new ideas, to meet new people, and to take chances generally has a positive effect.

For the Cohans, they stopped laying off just as soon as George got out of the picture. A change in the combination, or in perception, can make all the difference. George, of course, succeeded on his own, too. He became the toast of Broadway: a successful playwright, producer, performer, composer, dancer, and director. There's a statue of Cohan on Times Square.

Sure, you might not be as talented or as lucky as George M. Cohan. But if you have even the slightest confidence in yourself, you will pull through. And if you need to take a job outside the business for a while to stay alive, you wouldn't be the first creative professional to do that, either, regardless of how much it hurts.

Mom and Dad

Actor and writer Steve Martin told these stories about his father:

"Generally, my father was critical of my show-business accomplishments. Even after I won an Emmy at twenty-three as a writer for *The*

Smothers Brothers Comedy Hour, he advised me to finish college so I would have something to fall back on....

"Years later, my friends and I took him to the premiere of my first movie, *The Jerk*, and afterward, we went to dinner. For a long time, he said nothing. My friends noted his silence and were horrified. Finally, one friend said, 'What did you think of Steve in that movie?' And my father said, 'Well, he's no Charlie Chaplin.' My father did not believe he was hurting me. He was just being honest....

"I walked into the bedroom where he lay, his mind alert but his body failing. He said, almost buoyantly, 'I'm ready now.' I understood that his intensifying rage of the last few years had been against death and now his resistance was abating. I stood at the end of the bed, and we looked into each other's eyes for a long, unbroken time. At last he said, 'You did everything I wanted to do.' I said, 'I did it because of you.' It was the truth."[27]

Filmmaker Jim Jarmusch had no easier time with his dad:

"My father saw my first film, *Permanent Vacation*, and said he thought that there was a reel missing somehow, that there wasn't a story there. He said, 'I don't think I saw the whole thing, did I?' And I said, 'Yeah, that's it.' And he said, 'Well, I think something's missing from the story.'"[28]

Neither did Ravi Shankar, one of many creative people who was nurtured (as many creative people are) by his mother:

"I have to talk about my father a little. See, he was a seeker. In the sense that he was always seeking for knowledge. And he was such a learned person. In every subject. Starting from Sanskrit, to music. He was a lawyer by profession, he was in the Privy Council in London, he was with the League of Nations when it started in Geneva.... He earned a lot on different occasions, but he never saved.... My mother was separated from him at an early age.... So from my childhood on, I saw my mother very unhappy and very lonely.... She spent all her energy,

[27] SOURCE: Steve Martin, "The Death of My Father," *New Yorker*, June 17 & 24, 2002.
[28] SOURCE: Quotes from Jim Jarmusch Interviews by Ludvig Hertzberg.
Film Comment, Vol. 21, No. 1, January/February 1985, pp.54-60-62, interviewed by Harlan Jacobsen, 1984.

time and everything for the sake of us children.... So I had nothing to do with my father, unfortunately, though I respected him and liked him very much. But I grew up very lonely myself because I was the youngest. My mother was my best friend."[29]

Taking Control of Difficult Situations

Anger, frustration, sadness, insecurity, inadequacy, and other psychological pinball games can be extraordinarily difficult to overcome, even with help from a professional, and with extraordinary dedication to change.

Miles Davis's solution was to tough it out. He told *Ebony* magazine:

"I made up my mind I was getting off dope. I was sick and tired of it. You know can you get tired of anything. You can even get tired of being scared. I laid down and stared at the ceiling for twelve days and I cursed anybody I didn't like. I was kicking it the hard way. It was like having a bad case of the flu, only worse. I lay in a cold sweat. My nose and eyes ran. I threw up everything I tried to eat. My pores opened up and I smelled like chicken soup. Then it was over."

Eric Nisenson describes John Coltrane's struggles:

"Despite Coltrane's devotion to his health, he had tremendous difficulty controlling his weight, even to the extent of having two wardrobes, one set of 'fat' suits and another set for when he had his weight under control. His use of the latter became increasingly rare as the sixties wore on.... The cause of his weight problem was his love of sweets, which also wrecked his teeth.

"He often fell victim to his sweet tooth, however, and despite his interest in good nutrition and regular workouts with weights, as the sixties went on, he was overweight more often than not. He was able to kick alcohol and heroin, but could never get his craving for sweet potato pie out of his system."[30]

---

[29] SOURCE: Mihaly Csikszenmihalyi, *CREATIVITY,* p. 169.
[30] SOURCE: Eric Nisenson, *Ascension,* pp. 134 and 193.

Scientists aren't altogether clear on the psychology and neurology of joy, or its frequent companions, love and laughter. We know what happens when a body laughs, but nobody's sure why people laugh, or love, or experience joy. Or why some people seem to experience joy more easily than others.

To say that joy is about being happy is just playing with synonyms. Joy seems to rise above self-satisfaction and a high comfort level with the task and the people involved. There's an ecstatic feeling that comes with making music, or dancing, or even thinking in a profoundly exciting way. Joy can last moments, or it can float along for weeks as life and work couldn't be better. Sometimes you just stumble into it: You've created something, and you realize that you have just caused somebody to laugh, or to finally understand an idea. Teachers experience this sense of joy with the best possible audience: children.

Joy is also a force that must be present in order to achieve consistently excellent creative work, but the utter lack of it can be an equally powerful force in writing, art, music, comedy, filmmaking, and other forms.

Some creative people—myself included—are very sensitive to the "joy" factor. Walking into a business where people just don't seem to be having a very good time is a good reason to either: (a) consult with the organization and help these people, or (b) to work somewhere else. In other words, creative work is way too time-consuming and challenging to deal with an environment where people don't love what they do. If people aren't laughing, at least sometimes, you probably want to work someplace else.

In her many delightful books and on her posters, SARK[31] suggests plenty of ideas to stay loose and creative. Here are some of my favorites:

- Cultivate moods
- Take lots of naps
- Laugh a lot
- Draw on the walls

---

[31] SARK, *A Creative Companion*, various pages.

- Do it now
- Read every day
- Believe in magic
- Play with everything
- Be ridiculous
- Keep toys in the bathtub
- Believe in everything
- Do everything with your least dominant hand

I think joy keeps the gods happy. As a matter of fact, you'll meet those gods in the next two chapters: first, the mythological muses, and then, the lawyers and accountants, who are no less demanding.

Chapter 6 - The Creative Mind

What's going on inside your head? Is your creative brain somehow different from other people's brains? Do creative people think differently? If so, is the reason physiological or neurological? Is the difference related to genetics or personality, or does environment play a significant role? Were you born creative? Can you learn to be more creative? Can anyone learn to be creative?

Do we know the answers? In fact, the past few decades have been extraordinarily productive, and we know more than we've ever known before. We have some answers, or at least some hypotheses confirmed by scientific research. But as more is learned, new questions and unresolved issues enter the discussion. This is nothing new.

Greeks and Their Muses

A most excellent combination of safety, relative isolation, enlightened thinking, and a perfect climate allowed Greek culture to be blessed with an extraordinary level of creativity. What's more, the Greeks were entirely clear on how and why the creative process worked.

There were two chambers in the Greek mind. One was used for everyday human activities. The other was controlled by the gods, a place where new ideas were born. In order to activate the brain's second chamber, an individual invoked the assistance of a muse.

There were nine muses, each a nymph who communicated with both the individual and the gods.

If you were creating epic poetry, you would invoke *Calliope*, for her eloquence and her fine voice. Epic poetry was a significant art form, so Calliope was the lead muse.

Writing a lyric poem? Not without the help, inspiration, and passion provided by *Erato*. She's the muse who is often seen holding a lyre. Erato was not the music muse, though. That would be *Euterpe*, who apparently invented the flute and is often seen with a garland of flowers in her hair. If the music was vocal, that was *Polymnia's* department; she invented the lyre and can be identified as the woman in a pearl crown with a scepter in her left hand. She also wears a veil. Polymnia also helped writers, mathematicians specializing in geometry, meditators, and farmers. For assistance in dancing, *Terpischore* was the one to contact. She dances and plays the harp. Terpsichore is also mother to the Sirens.

You'd recognize *Thalia*, the music of comedy, by her mask. Her other familiar symbols: ivy garland, ankle-high boots, and shepherd's staff. Thalia is also charged with pastoral poetry (the Greeks enjoyed various types of poetry, with a muse for each type).

The dark skies contained wondrous mysteries. To better understand and imagine what was up so high, there was *Urania*, the virgin with the bar and the globe. With a trumpet in one hand and a book in the other, *Clio* was the muse who helped Greeks when they recorded or interpreted history.

Each muse was a goddess, a daughter of Zeus and Mnemosyne; they were a marriage of power (Zeus) and memory (Mnemosyne). Since written or recorded media were uncommon in ancient Greece, people relied on memory: *power + memory = muse.*

If you're planning to invoke muses for your own contemporary work— we can all use all the help we can get—you might also jot down the names of some earlier muses, notably *Melete* (for meditation), *Mneme* (for memory) and *Aoede* (for song); and at the Delphi oracle, *Nete, Mese,* and *Hypate*.

Ancient schools showed their respect for muses with a shrine called a *mouseion* (yes, inspiration for our *museum*). "Before poets or muses recited their work, it was customary to invoke the inspiration and protection of the muses"[1] at a temple connected to the Museum of Alexandria; I think we should encourage today's schools and businesses to do something similar.

Creation and Hero Myths

The mythology of heroes runs deep. After thousands of years, hero myths continue to dominate popular entertainment. Fundamental myths describe prototypical human struggles; no doubt, you will recognize many from movies, television, books, and video games.

Mythology scholar Joseph Campbell[2] described the hero's journey in terms that will be clear and familiar to any creative professional who has taken on an exceedingly difficult, imaginative project.

1. The mythological hero, setting forth from his "commonday" hut or castle, is lured, carried away, or else voluntarily proceeds to the threshold of adventure.
2. There he encounters a shadow presence that guards the passage.
3. The hero might defeat or conciliate this power and go alive into the kingdom of the dark (brother-battle, dragon-battle, offering, charm) or be slain by the opponent and descend in death (dismemberment, crucifixion).
4. Beyond the threshold, the hero journeys through a world of unfamiliar yet strangely intimate forces, some of which severely threaten him (tests), or give him magical aid (helpers).
5. When he arrives at the nadir of the mythological round, he

---

[1] SOURCE: http://www.eliki.com/portals/fantasy/circle/define.html.
[2] SOURCE: Joseph Campbell, *The Hero with a Thousand Faces*, pp. 246-247, Bollingen Series / Princeton, 1949 and 1972. (Originally presented as a single paragraph; numerical breaks mine.)

undergoes a supreme ordeal and gains his reward. The triumph might be represented as the hero's sexual union with the goddess-mother of the world (sacred marriage), his recognition of the father-creator (father-atonement), his own divination (apotheosis), or again—if the powers have remained unfriendly to him—his theft of the boon he came to gain (bride-theft, fire-theft). Intrinsically, it is an expansion of consciousness and therewith of being (illumination, transfiguration, freedom).

6. The final work is the return. If the powers have blessed the hero, he now sets forth under their protection (emissary); if not, he flees and is pursued (transformation fight, obstacle fight).

7. At the return threshold the transcendental powers must remain behind; the hero re-emerges from the kingdom of the dead (return, resurrection). The boon that he brings restores the old world (elixir).

When charged with a new major project, it is not common to find the creative leader struggling through her personal role as the central hero in a workplace version of this myth.

Thrust from the commonday, she finds herself on the threshold of adventure, battling the shadowy presence of network executives or anxious clients. Often, a project or adventure of this magnitude is encumbered with strangely intimate forces, such as self-doubt, or friends who become jealous and dangerous enemies. Only by overcoming this darkness can the hero emerge, but not without stepping into the light for an encounter with the father figure who insidiously set the stage, and/or the establishment of the hero's own place as a transfigured or divine being. The hero might emerge from this scene and return home to accolades and adoration, but as often, the hero now sets herself up for the fight of her life; the tremendous risk and bounty might be taken from the hero at the final moment, or she might be required to fight to maintain its integrity.

As I wrote that paragraph, I thought of the composer who insists on keeping the integrity of his motion picture score; the photographer who has been to hell and back to make images that an editor now wants to publish in the smallest possible size; the creative director who has put his agency's future on the line for a campaign that the client must implement in order to insure its own survival; the architect who keeps flashing on Ayn Rand's *The Fountainhead* as he fights for the building to be constructed as it must be.

The hero's journey is a sacred adventure. Few are chosen for the journey. Few are willing to sacrifice their careers, their emotional stability, and all their time and energy. This journey is not a part-time gig. My most memorable journey was the development of *Where in the World Is Carmen Sandiego?*, which sounds rather silly because it was a public television series and might easily be perceived as a road with baby bumpers. Every journey isn't *City Slickers*; not everyone rescues the beloved calf from the rushing, raging river waters or recognizes his role as a replacement for the once-despised, now-deceased father figure and manages to herd the cattle safely home.

Carmen Sandiego was the largest project I had ever attempted. I was sitting at a Manhattan restaurant when the waiter came over to the table— this hasn't happened to me before or since—and told me that my wife was on the telephone. I knew it was an important call, but I also sensed that this was a call to opportunity, not for a family emergency. She told me that I was to interview for the producer job, on a new PBS children's series based on the successful computer software product, *Where in the World Is Carmen Sandiego?* In an instant, I knew that I would get the job; the series would be one of the biggest projects of my career, and it would be an excellent adventure (thank you, Bill and Ted). I was truly plucked out of a commonday existence: My life was about writing books and marketing/consulting at that time, not about making television shows.

The journey began slowly, with visits to dozens of classrooms, meetings about budgets and creative concepts, and an impending sense that a shadow presence would make the journey difficult. Like Billy Crystal's character in *City Slickers*, I made the journey with friends beside me. And they remained beside me as this project engulfed every emotional and intellectual moment of our lives. We went to work on a Sunday evening in January, and didn't come home again until April. We worked seven days a week, mostly from 8:00 A.M. until midnight, leaving the office only to eat and sleep, and then, only in a nearby hotel. Families came to visit but were allowed to stay for a short time, and then mainly to bring clean clothes. The staff put *Carmen* hostage signs on their office doors and counted the days since they'd seen daylight. Dragons kept coming: The old Manhattan office building's roof opened during torrential rains that flooded our offices; two policemen, who were to protect us during our late nights, were found chained and gagged downstairs with pig masks pulled onto their faces; scripts were rewritten a dozen and more times causing endless delays in every department.

There was fear and doubt. There was a primal scream room next to the studio for the exclusive use of the cast members for whom traditional means of relaxation proved wholly inadequate.

And then, we recorded our first episode. And it was good. And the crew laughed. And the children smiled. And the adults hated it.

The final battle. Would a series designed for children be destroyed by the adults who had forgotten what being a kid was all about? The market research provided the ammunition for the naysayers: the show tested badly. The money had been spent; the shows had been edited. Despite the research, the shows went on the air.

And there was redemption, in the most unexpected places. I happened to wear my *Carmen Sandiego* tour jacket—we had jackets with embroidered logos made for the cast and crew—as I entered a commuter train. And the children sang. Every word. They sang every word to the theme song! They knew the words, they knew the melody, they said, "We love what you did." And that was our elixir.

How Your Brain Works

The brain is a mass of tissue, nerves, and muscle inside your head. Your mind is a theoretical construct that attempts to explain the elusive science related to thinking.

At a cellular level, you'll find neurons (nerve cells) throughout the brain. Unlike other types of cells, neurons have thin fiber extensions that form a network. Signals are sent from the cell through axons and received by the cells through dendrites. Every neuron contains several dendrites. These fibers are contained within electrical membranes, whose tiny charge makes it possible for a signal to pass from axon to dendrite across synapses, or gaps, throughout the brain. The interconnected network includes over ten billion neurons, each with an average of 100 connections (in case you're curious, that would be 1,000,000,000,000, or one trillion, connections in an average adult).

This network is described as a macroneuronal system. In addition, microneurons are generated to make the overall network even more durable, powerful and dazzling. The result is the complex variations of human thought.

Shifting the magnification so we can now see the entire brain, most of the wavy, convoluted gray mass is called the cerebral cortex, and it's about an inch thick. What you're seeing are billions of neurons responsible for thinking, perception, and other functions.

Beneath the cerebral cortex, the cerebrum's larger white mass of cells is apparently separated into four sections, or lobes, by various fissures, folds, and lines. The frontal lobe is responsible for speech, and other "precise, willed movements."[3] The small lobes toward the bottom rear are called the occipital lobes—the brain's vision center. The temporal lobes interpret what we see and hear. The left temporal lobe plays a significant role in language interpretation. The parietal lobes are related to parts of the perception process.

The cerebellum controls and monitors movement and equilibrium. Moving down toward the neck, you'll find the pons and the medulla, an extension of the spinal cord. The tiny hippocampus (which resembles a

---

[3] SOURCE: James H. Austin, *Zen and the Brain*, p. 149.

seahorse, the basis for its name) is integral to memory operations. Nearby, the amygdala deals with fear, anger, and your dark side.

These regions do not operate independently; instead, there is constant interaction during the processes of thought, action, memory, and other human activities.

Among the various components of thinking, the physiology of perception is perhaps the best understood. As perceived images and sounds (and input from other senses) are received, every human filters the input through various emotional, intellectual, and memory structures. The limbic system's amygdala serves as a perception control center and triggers emotional reactions from fear and lust to hormonal secretions. Nearby, the hippocampus acts as a clearing house, determining what should and should not be remembered, and so it is a key to behaviors associated with learning. The hippocampus also plays a role in emotions. The limbic system's other components demonstrate the complex relationships between perception, memory, emotion and sexuality—all of which are likely to be significant factors in the creative process.

So, what happens in your brain during the creative process? We have a few pieces of the puzzle: Perception is widely understood, but the interaction of perception with various types of memory, and the reasons some people can create or synthesize more readily than others, remain vague and obscure. There is the occasional specific—a bit of decay in the physiology of the limbic or related systems that causes either unconventional behavior or encourages learned behaviors to cover for the mismatch with society's perception of normalcy—but these knowns tend to be special cases that do not broadly apply.

Are creative people born different, or do we learn to think differently?

This nature versus nurture question has long defied scientists. Certainly, genetics plays a role: Both of my children's grandfathers were artists, so it's no surprise that my children can draw. Then again, for every example of genetic continuity, there's another that presents a break—a musician with no apparent family background. Similarly, environment is a strong factor—and is no more definitive factor. Some brilliant artists are nurtured by their upbringing and their surroundings; for others, this is an insignificant factor. It seems as though nature and nurture sometimes play a role and sometimes do not.

The Mind

The human brain is an organ designed for several specific purposes: managing critical processes, such as the operation of the circulatory, respiratory, and digestive systems; basic body functionality, such as movement and responses to danger; perception, including the management of our senses; and the process that seems most unique to human beings: thinking.

Other animals think. Other animals communicate. Other animals remember. Other animals can solve problems. Humans possess something else: the conception of a mind. Much as I love her, I do not believe that my dog has much of a mind.

Then again, after doing a whole lot of research for this book, I cannot honestly say that I can explain what a mind is. If there is such a thing as a mind, I'm guessing that it:

- Thinks
- Learns
- Remembers
- Perceives and filters input and stimuli
- Responds to stimuli with emotions, such as laughter
- Responds to interpersonal situations
- Stores values, beliefs, habits, and behaviors
- Possesses and generates ideas
- Can change
- Likes, dislikes, and loves other people
- Enjoys itself

- Likes itself
- Struggles because it does not like itself
- And more (or less?)

To some extent, Karl H. Pfenninger's functions of the nervous system[4] help define the functions of the mind. At the lowest level of functionality, there's *Autonomous Control* of the most basic bodily functions, and one level up is *Instinct*, or inherited behavior. The next level is *Memory of Learned Behavior*, followed by *Language*, which allows information exchange between species. Our conception of "mind" might begin with *Memory and Language*, though it might be argued that parts of Instinct also define the mind. Certainly, the top two levels are mindful: Intelligence, which involves learned adaptation and the learning of concepts, and *Creativity*, which envisions novel concepts.

The mind is subject to a variety of influences. In *Understanding Creativity*, John S. Dacey and Kathleen H. Lennon describe several "biopsychosocial" effects on creativity, which apply equally to about any of the mind's theoretical functions.[5] There are biological factors, which include the structure and operation of the brain and neural network, genetic makeup, and more. Environmental factors, from quality of life and neighborhood safety to the quality of light, have a big effect, as do education, ethnic background, economic and social conditions, religious beliefs, and family situation. And then there are the vagaries of personality, intelligence, and situational factors, like workplace issues and relationships.

The Magic of Imagination

Perhaps one difference between the brain, which perceives and processes, and the mind, which is a made-up construct, is the mind's ability to imagine ideas that do not exist. Humans are storytellers; maybe this is

---

[4] SOURCE: Karl H. Pfenninger, "The Evolving Brain," in *The Origins Of Creativity*, Oxford U Press, 2001, p. 91.

[5] John S. Dacey and Kathleen H. Lennon, *Understanding Creativity*, Jossey-Bass, S.F. 1998.

unique in the animal kingdom.

What is imagination? How does it work? Once again, there is no meaningful definition of this made-up idea. There is no real measurement of the depth or power of imagination.

As creative professionals, we, perhaps more than any other segment of the population, ought to be able to recognize the real thing, the right stuff, the gold.

Within the professional world, it's clear to me that imagination in action combines two key components: the freedom, the uncluttered thinking and sheer joy of a child at play; and the extraordinary craftsmanship that comes from superior thinking, technical skill, and artistic ability. I think I know when I'm seeing imagination in action at work. And I know when I'm experiencing real imagination in the end product. It doesn't happen often. When it does, imagination and magic are one.

So when have I experienced pure imagination? The first time I saw a Cirque du Soleil, but only the first time. When Disney returned to the animation business, I thought a great deal of the imagination that made *The Little Mermaid* and *Beauty and the Beast* so delightful. I'd give children's illustrator David Wisner points for his book *Tuesday*, and Chris Van Allsworth as many points for the magic of his artistic imagination, and certainly Lewis Carroll for his extraordinarily crazy adventures of Alice. Among adult conceptions, *Being John Malkovich* helps me to define imagination in terms of contemporary culture; imagination transports me to another place, one that does not exist or does not follow the rules of the real world. A really fine work of fiction does just that. Most other forms of entertainment do not—they are, instead, purely commercial products that skillfully employ techniques, technologies, and processes to cause consumers to spend money. Imagination need not be a part of the formula.

In truth, most creative professionals are not required to demonstrate any particular magic or imagination. We're mainly hired for the craft, less for the art. In order for true imagination to prosper, it requires the proper atmosphere. The marketplace does not typically reward outstanding imagination. Booksellers do not sell more books because they are imaginative (except, perhaps, in children's books, where imagination is more directly connected to commercial value). Instead, booksellers sell more books because they are written by established authors and celebrities. Television networks do not especially value imagination; if a program is too clever, it distracts from the commercials. Architects are dissuaded from too much imagination, from taking chances with buildings that are intended to either send a message or provide years of functional utility. It is more important for a marketing campaign to be "on message" than extraordinarily creative or imaginative.

So what is the role of imagination for the creative professional? Imagination becomes a tool that's either used broadly when the platform is appropriate (Cirque du Soleil), or one that's to be used subtly to enhance or improve the quality or attractiveness of a commercial product. Imagination can also provide a market breakthrough, even if the odds are often against the creative perpetrator. Art Spiegelman's *MAUS* was a comic book telling of the Holocaust nightmare that benefited enormously from the artist/writer's imagination. Unfortunately, commercial pressures— called "commercial realities," which thereby snub their noses at the "unrealities" that define imagination—rarely nurture the unusual, the ultra-creative, the imaginative.

The Role of Fun

I am not sure why, but most business people have trouble with the creative professional's attraction and adherence to fun. (Maybe it's jealousy.) I cannot understand why—given the opportunity to have a choice— anybody would devote forty hours a week, or 2,000 hours a year, or nearly 100,000 hours in a working lifetime, to an activity that they did not personally enjoy.

Certainly, there are financial challenges and family responsibilities. Not everybody is fortunate enough to choose their particular job or career. Those struggling to make ends meet address other priorities before fun enters the picture.

For the working creative professional, however, fun is a part of what makes work a worthwhile endeavor. So what's fun? And how does it apply to the working life of a creative professional?

For me, fun is the childlike pleasure in discovering new ideas, in playing with them until they fit my dreamlike conception of what a creative project ought to become. For example, writing this particular chapter has been fun. I started out with a rough idea of talking about the Greeks, the way the human brain functions, and, perhaps, faith. As I did my research, the connections laid out before me: Learning fits into the picture, so do adult relationships with mom and dad. I started reading more about Eastern religions. My fifteen-year-old son and I got into a deep discussion about how human brains work; why humans seem to be the dominant species (he led the discussion); and how a combination of tools, hands, and feet have allowed humans to dominate (and really screw up) the planet.

Fun is also the laughter that comes naturally, or ought to come naturally, when working with others to explore and establish a new domain. Some of it is nervous laughter, masking fear and insecurity, but most of it comes as a result of the clever people who tend to congregate around high-impact creative endeavors. We laugh loud and often—which makes the non-creative professionals wonder how and why we are having so much fun at work.

Fun is also about being with people who know how to be funny. Comedian Colin Quinn talks about an older comedian, Pat Cooper, with enormous respect. Why? Because Cooper is authentic, a person who is genuinely funny. Cooper is not a poser. He is the real thing.

Fun is also being silly, feeling a little stupid sometimes, unlatching the impulse control so that you can travel freely, playing with toys, inventing new toys, role playing and play acting, and trying out crazy ideas.

To put all of this another way, fun is a critical component in the work of a creative professional. If you are not laughing regularly, and you are not having fun nearly every day, then you either are not a creative professional or you've managed to find a group of people who ought to be banished from our club.

Learning and Education

Most organisms learn. At learning's most basic level—instinct— organisms seem imprinted with behavior patterns. Many animals with limited cerebral capacity also learn by sensing the environment, repeatedly trying until a problem is solved, and so on. When my dog sees food she wants but cannot easily get, she tries various solutions. And the next time the food is in that place, she will immediately go to the step that worked the last time. That's learning.

Humans have elevated learning to a considerably higher level. We have recorded the most important aspects of our existence and codified this information so that it can be imprinted on our young. Unfortunately, we've combined the pure and useful conception of learning with the more cumbersome formality known as education.

Education

A Mark Twain quote sets the stage: "Never let formal education get in the way of your learning."

His folksy quip turns out to be pretty smart. Dr. Teresa Amabile, one of the most respected researchers in the field of creativity, childhood, and education, filled in the details when she wrote about "creativity killers" associated with classroom learning.[6]

The first killer is *surveillance*. The teacher hovers over the students, making them feel as though they are being watched while working. In fact, this is precisely how most classrooms operate. The second is *evaluation*, the basis of mass education. From gold stars to achievement awards, teachers regularly *reward* students. This misguided motivation technique

---

[6] SOURCE: Daniel Goleman, Paul Kaufman, Michael Ray, *The Creative Spirit*, p. 61.

puts children into a desperate win-lose situation, punishing children who do not succeed in accordance with the evaluation criteria. *Overcontrol* leaves children with the feeling that their originality is a mistake, and that exploration is a waste of time. *Pressure* from teachers, parents, and peers completes a nasty picture.

This list applies not only to schools but to work as well. In *Creativity in Adults,* Sandra Kerka adds several items to Amabile's list: "... restricting choices; fearing failure; judgment, or appearing foolish; having to find the "right answer; ... working under time pressure ..."[7]

Mihaly Csikszenmihalyi adds "... schooling also inhibits creativity by imparting low tolerance for failure; schools therefore make students risk-averse.... For one thing, failure is often punished in some way, whereas good work is rewarded. Failure might result in students having to do makeup or remedial work or might cause them the humiliation of appearing unmotivated or dim-witted. Risk-taking in school is discouraged, both explicitly and implicitly." [8] Csikszenmihalyi continues: "Schools suppress creativity....Teachers, peers, and the educational system as a whole diminish children's urge to express their creative possibilities."[9]

Says Laurence G. Boldt, "We rejected the Mystery of the whole and came to rely on rational consciousness as the sole means of experiencing the universe. This gave us the one-at-a-time (abstract, linear) sense of reality—a world of different things. (We imposed) law and order on this chaos. We put faith in political laws to control the wills of others and natural laws to regulate nature. Politics and science became the religions of the modern era."[10]

School and education are designed to satisfy a norm, to provide a general education and day care for millions of young humans whom we

---

[7] SOURCE: (Amabile 1996, Grupas, 1996) -- ERIC EDO-CE-99-204 — "Creativity in Adults" by Sandra Kerka.

[8] SOURCE: Mihaly Csikszenmihalyi, *Understanding Creativity*, p. 72.

[9] SOURCE: Mihaly Csikszenmihalyi, *Understanding Creativity*, p. 69.

[10] SOURCE: Laurence G. Boldt, *Zen & The Art of Making a Living*, p. xxxix.

have deemed too young for the workplace and too irresponsible to be allowed freedom without adult supervision.

Between the ages of three (when pre-school begins) and eighteen (when high school thankfully ends), students spend over 13,000 hours sitting in classrooms and 4,000 more doing homework to reinforce what was learned in school.

A roughly equivalent number of hours are spent watching television.

And none of these activities encourages creativity, individuality or divergent thinking.

It's no surprise, then, that children tend to lose, submerge, or forget about their creativity as they grow up. Sandra Kerka points out,[11]"Although most young children are very creative, it is estimated that creativity diminishes by 40 percent between the ages of five and seven.[12] At these ages, formal schooling begins, and there is some agreement that education inhibits the transformation of early talent into adult creativity.[13] It may be that schooling and/or the stage of cognitive development at that age emphasizes logical rather than divergent thinking, or that schools (and families) value conventional behavior, well-defined problems, and good grades."[14]

High-achieving creative people, who possess superior skills that match their formative divergent thought patterns, may be rewarded. Other students, whose skills are still forming and whose thinking is unsophisticated, may be perceived as lazy, uninterested, disruptive, or otherwise unsuitable for the classroom machine.

"People like me are aware of their so-called genius at ten, eight, nine.... I always wondered, 'Why has nobody discovered me? In school, didn't they see that I'm more clever than anybody else in this school?

---

[11] SOURCE: ERIC EDO-CE-99-204 – "Creativity in Adults" by Sandra Kerka.

[12] SOURCE (as quoted in Kerka): (Grupas, 1990; McCormick and Plugge, 1997).

[13] SOURCE (as quoted in Kerka): (Albert, 1996, Amabile 1996).

[14] SOURCE (as quoted in Kerka): Albert 1996.

That the teachers are stupid, too? That all they had was information I didn't need.' It was obvious to me. Why didn't they put me in art school? Why didn't they train me? I was different. I was always different. Why didn't anybody notice me?" This from John Lennon,[15] who sounds very much like Picasso or Mozart:

"The story of his (Picasso's) formal artistic education is reminiscent of Mozart's—a series of virtually unnecessary enrollments in formal classes, contempt for mediocre teachers, unpleasant personal clashes, and a reversion to self-education at the feet of favorite masters...."[16]

Few schools and teachers provide the resources needed to nurture the creative student. Most teachers lack the training and fear a loss of the control that is an essential component in classroom education.

Paul Torrance explains, "The creative teacher is involved in discovery, risking, pushing the limits and taking a step into the unknown. This is serious business—dangerous business. When you challenge students to be creative, you lose control."[17] As a result, "students never learn how to take sensible risks, a skill that will be needed if they are going to do genuinely creative work,"[18] explain Sternberg and Lubart.

Multiple Intelligences
Thank goodness for Howard Gardner!

In 1983, Harvard educator Gardner published *Frames of Mind: The Theory of Multiple Intelligences*. In his book, he expanded the definition of intelligence and questioned the fundamental structure of the education system (he continued this line of thinking in 1991's *The Unschooled Mind: How Children Think and How Schools Should Teach*).

---

[15] SOURCE: Howard Gardner, *Frames of Mind*, p. 115.
[16] SOURCE: Howard Gardner, *Creating Minds*, p. 146.
[17] SOURCE: Paul Torrance, "The Beyonders" in *Why Fly: A Philosophy of Creativity*, p. 107 as quoted in *Understanding Creativity*, p. 71.
[18] SOURCE: Sternberg and Lubart, *Defying the Crowd: Cultivating Creativity in a Culture of Conformity*, pp. 48-49.

Gardner said: "I believe that we should get away altogether from tests and correlations among tests, and look instead at the more naturalistic sources of how peoples around the world develop skills important to their way of life....

By studying child development, the diversity of skills found in various populations of children, brain-damaged patients (who retain certain capabilities while losing others, allowing researchers unusual insights), and "special populations... all of whom exhibit very jagged cognitive profiles," Gardner worked out an expanded definition of intelligence.

Employing relatively strict criteria to define precisely what constitutes an intelligence,[19] Gardner described seven and readily admitted that there are likely to be more:

Linguistic Intelligence
* Sensitivity to meaning of words
* Command of language mechanics and dynamics
* Use of language to persuade others
* Memory aspect of language: recording and remembering information
* Explanation and clarity of expression
* Meta-linguistic analysis: using language to clarify language

Musical Intelligence
* Pitch sensitivity (including melody)
* Rhythm sensitivity
* Emotional connection
* Structural understanding
* Memory aspect of sound
* Performance capability

---

[19] SOURCE: Howard Gardner, *Frames of Mind*, pp. 62+.

Logical-Mathematical Intelligence
- Sensitivity to links between various mathematical and logical concepts
- Pattern recognition
- Ability to deal effectively with abstraction
- Ability to skillfully handle long chains of reasoning
- Ability to deal with complexity
- Problem solving, a high level

Spatial Intelligence
- Ability to perceive the world accurately
- Ability to perform transformations and modifications upon one's initial perceptions
- Ability to recreate aspects of one's visual experience, even in the absence of relevant physical stimuli

Bodily-Kinesthetic Intelligence
- Control of one's bodily motions
- Capacity to work skillfully with objects
- Gross and fine motor skills

Intrapersonal Intelligence
- Capacity to notice distinctions among others (such as contrasts in moods, temperaments, motivations, intentions)
- Capacity to communicate effectively with others

Intrapersonal Intelligence
- Knowledge of internal aspects of a person
- Aspects to one's "feeling life"
- Understanding, identification, labeling of emotions
- Guide one's behavior based upon model of self

You may sense a kinship between these intelligences and the Myers-Briggs Type Indicator classifications in the first chapter. Instinctively, people seek work and are hired in roles that match their intelligences.

Learning Creativity

Can creativity be learned, or taught? In a word, yes. One word states the case but oversimplifies the answer.

It is certainly possible to learn any of the crafts and artistic techniques associated with creative endeavors. One can learn to act, dance, direct, design, compose, arrange, harmonize, or do any number of other things that creative people do. You'll find teachers for all of these subjects in just about every major city. You can acquire a complete set of necessary skills; whether you then bring art and talent to those skills may or may not be related.

It's also possible to learn new ideas, through books or formal education. These ideas are likely to teach you something else of value: how to think differently. Extensive training is available to train your toward divergent thinking, abstract conceptualization, thinking in three dimensions, and on other theoretical topics that might have practical applications. Here, the quality of the teacher is critical, and one might need to travel to a particular university or private facility in order to learn effectively.

Creative workshops are also available. Some grow from the new age and holistic health communities; others are focused on innovation for corporations or other groups. Writing workshops; art, music, dance, and theater workshops; photography workshops—all these can be valuable if you're fortunate to find a good teacher and good classmates.

If you were still in public school, your parents could seek out a school that's based, at least in part, upon Howard Gardner's multiple intelligence theory. This discipline is much more difficult to find at the college or university level, and rarely infiltrates any forms of adult education. More often at the adult level you will find coursework specific to a particular type of creative skill (most often found at nearby colleges or universities).

By all means, take these courses. I take courses in art and photography on a regular basis. I am not a wonderful student. I do not have time to attend every class, nor have I time for the homework. Still, these courses are enormously instructive because they force me out of the world in which I am, typically, a creative leader. They place me back in the position of a student with much to learn.

My son Michael is now seventeen. He has spent over a dozen years of his life in classrooms. So far, Michael's classroom learning has been very traditional: math, science, English, a foreign language, health/gym and marching band. Next year, his senior year, he will have satisfied the school's requirements, and so he is taking the courses that he wants to take: creative writing, filmmaking, drawing, and psychology.

As I write this paragraph, he's looking at possible colleges on the Web. A solid B student (who might be an A student if more of his varied intelligences mattered to those who design curriculum), he is a typical candidate for a career as a creative professional. In his early stages, he writes, draws, plays several musical instruments, designs, makes up insightful jokes, and so on. Michael is facing what has become a standard set of choices for his college education. The basis and criteria for his decisions are common among many high school students who are considering careers as creative professionals and should prove helpful for adults who are moving into the creative field or contemplating a new career.

Enroll in a Liberal Arts College
• Major in one of several available creative majors, such as art, theater, communications, or music.

• Take the core courses in science, math, foreign language, etc.

• Minor in another creative domain or expand his thinking into psychology, sociology, philosophy, or other intellectual pursuit.

• Major in a more traditional subject, such as psychology or English. But take as many creative courses as possible as electives.

• Become involved in one or more student organizations that are closely aligned with his creative interests, such as a club that produces student films, or the campus TV station.

There are several positives associated with the liberal arts approach. He will interact with lots of students with varied interests. Most students will not be majoring in creative areas, so this microcosm more closely resembles the real world and prepares him for real life. He can earn a degree that will allow him to get any kind of job, not just a creative one. He can take whatever coursework in creative topics that he wants, without the pressure of completing all the work in a creative-only curriculum.

Selecting a college or university with a distinguished arts program could be the best solution. Unfortunately, institutions vary in the quality and commitment of their creative departments. Financing for these programs varies widely. Therefore, it is vitally important to visit prospective institutions prior to applying for admission.

Attend a College Specializing in the Arts

• Major in any of the many available creative majors, such as art, theater, communications, or music.

• Take the core courses in science, math, foreign language, etc.

• Minor in another creative domain or take a few courses in other stimulating topics.

• Become involved in one or more student organizations that are closely aligned with his creative interests, such as a club that produces student films, or the campus TV station.

Compare this list with the previous one. There are few majors outside the creative fields. This type of institution is typically a music conservatory or an art/design school.

The student population will be composed mostly of creative people. Often, students who felt out of place in high school speak of finding a home in art school. At home, they were odd. Here, they're normal.

Is it a good idea to spend four years in a totally creative education environment? For those who will rely on craft, the four-year equivalent of an apprenticeship can be valuable. Musicians who focus through an undergraduate and a graduate education develop a tremendous understanding of repertoire, technique, history, and possibilities. Photographers who develop their eye and their skills under master teachers can benefit enormously from an art school education. Filmmakers often talk about the benefits of film school.

Often these institutions are tied into the professional artistic communities. They might offer spectacular apprenticeships, internships, and interactions with impressive faculty members.

For budding creative professionals who are not passionate about one very specific discipline, these colleges can be limiting. Few art schools, for example, also boast a superior curriculum outside of the creative domains. The number of psychology or English classes might be limited, and the faculty might not be so impressive in these fringe areas. Many such classes exist only to satisfy state requirements.

Social life could also be limited. These are the latter-day equivalent of trade schools and conservatories; the reason for attending these schools is more professional than social. All day, all night, the buzz is about creative endeavors, pressure to get the next project right, and professional possibilities. Not much time or attention for dating, not much discussion about the school hockey team because there is rarely a team to talk about. Most such schools are located in urban locations, close to the local arts scene. This, too, might not be for everyone.

What Matters?

Over time, I've probably hired a few hundred creative professionals. Their choice of college or university was rarely a consideration. My main concerns are whether the person will get along with the team and whether they can do the work. I'm not sure that a Princeton or Stanford education is more valuable than four years at Rhode Island School of Design, Syracuse University, or Ohio State.

If I'm hiring someone right out of school, it's almost always on the basis of a personal recommendation. When that happens, so long as the person has graduated college, I can't say that I care which one she attended. I care about what happens during the interview, and if her work sample is especially impressive, I care about that, too. I also notice internships and deep involvement in extra curricular activities (I don't care that you were a disc jockey on the college station, but it matters if you were a music director who changed the station and doubled its popularity).

If I'm hiring someone with experience, I care about the experience, not about their education. Sure, during the interview we might talk for a moment about a particular college or university, but the subject is mentioned in passing.

What about graduate school? In art and music, graduate school probably matters. In most other creative professions, it's better to start work and take some coursework along the way. Even those with a particular interest in, say, products or services for children, are better off entering the work force and then completing a master's degree in childhood education or child psychology with the benefit of real world context and experience. Learn what you can in four years, get out into the arena, then go back for more education if you think it will help you or simply because you want to learn.

ADD, Learning Disorders and Mental Diseases

Educators, psychologists and neurologists have identified a broad spectrum of conditions that describe abnormal behaviors. Some of these, such as ADD and ADHD, feel more like convenient labels than diseases. Others can be debilitating. Many have been associated with creative people.

ADD / ADHD

Attention deficit disorder is not a recognized psychological condition. It is not a disease and cannot be precisely diagnosed. In children, who are by nature easily distracted, impulsive, and restless, it's the skilled psychologist who recognizes divergence from normal behavior. Still, the judgment can be made only in comparison with a peer group; the symptoms are relative.

Discussions of adult ADD began in 1978, at a conference about what was then labeled MBD (minimal brain dysfunction). In 1990, the respected *New England Journal of Medicine* published a paper by Dr. Alan Zametkin of the National Institutes of Mental Health. "In brief, what Zametkin proved was that there was a difference at the cellular level, in energy consumption, between parts of the brain that regulate attention, emotion, and impulse control in subjects with ADD as compared with subjects without ADD."[20] Further biological evidence followed. As a result, school psychologists began working with teachers, supporting children with a range of learning disabilities, and developing specific strategies to help them learn. Roughly 5 percent of children are "LD" (learning disabled) kids, and in many schools, these programs meant the difference between confused, lost, and sometimes troublesome students and children who gradually found their way back into mainstream programs.

At the same time, many adult parents were exposed to symptoms associated with ADD and the strategies used to counteract their negative effects. Some adults began to understand their own behavior through their exposure to children's ADD. The genetic component seems real: If

---

[20] SOURCE: Edward M. Hallowell, M.D., and John J. Ratey, M.D., *Driven to Distraction: Recognizing and Coping with Attention Deficit Disorder from Childhood through Adulthood*, p. 71.

one parent has a form of ADD, at least one child is also likely to suffer from some of the behaviors.

In its gentler manifestations, ADD can be understood and aided by a self-help guide, like *Driven to Distraction* or its many competitors. To deal with a high score on the above guide, a therapist is probably essential, at least for a period of time.

Many creative people believe that they have ADD. In fact, I've now worked in several companies where the creative departments refer to themselves as "the ADD ward" or by a similar self-deprecating label. Creative people will try anything to explain how and why they are different from other people; this difference becomes a badge. Although I've always thought of the "ADD defense" as a stupid and childish reduction of the creative process, I've been too quick to judge. In fact, ADD and creativity correlate, as Hallowell and Ratey explain:

• "People with ADD have a greater tolerance for chaos than most.... In order to rearrange life, in order to create, one must get comfortable with disarrangement for a while...."
• "One of the cardinal symptoms of ADD is impulsivity.... One does not plan to have a creative thought ... it is out of nowhere, on the wings of impulse, that creativity flies in."
• "The ability to focus or hyperfocus at times ... The term "attention deficit" is a misnomer. It is a matter of attention inconsistency. While it is true that the ADD mind wanders off when it is not engaged, it is also the case that the ADD mind fastens onto its subject fiercely when it *is* engaged.
• "People with ADD are always reacting. Even when they look calm and sedate, they are usually churning inside, taking this bit of data and moving it there, pushing this thought through their emotional network, putting that idea on the fire to burn, exploding or subsiding but always in motion."[21]

---

[21] SOURCE: Edward M. Hallowell, M.D., and John J. Ratey, M.D., *Driven to Distraction*, pp. 176-178.

Certainly there is a high correlation between creative thinking and these four factors. Creative professionals do work within the imaginary unknown, and we tend toward impulsive thinking because it either comes naturally or because we've been trained that way. We're not the only population who can hyperfocus, and we're not the only ones who are always thinking. Take a moment and compare the list of creative traits on page 000 to the exercise you've just done, and you'll find a relatively small number of common characteristics.

DO YOU HAVE ADULT ADD?

Many creative people believe they do—are you one of them? Here's a short adaptation of the checklist that appears in *Driven to Distraction*. Rate your tendency with a 0, 1, 2, or 3 (0 = very uncommon or very low intensity behavior; 3 = persistent, high-degree, chronic behavior).

0,1,2,3	BEHAVIOR
	A strong sense of underachievement, a sense of not meeting one's goals—regardless of how much is actually accomplished.
	Difficulty getting organized.
	Chronic procrastination, trouble getting started.
	Many simultaneous projects, most or all of which are never completed.
	Tendency to say what comes to mind without necessarily considering the timing or appropriateness of the remark.
	A frequent search for high stimulation.
	An intolerance of boredom.
	Easy distractibility, trouble focusing attention, tendency to drift in and out of conversations—often coupled with extreme hyperfocus at times.
	Trouble in going through established channels and/or following proper or appropriate procedures.

	Impatient, low tolerance for frustration.
	Very impulsive, either in spoken words or in action. Often linked with significant, unexpected changes in plans, career paths.
	Tendency to worry needlessly and endlessly, alternating with disregard for actual dangers.
	Sense of insecurity, no matter how secure life situation may be.
	Significant mood swings when disengaged from a person or a project; might experience extremes of happiness and sadness within hours.
	Restlessness.
	Tendency toward addictive behavior.
	Chronic problems with self-esteem.
	Inaccurate self-knowledge; poor understanding of interpersonal or group dynamics.
	Family history of mental illness, such as depression, poor impulse control, mood swings, substance abuse.
	TOTAL (add all 0, 1, 2, 3)

If you score is under 30, you probably do not have ADD. Scores in the 31-42 range indicate some aspects of adult ADD. If you score was 43 or higher, you may be an ADD candidate.

Some creative people have ADD. Most of us do not.

If you need a cover story to explain yourself, you will not find much help in other learning disabilities or other unusual behaviors. Left-handed people are no more creative than right-handed people. Dyslexics are no more or less creative than the rest of the population.

Creativity and Mental Illness

Still, it is unwise to dismiss any possible connection between creativity and mental illness.

"An excellent study by Arnold Ludwig of persons whose biographies had been reviewed by the *New York Times Book Review* between 1960 and 1990 revealed that poets had the highest rate of mania, psychosis and psychiatric hospitalizations and that 18 percent of them committed suicide. He also found, in his comparison of those in the creative arts to those in professions such as science and business, that members of the arts group were at least twice as likely to suffer from some form of mental illness and were six times as likely to have been hospitalized for psychiatric reasons."[22]

Let's define terms. Mental illness includes a wide range of diseases, symptoms, behaviors, and other abnormalities that include: anxiety disorders (panic, obsessive-compulsive, phobias); depression and mood disorders (including bipolar disorders); eating disorders; codependency; anger; various types of stress; issues related to loss; personality disorders; schizophrenia; abuse and addiction; and more.

For the most part, creative people are no more or less likely to suffer from these problems than the rest of the population. Several studies indicate a higher likelihood of schizophrenia and bipolar disorders among the creative population, offering up the painters Vincent van Gogh and Edward Munch and writer Sylvia Plath as stunning examples.

Certainly, this description of Beethoven suggests something decidedly different from those who work in more traditional jobs: "Music seems to have acted on Beethoven as a drug. He literally seems to have lost control as sheer sound seized him. We can imagine him seated at the piano, conducting one of his orchestral works. As the music progressed, he would quite forget the purpose of his job. He would rise, be carried away, make motions that might be understood today but were the equivalent of gibberish then."[23]

I believe there is a different explanation for the link between creative work and mental illness.

---

[22] SOURCE: Mihaly Csikszenmihalyi, *Understanding Creativity*, p. 141.
[23] SOURCE, Harold Schoenberg, *Great Conductors*, p. 59.

Often, an individual with mental illness issues finds traditional work to be a frustrating challenge. Tolerance for those with anxiety disorders, depression, codependency or anger is very limited in workplaces. As a result, individuals with these and other disorders tend to do one of three things: (a) they work alone; (b) they seek out a workplace where they are accepted; and/or (c) they do not work, or do not work with any regularity.

As it happens, many creative professions are solo acts: photographers, fine artists, writers, poets, sculptors, and so on. Each of these professions provides an extraordinary opportunity for self-expression through work, which might serve as a focused outlet for mental energies. Minimal involvement with others may be possible, and yet, the individual might be both productive and creatively satisfied. In fact, the individual might be quite successful despite personality disorders, addiction, codependency, or depression. It is no wonder that Arnold Ludwig found such a high rate of psychological problems among poets and other individual creative talents—more than likely, many people in his profiles selected creative professions precisely because they were mentally unstable. In other words, his sample was self-selecting.

Mental illness can be skillfully masked, particularly in a high-tolerance environment or industry. For example, rock music, jazz, and theater are especially tolerant. And it is not uncommon to find a rock or jazz musician with a substance abuse problem. Stories about depression, panic, anger, and other personality disorders are common in theater legend. If the individual is a key creative talent central to the success of a project, the television and motion picture industries might also be tolerant. Some individuals have managed long, successful careers in these sectors while managing to keep their mental illness issues in check through a combination of sheer will, therapy, and medication. Others have been less successful; unfortunately, some of these failures are well-publicized. In some situations, particularly in rock music, the disorder becomes part of celebrity lore; more often, the career falls apart.

Knowing and Nurturing Your Muse

Regardless of how much science and rigorous research contribute to the discussion, I keep wondering if the Greeks were right. Every once in a while, a muse enters my head. I have this feeling of confidence. Time just flies by. The work is good. I feel good about what I am doing.

He, she, or it doesn't visit me when I am in one particular place. There's no single time of day when it's more or less likely to happen. No one piece of music inspires me.

I do better work with some people than with others. I select my creative partners carefully. That seems to matter. Maybe when I create something with my friend Dorothy, our muses are especially well-suited to one another. My muse gets a great deal of respect from me. I don't even begin to understand the relationship, but I am very careful not to do anything wrong.

For me, the most significant factor is getting enough sleep. When I am working with less than eight hours of sleep, my muse is not wild about hanging around with my cantankerous self. My muse is more tolerant of the pressure that sometimes comes with deadlines or impossible situations; the muse helps me to deliver regardless.

I also know when to stop. My muse cannot work twenty-four hours a day. We go through a cycle together. In the morning, ideas are percolating and we're anxious to get to work. We pace ourselves, though, and maybe take a walk before diving into the project. Work for a few fluid hours, then take a break for something to eat. From time to time, a little hit of chocolate seems to help us both. Pretty regularly, the muse tries to cut out just a few hours after lunch. I encourage her to stay, mainly by setting an example for myself. I just keep working, and without saying a word she stays. (Okay, I see I'm using "she" and not "it" or "he," so I'll assume that my muse is some sort of a feminine presence.) Then, I get a little bored with the work. I want to finish the section or that part of the project, but she's no longer interested. I can skate for a while on my own, and then I stop. I very rarely insist on a hard push in the evening or on a weekend; I know she'll be too weary to come back for the following week's work, and it's not worth the potential sacrifice. Besides, those are feeding times: hours to read, take walks, look at art or sketch some of my own, talk to friends, travel, taste interesting foods, or immerse myself in a dark theater watching a movie that's somebody else's fantasy.

Abusing the Muse

The muse is a fragile being. I think of her in a gossamer form, one that solidifies when we need to get down to work, but essentially floating and billowy when ideas are drifting through my mind. The muse is not a critical thinker; that's my job. She glides along the neural pathways inside my mind or brain (I get confused about which is which, but she seems to know where to go). She's childlike enough to pick up on bad habits, and if I'm not careful, she'll slide into my work as well. She's sufficiently shapeless, formless, and colorless to be capable of transforming herself based on the most random factors. Once she changes, it's not easy to shift her shape back into what it needs to be. That's why I don't mess around altering my muse at all. She's been with me, doing good work for decades. We can learn together, sure, but I am extremely careful not to abuse her.

I am astonished when a creative person attempts to alter his muse. I'm pretty sure you're not supposed to do that. If you do, maybe you'll never get her back (if I have a female muse, do female creatives have a male one?). Then again, I'm a reasonably optimistic guy with a Tinkerbelle muse. What happens if your muse is like Al Capone or some other bad guy? In those situations, you might do everything you can to get away from the muse, to destroy the muse, or to change it in any way you possibly could.

One popular way to abuse the muse is with alcohol or drugs. Some people speak of enhanced awareness, sensitivity, and relaxation as a result of enjoying drugs or alcohol in small quantities, but that's risky. When the quantity becomes larger, these sensations are confused or overshadowed by the drug's tendency to confuse the mind or decrease motor coordination. As Csikszenmihalyi explains, "Many literary figures and some artists have believed that they were most able to contact their unconscious and produce their best work while under the influence of a psychoactive drug....Many others, however, found that the work they produced while using alcohol was inferior to their standards, and they ceased drinking specifically to improve the quality of their work.... Jackson Pollack ... actually produced the works considered to be his best during the three years when he was sober."[24]

Then again, there's the wisdom of Louis Armstrong: "Marijuana was not merely a diversion for Louis, it became an obsession, an inspiration, and a necessity. 'I smoked it a long time,' he wrote about the substance he called gage, 'it's a thousand times better than whiskey. It's an assistant, a friend, a nice cheap drunk, if you want to call it that, very good for asthma, relaxes your nerves.' It was so important in his life that in later years, when he began to prepare a third volume of memoirs for publication, he planned to call it *Gage*."[25]

Armstrong questioned whether marijuana should be considered in the same class as other narcotics; others have repeatedly asked the same question.

Whether or not marijuana leads to other drugs, it's not unusual these days to find the *bon vivant* writer or artist or producer who loves his food, her drink, his cocaine, her sexual partners. It's L.A., it's Paris, it's London, it's the country place, it's the cabin by the lake, and it's okay because it's both discreet and commonplace. Danger and a feeling of "getting away with it" heightens the experience. It's a privilege that's part of fame. It's tradition. And besides, I only drink when I'm not working. Or when I need to get started in the morning.

We've all read that play, seen that movie. But where's the line? Certainly, it's not just skipping out on the gym for a few months, certainly it's not the few extra pounds or anger at the wardrobe assistant who's secretly tightening every costume's waistline. The muse requires nourishment. The muse works best when she is pampered. And when I

---

[24] SOURCE: Mihaly Csikszenmihalyi, *Understanding Creativity*, p.145.

[25] SOURCE: Laurence Bergreen, *Louis Armstrong: An Extravagant Life*, pp. 282-3.

stand in front of the mirror, the extra weight can hardly be seen at all.

Anyway, it's not my fault that things aren't going well. I hired the wrong director. And that argument that we had last night, well, it wasn't as severe as the one we had the night before. I'm beginning to feel as though I'm the only one I can really trust.

Unchecked, it is remarkably easy to make mistakes. Unchecked, the insecurities and the dark side can conspire with the muse and lead just about any of us astray. We live in these fantasy worlds where we get paid, sometimes richly, for what we think, or how we act, or how we sing or dance. We begin to take ourselves seriously. The muse remains, but only because she's chained. People are watching. People will remember. It doesn't matter; only the talent matters. Nobody can do it the way I do. If they want what I do, nobody does it better.

Maybe not. But there are those who do it their own way. And that might be good enough.

Are We Different From Other People?

As children, many creative people exhibit particular skills, natural abilities, or talents. Positive reinforcement encourages us to pursue these specialties. Sometimes we respond, sometimes we don't, and often we don't until much later on. Unless we turn out to be prodigies, or we suffer particular abuse, most of us live pretty normal lives.

Csikszenmihalyi wrote, "None of the (creative) people we interviewed remembers being popular in adolescence. Some of them seem to have had a reasonably untroubled time, and others think back on those years with barely disguised horror; however, nostalgia for teenage years is almost entirely absent. Marginality—the feeling of being on the outside, being different, of observing with detachment the strange rituals of one's peers—was a common theme."[26]

Early in a career, parental approval might seem significant, but with success, most parents learn to accept their adult child as a creative

---

[26] SOURCE: Mihaly Csikszenmihalyi, *CREATIVITY*, p. 187.

professional. Director Jim Jarmusch said: "Certainly my father it bothered a lot. Because he wanted me to go to law school or enter business or something like that. And it caused a lot of problems, a real separation between my father and me. But for some reason now, I think because my father is older, he accepts things much more easily than he used to. And he's proud that the film is doing well."[27]

All grown up, it's often difficult to distinguish creative professionals from other types of professionals and other types of adults. Comedian Chris Elliot talks about his father going to work in a shirt, tie, and a suit, carrying a briefcase; it didn't occur to him until years later that his father's job was extraordinary (his father was a very popular radio and stage performer, half of the comedy duo Bob and Ray). Years ago, some creative professionals wore suits, but as many were easier to spot because of their relaxed dress; now casual dress is common, even in offices.

Finding the true creative professional requires a more thorough understanding of our distinguishing marks, and even these can be misleading: unusual or highly evolved communications skills; highly evolved use of colorful, imaginative, non-traditional words and imagery; above-average combinations of spatial, musical, interpersonal, intrapersonal, and logical-mathematical intelligences. Look for the person in the meeting who seems skillful in synthesizing ideas rapidly, who regularly suggests highly logical or highly divergent paths, who asks questions and then quiets down for a while. Look for the person who makes the others laugh. Look for the ones who experience emotions deeply but easily shift from one mode to the next, then get to down to work without allowing problems to get them down. Look for some or all of these characteristics and you're likely to identify a member of our clan.

---

[27] SOURCE: Quotes below from *Jim Jarmusch Interviews* by Ludvig Hertzberg. *Film Comment*, Vol. 21, No. 1, January/Feburary 1985, pp. 54, 60, 62, interviewed by Harlan Jacobsen, 1984.

Eastern Views

For many creative people, Eastern thought offers meaningful resonance. Acknowledging the growth and popularity of all things Eastern, ways of thinking that evolved in Asia are substantively different from the ways that westerners look at the world, in general, and at creativity, especially.

Zen Buddhism

Since the 1950s many creative people have felt an especially strong connection with Zen Buddhism. Historically speaking, Buddhism is over 2,500 years old,[28] but the Ch'an techniques did not become influential until the T'ang Dynasty (618-987 C.E.[29]). Over the next several hundred years, Buddhism expanded to Japan, and around 1200 C.E. Zen Buddhism became a part of the Japanese Imperial culture in Kyoto, then the capital city. After World War II, Zen Buddhism became popular in the West, largely through the writings of D.T. Suzuki and Alan Watts.[30]

Zen emphasizes living in the present, but like the creative process, it is a mass of seeming contradictions. As I summarized this list from its source, I found that many aspects of Zen are consistent with the way I think about creativity. In fact, as you read each bullet point, try replacing the word "Zen" with the word "creativity" or "the creative process." Some Zen fundamentals:[31]

• *"Zen emphasizes meditation as a way to enlightenment.* Power is not from above; it is within ourselves and around us. Meditation opens the universe to us, and opens us to the universe."

---

[28] By comparison, Christianity is about 2,000 years old, Judaism is about 4,000, and Islam is about 1,500 years old.

[29] Curent Era, a more socially acceptable alternative to Anno Domahi, the year of our lord.

[30] For an introduction, read *The Way of Zen* by Alan Watts and/or *Zen Buddhism: Selected Writings* by D.T. Suzuki (William Barrett, editor).

[31] SOURCE: James H. Austin, M.D., *Zen and the Brain*, pp. 11-14.

• *"The intellect is not at home in the province of Zen.* No abstract theories, complicated rules, challenging philosophies, or reliance upon words and their cloudy meanings. Instead, there is only what is."

• *"Zen values the simple, concrete, living facts of everyday direct personal experience.* Instantaneous, uncluttered awareness throughout everything else is? in the here and now."

• *"Zen is intensely pragmatic.* Wary of moralistic judgments, of manmade distinctions between good and bad. People will naturally act in accord with the right way of things; behavior becomes increasingly selfless."

• *"You learn Zen in zazen, Zen meditation.* It is essential, fundamental practice for ripening the brain's intuitive faculties."

• *"You needn't sit on a pillow to practice Zen.* Aspirants flounder until they finally let go of their attitude that enlightenment is something to 'achieve.'"

• *"Zen stresses self-reliance, self-discipline, and personal effort.* Zen de-emphasizes, even-handedly, not only those behaviors that are self-centered from the inside but also any authoritarian doctrines from the outside that might interfere with self-realization."

• *"The inner journey is but a prelude to going out.* What does the herdsman do in the old Zen story after he finally becomes enlightened? He does not retreat from the world to become a hermit. Instead, he goes forth with joy and compassion to mingle in the world 'with helping hands.'"

Austin's analysis[32] of the seemingly contradictory aspects of Zen Buddhism also correlates with my view of creative people at work. We

---

[32] SOURCE: James H. Austin, *Zen and the Brain*, p. 678.

must rely on ourselves, but we are at our best when doing so without ego. We must exercise enormous self-discipline and restraint, and yet our stock in trade is behavioral freedom and spontaneity. Simplicity is sophistication. We must participate directly in the here and now while simultaneously detaching ourselves from the present. We must pursue goals, and yet we are most powerful when we are goal-less. We must stay attentive, but we must let go.

Chakras[33]

In Chinese and Indian thought, and in their meditation, the movement of energy through the body and the universe is a central idea. In the body, this life force moves along invisible lines called meridians. The energy centers of the body are known as chakras. There are seven key chakras, each one controlling an aspect of physical, emotional, and mental function, each one closely related to the others. Each chakra is located at a place in the spinal column that is connected to key bodily functions.

The role of meditation is to keep the energy flowing to, through, and from those chakras. Their efficient operation is the key to health, happiness, learning, and creativity. The relative strength of each chakra varies with each person, and the times in their lives.

• *Crown Chakra*—Located on top of the skull, the crown chakra connects personal consciousness to the outer world. Here, knowledge, wisdom, understanding, spirituality, and bliss develop.

• *Third Eye Center (or, Brow Chakra)*—Located on the forehead between the eyes, this chakra relates to seeing, both physically and intuitively. When this chakra is well-developed, it is possible to visualize and understand a wide view.

---

[33] SOURCE (OF LIST): http://www.sacredcenters.com/chakras.html.

• *Throat Chakra*—This chakra includes the throat and the mouth; as such, it is concerned with self-expression, communication, and with food intake.

• *Heart Chakra*— "...provides the true understanding that people are interconnected. The heart knows that no one person or one group can truly benefit at the expense of another." Located at the symbolic center of the seven key chakras, the heart chakra "allows us to love deeply, feel compassion, have a deep sense of peace and centeredness."

• *Power Chakra*—Located in the solar plexus. "It rules our personal power, will, and autonomy, as well as our metabolism. When healthy, this chakra brings us energy, effectiveness, spontaneity, and non-dominating power."

• *Second (sometimes, Third) Chakra*—Located in the abdomen, lower back, and sexual organs, it "is related to...emotions and sexuality. It connects us to others through feeling, desire, sensation, and movement. Ideally this chakra brings us fluidity and grace, depth of feeling, sexual fulfillment, and the ability to accept change" (the latter related to digestion).

• *Base Chakra*—Located at the base of the spine, "this chakra is related to our survival instincts, and to our sense of grounding and connection to our bodies and the physical plane." It is associated with family. Ideally this chakra brings us health, prosperity, security, and dynamic presence.

For those who believe strongly in the power of mediation and in the clarity of Eastern thought, the chakras provide a very clear picture of how human beings operate. For others, it's yet another map of the mind-body connection, useful but perhaps just another in a series of such attempts at mapping the unmappable.

Sacred and Scholarly Texts

As a Westerner explores Eastern thought, several key documents are essential scholarly pursuits.

Is the answer in the *Tao Te Ching*, or the *Bhagavad Gita*, or the *Q'ran?* For some creative people, this literature contains extraordinarily clear answers to essential questions. For most people, though, they are exceedingly long documents that are difficult to navigate for any practical information or advice. They demand study and illumination. The documents themselves play a very specific role within their religious contexts; they are not purely literature but part of a connected system of ideas, beliefs, values, and cultural behaviors.

Faith

Over 2,000 years ago, the Greeks helped move mankind up the evolutionary ladder. No longer was our faith based upon the surface qualities and magic of God. We now looked to the philosophers for a verification of what we believed to be truth. Discourse led to deeper understanding as individuals began to trust their own perceptions and beliefs.

This evolution roughly parallels the way in which humans teach themselves about faith.[34] At three or four or five years old, children accept the magic of God and see faith in its surface qualities. By age five or six or seven, they rely on the credibility of storytellers, such as teachers, parents, and books, to verify the truth of faith. By twelve or thirteen or fourteen, children begin to think for themselves, become aware of alternative ways of thinking. They deconstruct symbols and wonder about the credibility of the elders. They begin to trust their own judgment but continue to rely on authority figures to answer their questions and to show them the way.

---

[34] SOURCE: *Understanding Creativity*, p.130, originally from theologian James Fowler, "Stages in Faith Consciousness" in *Weaving the New Creation*, J. Fowler, editor.

It's interesting to parallel the development of confidence or faith in one's own creativity. At three or so, the creativity is natural and without need for verification. At five or six, the drawing isn't good unless the teacher or the parent says it's good. By twelve or thirteen, most children have stopped drawing completely, for those whose creativity has not been smothered, exposure to alternative forms and the wider world does tend to bring one's faith in one's own skills into question.

By age eighteen or so, one assumes responsibility for one's own beliefs, attitudes, commitments and lifestyle. Those who continue to require the dogma figure might join a religious organization or club. By age thirty or so, the view changes. The symbols, rituals, and beliefs begin to make sense, not as disparate parts but as a coherent whole. Relationships become clear. We begin to explore the supernatural in a meaningful way, to experience a Supreme Being or a force in its glory, and feel a part of a universal community. At forty or so, these discoveries become part of existence. And around fifty, we rely on them for sustenance and to make sense of the universe.

When I think about the evolution of creativity in my own life, and in the lives of others I know, I see these changes again paralleling the faith stages. That, however, is just the beginning of the realization. At some point, typically in the late thirties, forties, or early fifties, the lines of faith and creativity seem to converge.

Once again, I return to my *Carmen Sandiego* experience. I recall sitting in a religious study group—not something I have done often in my life. I was trying to explain what happens when an idea takes shape during rehearsal—an embarrassingly show-business-y take on the world, to be sure. I explained that the room would typically be filled with two or three performers, a director, a writer or two, several producers, an art director, a wardrobe designer, and maybe a few departmental assistants. The script is okay, a funny idea but one that could use improvement. We struggle a bit, and then there is this moment when the right idea materializes. It's not exactly a *Eureka!* moment but more like a "yeah, we ought to try that … okay, let's run the bit … hey, that was really funny" series of moments. At that moment, everyone in the room feels the presence of something, a superior force, a collective consciousness. *We* did that. Or, our muses all convened above us, and filled our second brain chambers at the same moment. We all laugh at the same instant. We laugh together. We remember the laughter. We record the bit, and people at home share the religion. They laugh, too.

We develop a belief that we can repeat this experience. We are not always successful, but when we are, and we see that we made someone laugh, we get that special feeling again. This is not just craft, we think this is something closer to faith. There is a force; energy at play.

Which makes me wonder about faith, religion, and (oh, what the heck), slapstick comedy. I think I understand the faith concept: It is a belief in magic, in a force that rises above daily existence. The more I learn about religion, the more I believe that religion is the institutionalization of faith, just as education is the institutionalization of learning. Which brings us to Buster Keaton.

Buster Keaton always makes me laugh. He makes my wife laugh, he makes my kids laugh. He's made us all laugh, even when the children were very small. Charlie Chaplin makes us laugh, too. So do the Marx Brothers. My kids were brought up on black-and-white comedies. When Turner Classic Movies schedules a Harold Lloyd film, my kids don't do their homework that night. My wife fed my kids a diet of Hope and Crosby *Road* pictures. Why? We didn't think about the reason at the time, but looking back, I see the reason. It was because these people are magical, and magic is an essential ingredient in childhood education. As it happens, this magic also helps cancer patients to live a little longer; sometimes, it helps to cure them. What causes laughter? This is not a question that scientists have been able to answer (and I hope they never figure it out). Funny people know. When they look into a child's eyes, they can make those eyes brighter. I have faith in the clown.

Faith and joy seem like pretty closely related ideas to me. When I see a fat, jolly Buddha, he makes me happy. Faith works best when it's linked with happiness, I think. The elegant Hindu dancer, Shiva Nataraja, also expresses religious ecstasy (in the form of a victory of spirit over evil). I'm not so sure about religions based upon suffering; I like the part about rebirth, nature, the seasons, and the lessons we can learn from the religious mythology (or literal fact, if you like) in the Bible.

Maybe St. Augustine was wrong. Maybe creative ideas do come straight from God after all.[35]

The Role of Spirituality

"*A Love Supreme* has been described as a prayer, a work of devotion, a meditation on God, but it is much more than that. It is a searingly confessional, frankly personal piece based on (John) Coltrane's quest to reach and find God through seeking within."[36]

Browsing through H.W. Janson's massive *History of Art*, the role of spirituality and art seems to ebb and flow with the times. His story picks up around 3,500 B.C. The pyramids were probably built to celebrate some combination of "political power, religious ideology, and the development of high technology." Greek art celebrated gods and goddesses and the human acts made possible by them. Much Roman art is about power, not spirituality, which seems consistent with their culture. By the Middle Ages, the church is strongly in control, and for those several hundred years, Janson's book is filled with church architecture, or with mosaics, tapestries, or gilded paintings of Christ, his family, and his apostles. Many of the book's Renaissance images feature similar themes. Then, around 1500, the content of the book changes. No longer is spirituality the central theme. Hans Holbein the Younger paints Erasmus of Rotterdam, an author, and Henry VIII in the famous royal portrait. There's a landscape, a still life at the local meat market, where sausages are suspended above some dead

---

[35] "(Saint Augustine, bishop of Hippo), in his brilliant treatise The City of God, written between 413 and 426…was probably the first to discredit the idea that all creative ideas come straight from God, devout though he was."
—*Understanding Creativity*, p. 22.

[36] SOURCE: Eric Nisenson, *Ascension*, p. 152.

chickens and a disembodied cow's head. Bruegel the Elder painted *Peasant Wedding* in 1565. Halfway through Janson's thousand-page tome, God and Jesus seem to disappear. Some artists explore spirituality, but most are concerned with the quality of light or interesting local personalities (Frans Hals painted *The Jolly Toper* and *Malle Babbe* in the mid-1600s, both personalities ripe with local color). By 1734, William Hogarth is represented by a painting called *The Orgy* (tame by contemporary terms, but with a bit of skin). Royal families and bloody battles occupy the next hundred years. Then, it's the impressionists painting the common folk: Degas, Renoir, and Toulouse-Lautrec capturing the Paris nightlife, the ordinary folk living their ordinary lives.

What happened to God?

Dali answered the question by placing Christ on a slab-like crucifix in a 3-D painting. Others experimented less boldly. The connection between God and art—or Western art, anyway—has been more or less forgotten.

The issue goes deeper than a change in artist's patronage. At a certain point in time, probably just before 1500, Western artists freed themselves of the requirement that art celebrate God or Jesus Christ. A similar phenomenon occurred in Western music. Certainly, in modern times, nearly every culture has followed a similar path. Few cultures continue to demand that an artist's work be spiritual in nature.

Still, spirituality does play a role—and not only in contemporary religious music.

Sit down quietly with almost any creative person—creative professional or not—and you might find yourself engaged in a highly spiritual conversation. Listen carefully to the words. You might not hear the traditional terminology. Neither Jesus Christ nor the Old Testament nor Buddha nor angels might be mentioned, but something is happening inside that cannot be attributed purely to brain power and manual dexterity. Most creative people sense there is a spirit of some sort that eases the process along, paves the way, provides stimulation, makes concentration and focus possible, and lends emotional support. These ideas might be only vaguely drawn, but it's rare to find a creative person who explains himself or herself without them. And looking backward, the story is essentially the same as the one devised by the Greeks—a higher power plays a role in the brain's second chamber, perhaps eased by facilitators (who they happened to call muses).

"I don't ask for the full ringing of the bell.... I don't ask for a clap of thunder that would rend the veil in the temple. A scrawny cry will do, from far off there among the willows and the cattails, from far off there among the galaxies." So poet Wallace Stevens wrote[37] on the subject of his calling.

Author Gregg Levoy lists "song lyrics you can't get out of your head...instructions that arise unbidden from the silence of meditation... a dream that keeps coming back, or what pursues you in the dreams...a symptom that recurs and is exquisitely metaphoric, such as a pain in the neck from shouldering too much responsibility...a conversation that you overhear that seems as though it was spoken directly to you." I would add synchronicity: two or more connected coincidences. These are among the most common signs, the calls that you must be ready to hear, the stars that you must be open to see.

Levoy defines "disaster" by returning to the original Latin: "against one's stars." He writes of Theseus and the Minotaur: "After Theseus has slain the beast in the center of the underground labyrinth, he guides himself back to the surface by a length of thread given to him by Ariadne, the king's daughter, retracing his steps through the dark maze of tunnels."[38]

And he writes, "In his biography, Nikos Kazantzakis, author of *Zorba the Greek*, described an incident in which he came upon a cocoon cradled in the bark of an olive tree just as the butterfly was making a hole and attempting to emerge. Impatient for results, he bent over it and warmed it under his breath, by which he succeeded in speeding up the process. The butterfly, however, emerged prematurely, its wings hopelessly crumpled

---

[37] SOURCE: Gregg Levoy, Callings: *Finding and Following an Authentic Life*, p. 13.

[38] SOURCE: Gregg Levoy, *Callings*, p. 13.

and stuck to its own body, which needed the sun's patient warmth, not the man's impertinent breath, to transform it. Moments later, after a desperate struggle, the butterfly died in the palm of his hand."

And so, this book begins to end with the two themes associated with your own calling. Are you open to the call? Are you paying attention? Is the time right? Or is it too soon?

Some people describe very specific moments when they received a calling, and they knew, instinctively they understood, that the voice demanded to be heard, and that its words or ideas needed to be acted upon. And so, he quit his job on that very day and started work on the novel that very afternoon... she put aside her knitting and set off on a new path, teaching children... and so the stories go. Some are true, most were rewritten for the blurb on the back of a book.

The reality is: Creative people are always hearing voices, always open to new ideas, always ready to hear the calling. But which voice is the one telling the truth? Which voice will lead you to the correct path? Do you listen to the old voice that has always provided a means to feed your family, or to the new voice that could provide the personal satisfaction or creative joy that you continue to seek? The mythology of the trickster is ever present in the creative psyche: We ourselves are tricksters, agents of change who can alter the rules without warning. We are the clowns; we are the paradoxes. We speak loudly of the need for change, but require stability to do our best work. We demand freedom, for us and for everyone around us, but before we start a job, we always establish boundaries. We travel widely and encourage others to do the same, but the travels we like best are the ones that are taken through the imagination.

What is your calling? You probably know, but you're probably too busy right now to deal with the question. Your calling is almost certainly not a single song. More than likely, you will receive several callings through your life. Some, you'll sacrifice in order to pay the mortgage. Others will sing so loudly through your soul that you will be unable to silence them. The calling that returns, that transforms itself with mythical elegance and relentless resonance, the one that simply will not go away, that is the authentic calling, the one that cannot be twisted by the trickster, the one that begins your hero's journey.

You will be a pilgrim or a pioneer in pursuit of an idea or a company or a product or a vision that few people understand and most people discount completely. You will be tempted to give up, but you will not give up. You will persevere. You will lack the essential schooling, you will not have any idea how you will find the money or the market. People will tell you that you are wrong. You will listen, you will synthesize the criticism and make yourself stronger. You will fly too close to the sun, but you will be smart enough, and sensitive enough, to dive back toward the earth before any real damage has been done. But you will have felt the sun, you will have soared higher than any reasonable person should or would. Your calling is true. You have earned the right to call yourself a creative professional; to mentor others who wish to follow; to correct those who lack the perseverance or talent or childlike wonder. For now, you understand the magic and its secrets. You must keep the flame strong, for children are listening, and watching, and soon, they too will know how to draw. And you will have taught them well. And you will have changed the world.

Chapter 7 – The Law, Your Money

The caricature of a creative person is someone who lives in a world of ideas, but can't manage his own checkbook. This is old news. Armed with experience; media coverage of issues related to intellectual property; professional advice; books like this one; and access to answers via the Internet, creative people are no longer clueless.

Although a complete education in law and finance might be daunting for any individual, an understanding of the key concepts is certainly within reach. If you do not take the time to understand the basics, you run two risks: (a) somebody might take advantage of your ignorance for their own financial gain; and/or (b) you could learn about the law through your involvement in a lawsuit.

Disclaimer: I am neither a lawyer nor an accountant. This chapter is nothing more than an introduction. I strongly recommend that you work with a lawyer, accountant, or other professional in your real-world adventures.

Admittedly, not all of the legal concepts are easily understood on the first reading. Take your time. It's not as complicated as it may seem.

Exploitation

The noun "exploit" is related to successful deeds and outcomes (think of a knight's exploits). As a verb, Merriam-Webster first lists "to make productive use," a synonym of utilize, as one might "exploit your talents." The second meaning is "to make of meanly or unjustly for one's own advantage," as in "exploiting farm workers." While it's easy enough to replace "farm workers" with "creative workers" here, every creative professional's career is based on the productive-use definition. An individual's ability to think, for example, is essentially without value until the concept of exploitation is added. To restate the words that began this book:

"A creative professional is someone who utilizes imaginative skills to bring ideas, products, and/or services into existence. By definition, a creative professional is one who uses these skills to make money or create value."

Most business professionals perceive creative professionals as individuals who create the raw materials in the value chain—but do not, themselves, create value. Instead, the widely held belief is that the marketing and distribution process generates value for creative output. This is the fundamental reason why the author earns less than 10 percent of the cover price of the book that bears her name. It's why the record industry is falling apart—the Internet and other alternative channels are beginning to allow musicians to secure a greater percentage of the gross dollars earned by their recordings. When celebrity is part of the equation, the artist is the richest component in the value chain: Paul McCartney earned over $70 million (mostly from touring) in 2002, and he topped *Rolling Stone*'s "Richest Rock Star" for that year. The Dave Matthews Band was third on that list, with $31 million in combined touring revenues and record sales. The band grossed over $60 million in ticket sales, and so it received only a portion of the overall touring income. The power generated by its engine provided employment and wealth for the small businesses adjacent to its own (not unlike the large factory that provides revenue and employment for its vendors). When a network pays the stars of a prime-time series $1 million per episode, it is not significantly affecting its bottom line; each episode is worth many millions in advertising, syndication, and foreign distribution dollars. These performers also provide employment and create wealth for agents, lawyers, and, in the case of celebrity endorsements, for unrelated companies that benefit from their celebrity. Do creative professionals generate only the raw materials for the value chain? Sometimes, but the situation is constantly changing, almost always for the betterment of the creative side.

AFTRA and SAG are the two unions that negotiate collective bargaining agreements on behalf of television and screen performers. In both cases, the agreements detail work rules, short-term payments, and longer-term payments. Their basic model is a good one, worth a brief discussion because it ought to apply to other creative professionals, too.

First, the AFTRA or SAG performer is paid for the time spent rehearsing, on camera, and in post-production (doing voice work). The payment is determined by relative importance of the performer's role (lead players receive more than extras), and by the type of program (performers starring in made-for-TV movies receive more per day than local weathermen). These payments are essentially based on minimum day rates; some performers are paid "overscale," which means they receive more than the day rate negotiated by the union. These payments do not allow unlimited exploitation of the work product. Instead, the network or distributor is allowed only a specified number of plays. Additional plays mean more money for the performer. In addition, the producer pays a surcharge of roughly 12 percent into AFTRA's pension and welfare fund on behalf of the individual performer. These agreements also set work rules. If a performer plays a second role, for example, he receives a second fee. Payments must be made in accordance with a strict schedule. Work away from home or under potentially dangerous conditions guarantees additional compensation. Breaks in the work day are contractually assured, and when a work day runs longer than, say, eight hours, the performer receives overtime pay.

I wish every creative professional was similarly protected and compensated. Few creative professionals receive overtime pay. There is no limit on the use of their work; they are paid once, unless they happen to receive a modest royalty as a recording artist or an author. Sadly, there are too few benefits programs for creative workers.

Why would television and movie companies sign AFTRA and SAG agreements? These unions did the impossible: They organized creative workers! Following the model set by stage hands and technicians, the entertainment industry reluctantly allowed writers, actors, musicians, and directors to unionize. Unfortunately, these are the only creative professionals who are protected by a collective bargaining agreement.

A television network spends up to a million dollars, sometimes more, on an hour of television. This investment must be protected against claims that could prevent the network from exhibiting the program. An actor who appears without a contract is a time-bomb; if the contract is never signed, the network sacrifices the right to include the actor in the episode, which could destroy the storyline and make the episode unsuitable for broadcast. Potential claims go well beyond contract difficulties with star performers: The asset must also be secure with regard to copyright, trademark, various rights of privacy and publicity, laws regarding broadcast content, and other issues. This does not apply only to television—every creative asset must be considered to be a collection of rights that must be secure prior to market exploitation.

Laws Protecting Creative Property

In the U.S., there are three types of laws that govern the protection and use of intellectual property: copyright, trademark, and patent.

Copyright

The basis for U.S. copyright law is found in Article One, Section Eight of the U.S. Constitution: "Congress shall have the power... to promote the progress of science and the useful arts by securing for limited times to authors and inventors the exclusive right to their respective writings and discoveries...."

Over 200-plus years, the courts have interpreted copyright as an entitlement for large media businesses. One most dramatic interpretation of the law came in 2002, when the U.S. Supreme Court extended the rights claimed by Disney over Mickey Mouse despite the "for limited times" language found in the Constitution.

What does copyright law protect? In its most basic implementation, copyright law protects the right to make copies of a completed work, along with the right to make works derived from the copyrighted work. Copyright law also protects the right to publicly display, perform, or distribute the work.

Copyright law begins at the moment of conception. An idea is just an idea until it written, painted, performed, or otherwise "fixed in a medium." When the creator (or, in legal copyright lingo, the "author") sets the work in a tangible form, it is protected by copyright.

Why bother registering a copyright? To protect your rights later, you register a copyright to enter a specific date for the work in the public record, and you formally establish yourself as the author of the work. Both might be helpful in subsequent enforcement of your rights.

Under the current copyright law, a work is protected for the life of the author plus fifty years (if there are several authors, the fifty years begins when the last author dies). However, if the copyright was the result of a work-for-hire agreement, then protection runs seventy-five years beginning with the latter (what?) of the publication date, or a hundred years after the creation date. If you are being paid as a creative professional, the work is most likely a work-for-hire deal, and the resulting copyright belongs to your employer or client, not to you. (Yes, this concept runs contrary to the spirit of the U.S. Constitution, which was written before big companies existed, and which has since been interpreted by people whose careers are intricately tied to corporate America.)

Anything prior to 1923 is in the public domain.

Fair Use

For some commercial, non-commercial, educationa, and journalistic purposes, copyrighted material may be used without permission of the copyright holder. These instances are generally grouped as the Fair Use defense.

Under Fair Use, four characteristics are considered. Here, the scales of justice are a meaningful illustration of the process: Either factor is essentially weighed; wherever the scales tip at the end of the discussion, so ends the case.

The first is the character of the use. "The focus of this factor is 'whether the new work merely supercedes the objects of the original creation... or instead adds something new, with a further purpose or different character, altering the first with new expression, meaning, or message; it asks, in other words, whether and to what extent the new work is transformative.'"[1]

The second is the "nature and copyright status of the plaintiff's work." A work that is factual receives more protection than a work that is imaginative. Remarkably, an unpublished work is more likely to be protected than a published work.

The third Fair Use test is the amount of material used. Fair Use protection is more likely to be extended when the percentage of the original work used in the new work is comparatively small.

The fourth judgment is an evaluation of market impact. If the Fair Use was allowed, how might this use impact the market for the copyrighted material? If the copyrighted material is not currently in the market, or if its sales are minor and the use was otherwise fair, this factor could lead to judgment in favor of the defendant who claims that no infringement has occurred. However, if the material is not in the market, and sales are minor, but the use, based on the above three factors, was unfair, then discussion of this fourth factor might not enter in the decision at all. This becomes complex; whether you are defendant or plaintiff, you will want a smart lawyer who is well-schooled in the subtle features of Fair Use and copyright law.

When the A&E network used small portions of a science-fiction film entitled *It Conquered the World* for a Biography episode about Peter

---

[1] SOURCE: 2001 WL 725285 *4 (S.D.N.Y.), p. 4.

Graves, the court issued a summary judgment in favor of the network and the producer. Interestingly, no permission was secured for the use of the footage, and the court essentially confirmed that no permission was necessary. Why? A Westlaw Report on United States District Court, S.D. New York in the case of Susan Nicholson Hofheinz, Plaintiff v. A&E Television Networks and Weller-Grossman Productions Inc., Defendants, No. 00 Civ. 0623 (RWS), June 27, 2001 explains the case (note that these excerpts were selected to illustrate how a Fair Use case is decided, but the overall report contains considerably more information):

First (and this is alarming to those of us who own copyrights), the allegedly infringing work was a biography, which fits "comfortably" within the legal description of "criticism, comment, news reporting, teaching... scholarship or research." This part of the judgment favored the defendant because it "served to enrich the biography through the actor's perspective on his own performances." And "appearing in *It Conquered the World* was a fact of Graves's life." Following this logic, I could interview Stephen Spielberg about his making of *E.T.,* and then freely use portions of the movie without the studio or director's permission. Furthermore, the court made no distinction between a scholarly biography and one made for A&E's commercial purposes.

Second, the footage was excerpted from the film's trailer (which was not copyrighted) and not from the film itself (which was copyrighted), and the court weighed in favor of the defendant. However, because the film was not in general release, the court "slightly" favored the plaintiff.

Third, less than 1 percent of the film was used in the Biography episode. What's more, the clips were unrelated so it was "impossible to follow the storyline." The court weighed this "heavily in favor of the plaintiff."

Fourth, the court felt that there was little, if any, effect on the market for a film that was "not being sold or rented to the public." Here's the kicker: "Certainly, there is no reason—or evidence—to conclude that those who actually saw the only two showings of 'Peter Graves—Mission

Accomplished' that A&E ever broadcast... are now disinclined to see the plaintiff's film."

For those whose business is creating and marketing intellectual properties, a final insult: speaking of the defendant's use, "If anything, they likely spurred interest in the film."

Plagiarizing and Infringement

Students are discouraged from plagiarizing—essentially copying large amounts of text from copyrighted works with or without acknowledgement of the source—but few receive instruction about fair use. Plagiarizing is positioned as akin to cheating and generally carries similar penalties in the student's world.

In fact, each separate act of willful infringement can result in a penalty of well over $100,000, plus attorney's fees. The courts typically discount anything like a "but I didn't know I was breaking the law" defense. The courts do, however, weigh a variety of factors when assigning liability in cases of copyright infringement, many of which are detailed above, in the explanation of Fair Use.

Trademarks

According to the U.S. Patent and Trademark Office (www.uspto.gov), "a trademark is a word, phrase, symbol, or design, or a combination of words, phrases, symbols, or designs, that identifies and distinguishes the source of the goods of one party from those of others." What's more, "a service mark is the same as a trademark, except that it identifies and distinguishes the source of a service rather than a product."

In order to establish and protect your mark, you need only identify your product or service with the appropriate TM (for trademark) or SM (for service mark). You need not file any application to use these symbols. However, if you do file an application, and it has been accepted, you may claim a "registered trademark," which is represented by a circle-R: ®.

Why register? Again, the language of the government site is

reasonably clear as to a registered trademark's advantages: to serve "constructive notice to the public of the registrant's claim of ownership of the mark; a legal presumption of the registrant's ownership of the mark and the registrant's exclusive right to use the mark nationwide on or in connection with the goods and/or services listed in the registration; the ability to bring an action concerning the mark in federal court; the use of the U.S registration as a basis to obtain registration in foreign countries; and the ability to file the U.S. registration with the U.S. Customs Service to prevent importation of infringing foreign goods."

In creative professions, a trademark is typically associated with a brand name, or a product name, or identity. It is possible, for example, to trademark the identity of cartoon characters and the branding associated with cereals and children's toys. Service marks are less common, but as creative professionals play a larger role in the growth of our service-oriented economy, SM symbols are becoming more common.

Submitting a trademark application requires a degree of special skill and diligent research of potentially competitive marks used in similar or related industries. In order to increase the odds of an enforceable mark, work with an attorney who specializes in trademarks.

An employee who develops a trademark does not typically benefit from the trademark's value, at least not directly. The company owns the trademark. If the trademark, or the underlying product, proves successful, the company may (or may not) decide to reward the employee with a raise or new position. Ditto for copyrights and patents.

Patents

Once again, the U.S. government comes through with a comprehensive, searchable database of every patent issued in the U.S., and every current patent application on www.uspto.gov site. You will also find this overview paragraph of explanation:

"A patent for an invention is the grant of a property right to the inventor, issued by the Patent and Trademark Office. The term of a new patent is twenty years from the date on which the application for the patent was filed in the United States or, in special cases, from the date an earlier related application was filed, subject to the payment of maintenance fees. U.S. patent grants are effective only within the U.S., U.S. territories, and U.S. possessions."

The right conferred by the patent grant is, in the language of the statute and of the grant itself, "the right to exclude others from making, using, offering for sale, or selling" the invention in the United States or "importing" the invention into the United States. What is granted is "not the right to make, use, offer for sale, sell, or import, but the right to exclude others from making, using, offering for sale, selling, or importing the invention."

A patent application is a time-consuming and tedious undertaking. One must describe prior or predecessor inventions, then explain why the new invention is unique in terms of potential specific applications and very specific claims regarding uniqueness and utility. Black-and-white diagrams are also required.

The choice of specific language can make the difference as to whether a particular patent can be enforced. Working with an experienced patent lawyer increases the likelihood of an enforcement patent.

There are several different types of patents. A provisional patent application is completed in order to establish a submission date for a more complete patent application that is subsequently submitted. In general terms, "a *utility patent* protects the way an article is used and works...., while a *design patent* protects the way an article looks.... Both design and utility patents may be obtained on an article if invention resides both in its utility and ornamental appearance....," according to the USPTO Web site. Plant patents complete the story; they protect new varieties of asexually reproduced plants.

In general, patents are filed in the toy business and the software industry, but they're not as common in other media businesses (exception: equipment, such as a new stage-lighting instrument). While some patents have been granted for television game shows and other creative properties, a producer who pitched a patented game show concept would likely be perceived as a paranoid zealot. The protection that ought to be afforded many creative properties is simply overridden by decades of industry tradition (again, most often favoring the larger company, not the individual creator). Entrepreneurs with a technology orientation make better use of patent protection. Also note that the patent approval process could become more restrictive; some people believe that patents are too easy to get and as a result are not especially useful in the marketplace.

Of course, a creative professional who specializes in inventing can accomplish work equivalent to the Olympic gold medal in his field. Marvin Johnson is such a man: a seventy-four-year-old research fellow for Phillips Petroleum, he holds 212 patents, with eight more pending. He's a company man, loyal and conservative, working in an environment that most creative professionals could only joke about: a company research lab in Bartlesville, Oklahoma, "a place that will never be confused with Silicon Valley or Madison Avenue. What makes Johnson tick? He rarely meets a problem that he doesn't want to solve. 'You have to have the patience to return to it. Play with it for a while, go do something else, then come back every time you have a new idea. Each time you return to the puzzle, you pick up the same threads and weave a different cloth. Eventually, you get it right.'"[2]

Other Laws and Regulations

Fundamentally, every creative professional should be aware of his rights under the first amendment to the United States Constitution:

> "Congress shall make no law respecting an establishment of religion, or prohibiting the free exercise thereof, or abridging the freedom of speech, or of the press, or the right of people to peaceably assemble, and to petition the Government for a redress of grievances."

It's worth noting that religion comes first, and that freedom of speech

---

[2] SOURCE: *Fast Company*, June 2002.

is so closely related to freedom of the press. The paragraph is worth study, reflection, and discussion.

Defamation

Defamation combines the concepts of a falsehood, a medium for its dissemination, and negative consequences for a defamed party. *Slander* refers to spoken defamation. *Libel* refers to defamation in print (and, as the law is interpreted, on television). The defamed party need not be identified by name; if the public recognizes the description, likeness, or other identifying characteristics as the party claiming defamation, that is often sufficient to satisfy one of several legal tests to determine whether defamation has taken place. Another test is whether the statement was false; if the statement is true, then there is no defamation case.

Most creative professionals can avoid slander and libel by simply telling the truth and by steering clear of situations that might harm other people. Neither of these requirements seem like asking too much.

You might run into the term "prior restraint." This refers to a court or another party attempting to prevent potential defamation prior to the publication of the offending statement. Generally, prior restraint is uncommon in the U.S.

Rights of Privacy and Publicity

The right to personal privacy has not been codified in federal law. Instead, it is subject to various state and municipal laws. Privacy rights have also been studied by legal scholars. One scholar, William Prosser, outlined four essential personal privacy rights against:

- intrusion into one's personal life;
- unwanted public disclosure of private information;
- being presented in a false light;
- any form of identity theft.

A news organization interviews junior high school friends of a high-visibility personality. A movie producer or biographer discloses previously unknown aspects of someone's private life. A director restages a scene for more dramatic impact, interpreting the truth as she sees fit. A fictional character in a book is apparently based on a real person. How do these common media business activities fit into Prosser's view of personal rights?

The right of privacy is often considered in combination with, and in contrast to, the right of publicity. State law generally protects a person's life and likeness from appropriation for commercial purposes. However, laws do permit research and publication of facts about other people's lives for legitimate purposes by authors, journalists, and for other essentially non-commercial purposes. (And yes, there is some question here about what does and does not constitute commercial purposes.)

Satire and Humor

Fortunately, the courts have demonstrated not only a sense of humor, but considerable wisdom with regard to the value and importance of jokes, cartoons, and other funny stuff. Considerable leeway is given to the newspaper columnist, radio commentator, political cartoonist, stand-up comedian, and satirist—all creative professionals who help society to consider various sides of an issue or controversy through humor.

The definition of defamation is reasonably clear. Networks and newspapers, club owners, and owners of popular Web sites must be vigilant to guard that line and its associated right.

A satirical treatment also allows the satirist or humorist considerable play with copyrighted or trademarked material. It is recognized that the original intellectual property must often be the basis for the humor or satire or social comment—which is why *Saturday Night Live* can operate so freely as it spoofs other TV programs.

Obscenity Laws

The determination of what is and is not obscenity is often challenged in art and photography. The life and work of photographer Robert Mapplethorpe provoked numerous fights about obscenity laws. The art world's view is nicely expressed by Don a Matrix: "A photographer perversely proud of his lack of technical knowledge, Mapplethorpe had a brilliant but cold eye and ruthlessly objectified his sex partners and models. The truth is, Mapplethorpe was fixated on transgression, sadism, evil, and death. Incapable of love, he used and abused people, including himself, but these harsh truths don't detract from his impact as an artist or diminish the raw power of his images." [3]

In mid-1989, there was an uproar over the work of another photographer, Andres Serrano, whose "Piss Christ"—a murky, moody photograph of the crucified Christ submerged in the artist's urine—has been partially funded by a $15,000 grant from the National Endowment for the Arts. [4] The Associated Press covered a well-publicized story about New York's mayor. "Giuliani threatened to cut $7 million in funding if the Brooklyn Museum of Art goes ahead with the show on Saturday. He has called the exhibit, which also features bisected animals and a topless woman in place of Jesus at the Last Supper, 'sick' and offensive. When sexual or other troublesome material is presented in the context of art, community sensibilities are often aggravated." [5]

However, in most communities, sexually explicit material for commerce is acceptable, provided that access to the venue is limited for those under eighteen. In many communities, pornographic films can be viewed in hotel rooms, for example, or rented by adults from video stores. Most communities also permit the sale and purchase of pornographic magazines, but not to minors. Some continue to permit

---

[3] SOURCE: http://www.quertheory.com/histories/m/mapplethorpe_robert.htm
[4] SOURCE: http://www.quertheory.com/histories/m/mapplethorpe_robert.htm - *Robert Mapplethorpe's Extraordinary Vision* by Deborah A. Levinson. This is a review of "The Perfect Moment" exhibition for the Washington Project for the Arts at the Institute of Contemporary Art, 1989.
[5] SOURCE: Associated Press, September 28, 1999.

the exhibition of pornographic motion pictures in theaters; others allow strip clubs under the umbrella of acceptable adult entertainment. Standards vary by community.

Similarly, explicit lyrics and print materials are generally permissible, provided there is a warning label (on recordings, for example).

One must be extremely thoughtful about the use of any potentially obscene material in areas besides the ones listed above. Sometimes advertising agencies will push the boundaries with near-naked fashion models, or by other means to shock the system. Sometimes this is a strategic decision: Shock value can generate more publicity and public interest than the campaign itself. In a world where the once-conservative broadcast networks schedule prime-time programs like "Are You Hot?", a series in which panelists rated the sexual appeal of contestants wearing as little as possible, the line separating obscene from acceptable is difficult to understand. And yes, the line keeps moving.

Generally, the concept of obscenity is applied to explicit sexuality. Society is more accepting of most types of violence.

There are rules on the use of obscene language on broadcast media. If you require an education on these words, or the theory behind them, it's best to review the many commentaries by comedian George Carlin on the subject. Carlin's comedy is based on the mystifying inconsistencies in the way we think about obscenity (and many other topics). In many ways, Carlin's thinking is as valid and meaningful as the work of legal commentator Prosser (and maybe more so).

Laws and Rules Protecting Children

Specific laws protecting rights of children have been passed and often challenged. The Child Online Protection Act, or COPA, was passed in 1998. (See http://www.copacommission.org/commision/faq.shtml for the latest information.)

Generally, the legal system is vigilant in its pursuit and prosecution of individuals and companies who violate the rights of children. (Unless, of course, the issue is related to selling toys, candies, cereals, video games or other products to children; in these situations, society has permitted an extremely wide berth for marketers.)

Laws Protecting National Security
National security has become a priority in the United States, but no set of laws specifically bounds the behavior or output of creative professionals. Perhaps more significant than law are public perception and public attitudes that surround the laws. These perceptions are powerful and are likely to affect our work in unexpected ways.

Contracts
A contract is a formal document that details the terms of an agreement between two or more people or organizations. Contracts can be long, complicated and difficult to navigate, but over the past decade or two, there has been a movement away from complex legal language and toward plain language that can be understood and correctly interpreted without the benefit of a legal education.

There are many types of contracts. In the realm of the creative professional there are essentially three common types of contracts: employment agreements; contractor/work-for-hire agreements; and contracts related to intellectual property rights. Release forms and confidentiality agreements are also common.

Regardless of a contract's length, complexity, or formality, the purpose of a contract is to clearly describe the transaction: the exchange of goods and/or services in exchange for some form of "valuable consideration," most often compensation.

And, incidentally, there is no legal difference between the words "contract" and "agreement." The use of one or the other term is determined by the individuals and by common practice within their industry.

Parts of a Contract

Parties: Each party is clearly identified by name and with contact information. Often, each party is identified in the first paragraph of the agreement, with a current address. Sometimes parties are nicknamed to avoid the repetition of long names throughout the agreement, so that, for example "Phenomenally Creative Studios, Inc." might be referred to as "PCS." Sometimes, in an agreement between a composer and a publisher, the parties will be identified by name only in the opening paragraph, where they are labeled, simply, "Composer" and "Publisher." This sort of language is common when, for example, a publisher signs many such agreements each year.

Description of Goods and/or Services Provided: Typically, this is a brief description of the valuable property, the services to be rendered as an employee or contractor, or the rights to be transferred. Sometimes this section becomes very detailed and caught up in legalese. At other times, particularly when there is a list of deliverables involved, the list becomes a part of a contract attachment, called either an "attachment" or an "exhibit". Each attachment or exhibit is labeled with a number or a letter for convenience and brevity throughout the agreement. Sometimes each party to the agreement supplies goods and/or services, which must be fully described. At other times, one party supplies the goods and/or services, and the other simply pays the bill.

Description of Compensation: Typically this section states the amount of money that will be paid by one party to the other over a particular period of time. This money can be paid as salary, fees, royalties, stocks, bonds, stock options, warrants, exchange of other properties and so on. The key here is specificity: The agreement should very clearly state the amount of money to be paid, the trigger for each payment, the dates that payments are due, the penalties (if any) for late payment, the nature of any advance payments or special deductions; and if there's an employment or contractor agreement, a description of tax status (employee, independent contractor, etc.), and any definitions of gross versus net income (relevant to royalty payments).

This last item is worthy of further discussion, and this book provides the example. As an author, I do not receive a royalty based on the full cover price of every copy sold. Instead—and this is common practice—I receive a royalty based on the monies actually collected by my publisher, minus an allowance for books returned to the publisher from the bookstores or other customers. The total amount collected by the publisher is the publisher's *gross collected revenues,* which becomes, after the returns, the publisher's *net collected revenues.* These definitions can become very complicated and are often written to protect the movie studio, record label, etc., often at the expense of the artist. For example, if the net collected revenues definition allows for the deduction of marketing costs, these must be specified; and if these marketing costs include a trade show booth, then the determination of which motion pictures' marketing budgets carry those costs becomes a topic for negotiation. This is a vitally important discussion that should be pursued vigorously so that the resulting definition is fair to both parties.

Just because the language or the discussion can be complicated does not mean that the discussion should be dropped or dismissed with one party's statement, "Oh, that's just boilerplate language, it appears in all of our agreements." Your job is to read this language carefully and discuss what needs to be discussed—and/or to hire someone on your team who can not only read it and explain it to you, but negotiate on your behalf.

Term and Termination: The term of an agreement is the length of time that the agreement is in effect. This sounds simple enough: You're hired to do a job for a period of eight weeks, and when the eight weeks are over, you are no longer bound to the agreement.

What happens if the work requires nine weeks? Will you be paid for the ninth week, or can the employer or client rightly claim that you were hired for the period of time required to complete the project? If the agreement clearly stated eight weeks, and the employer really needs you for a ninth week, what happens? Sure, if you're available, you can agree to work the extra week. But what happens if you're not available, and the completion of the project depends on you and you alone?

And what happens if you complete the work early? You had agreed to complete the project in eight weeks, but you managed to get the job done in just six weeks. Does the agreement end early? Are you committed to the employer for the full term? Are you paid for the entire project, or for the period of time that you worked?

This leads into the related topic of termination. What happens if your work isn't satisfactory to the client? Can she terminate the agreement? Sure, but the issue is your rights under the agreement and the financial commitment involved. You can prenegotiate this scenario, or you can negotiate it later on, perhaps under more heated circumstances. Can you leave in the midst of the project? If so, do you still get your on-screen production credit? Do you still receive the royalty? What about the completion bonus or a percentage of it? This section of the agreement details who can and cannot terminate, the circumstances under which the termination can be activated, and the resulting changes in compensation or other rights and obligations.

Termination becomes an even more significant portion of the agreement if a severance package is involved. If you are asked to leave *for cause* (because you failed to perform your duties in a reasonably professional manner, or severely violated company policy or committed a crime), you could be asked to leave without severance. And if you elect to leave for cause, and it's because the company substantially failed to fulfill its obligations, you might well be within your rights to request severance pay. The opposite side of the coin looks like this: If you leave *without cause*, you might receive no severance; and if the company terminates you at its will, without cause, you likely will receive whatever has been previously negotiated. Admittedly, the language can be confusing. Unfortunately, severance packages are not common, except among senior leaders or highly valued special contributors.

Intellectual Property Rights: Although somewhat uncommon in the outside world, intellectual property provisions are common in agreements involving creative professionals. The principal consideration: Who owns the rights? As the creator, inventor, or author, you might own the rights, but the company paying for your employment or services is likely to demand that your rights be assigned as a fundamental part of the agreement. This is legal, and it happens all the time.

Generally speaking, any individual employed by a company automatically assigns rights to their creative output; no contract or other agreement is required. Furthermore—and be sure to read this next part very carefully—*your employer owns your work* if: it is created with other company employees; its creation used company facilities or property; it relies on concepts or secrets or processes discovered while you were or are an employee; *and/or* it was developed on company time. All of these conditions need not be met—only one can be true, but the creative output might be owned by your employer, not by you. Of course, most employers steer clear of pursuing legal action against employees—this is not the way to inspire trust and good work among company employees, nor is it inspiring for potential employees. Still, companies tend to know their rights (better than their employees do, which is shameful), and when there is a good business reason, they might well take action. In most cases, the creative professional dutifully surrenders the rights as a term of employment and agrees to sign whatever documents are necessary for the company to secure those rights.

The company's rights with regard to the output of an independent contractor must be explicitly stated. Otherwise, the court assumes that the independent contractor was working on his own behalf, not on behalf of the company. (This last statement might serve as an inducement for some creative professionals to avoid certain types of employment and instead supply services on a contract basis.)

In some cases, the creative professional receives a percentage of net collected revenues associated with the exploitation of certain rights, but this is uncommon, except in certain industries (royalties are paid in some sectors of the entertainment, toy and book publishing industries, but they're uncommon elsewhere).

Representations and Warranties: You might think of these as promises made by one party to the other. One common representation warrants that each party has the right to enter into the agreement and that no other agreement will be adversely affected as result of this agreement's terms. Another assures the other party that there are no specific known obstacles to fulfilling the terms of the agreement. Many more specific representations and warranties are common, but their content depends on the particular industry, deal, or project.

Indemnity: This paragraph adds teeth to the representations and warranties. If any of those assurances turns out to be untrue, the indemnity clauses may be activated. These might assure payment of damages, for example. As a rule, the indemnity paragraph is the one that requires the most careful attention by a lawyer. The language can be very tricky, and because you are on the hook for the indemnity clauses, not only for the agreement term but in some cases beyond it, you really ought to have it examined by a professional.

Breach: This clause details what happens if one or the other party cannot (or will not) fulfill the terms of the agreement. Typically, there is a period of several days or weeks for the problem party to "cure" or correct the breach. If the correction is not made, or not made to the satisfaction of the other party (the rules by which a party will be satisfied are typically outlined here), bad stuff happens: a claim for the return of funds plus a penalty; a claim for damages beyond the cash invested; and worse. Once again, this section demands a lawyer's attention.

Force Majeure, and Related Issues: Sometimes, the reasons a party cannot or will not fulfill its obligations do not supply the party with any reasonable remedy. For example, if the materials were destroyed by an act of God (a tornado, flood, etc.), there is typically no breach. Acts of war are also considered within the realm of "force majeure." So are labor disputes. Be careful here: These acts must truly be beyond the party's control. Acts of negligence and the like are not tolerated by the courts.

Signature Lines: A contract is considered binding *only* after it has been signed by both parties. An unsigned agreement, or an agreement signed by one party is not generally a binding agreement. It's convenient to have names printed along with dates, but this is apparently not essential for most agreements. In general, agreements involving creative people and/or properties are neither witnessed nor notarized, but there's no harm in these formalities, and in some situations, these might be useful additions. If a party is a company, then the agreement must be signed by a party authorized to act on behalf of the company (usually a corporate officer).

Other Clauses: The above describes some of the common clauses, but every agreement is different, and every industry has its own traditions. Some are minor, others are not. Read every agreement very carefully—and be sure to consult your attorney!

Some Key Legal Phrases

Although legal language has become less formal, some phrases have very specific formal meanings. Below is an introduction, but there is more to learn:

Best efforts usually means more than just doing a reasonably good job. Instead, this means that you will do everything in your power to accomplish the specified task.

Time is of the essence means that the schedule and delivery dates are key aspects of the agreement. Late delivery or inattention to the schedule could be the basis for a breach.

Review means that materials will be shown to the person with the right to review, but without any promise to consider input. *Approval* places the control of each element in the hands of the party with that specific right.

Consultation is little more than a version of review.

Sole discretion gives one party the exclusive right to make a decision.

Reasonable is one of several "wiggle words" that soften the impact of more hard-core terminology. If, for example, you agree to use "every *reasonable* effort to deliver the plans on May 1," then you must work diligently to achieve the promised result, but if the project requires a bit more time, you're probably fine (especially if you communicate your progress along the way).

Do You Need a Lawyer?

Every creative professional should develop a relationship with a lawyer, a specialist in her field. If you're an employee, you will have less of an ongoing need; if you're an independent contractor, you ought to have an attorney review any substantial agreement. Smaller agreements are always a judgment call—base your judgment upon the amount of money involved, the reputation of the other party, and how much risk you can tolerate.

Lawyers typically charge by the hour or partial hour. It's unusual to find a lawyer for less than $100 per hour, more common to find experience in the range of $125-$250 per hour, and for special expertise or clout within the industry, you'll pay $300-$500 per hour. Use these numbers as general guidelines; the rates differ by market and by the law firm's own priorities and policies. Lawyers typically do not work for a percentage of potential profits, but there are the occasional exceptions.

Legal Entities

As a U.S. citizen, you are a legal entity. You collect revenues (your salary, fees, royalties) and you pay expenses. You have a social security number, which also functions as your tax identification number. As a citizen, you have the right to do business under your own name. Many people do business in this way, both inside and outside the creative professions.

In order to separate business from personal activities, some people develop parallel systems: a second checking account or a second credit card used exclusively for business. If you adopt this way of working, you are still an individual doing business.

Sole Proprietorship

If you prefer to make the distinction more clear, and perhaps do business under a name that is different from your own, you can do so as a sole proprietor. When you hear about a *d/b/a*, the letters abbreviate "doing business as," and the business owner has filed a d/b/a certificate with the county clerk (or a similar entity). As a sole proprietorship, you can hire employees, arrange for loans on behalf of the business, and even accept some investment (under some very strict rules). Any profits that the business makes are taxed as personal income.

Partnerships

Although strategic and marketing relationships are sometimes called partnerships, the term has a very specific legal meaning. In a partnership, two or more parties own and operate a stand-alone business entity.

A *general partnership* is owned and operated by two or more parties; this is the traditional business partnership. The parties may own equal or unequal portions of the business. Each partner is individually responsible for the business's obligations and commitments. That is, one partner can commit the other to a business relationship. An operating agreement details the duties and the rights of each party with regard to investment, operating responsibilities, procedures for adding or eliminating partners, and ways in which decisions are made (particularly in the case of a disagreement among equals). Most agreements also include specific means of dissolving the partnership.

Some of the above characteristics apply to *limited partnerships* as well. In a limited partnership, there are two types of partners: one general partner and one or more limited partners. A general partner's role is typically operational; a limited partner is not involved in day-to-day operations but is instead a passive investor. As a result, liability risk is reduced for limited partners.

A *joint venture* is a type of general partnership, typically organized for a specific project.

A *limited liability partnership* and its kin, the *limited liability corporation*, combine some aspects of partnerships (see above) with others associated with corporations (see below). LLCs are more common in our field; LLPs are more closely associated with law and accounting firms.

As a rule, partnerships are not taxed. Instead, profits and losses are passed on to partners. This fundamental and seemingly simple fact has provided remarkable flexibility for clever financial advisors and stunning complexity for anyone who is attempting to select an appropriate business format. In other words, it is now nearly impossible to make an informed decision regarding choice of business format without paying both a lawyer and an accountant to guide you through the options, make recommendations, and prepare appropriate paperwork.

Corporations

A corporation is a distinct legal entity, responsible for its own assets, taxes, and business activities. A corporation is owned by its shareholders, who may own either "common" or "preferred' stock. *Common stock* is associated with both shareholder voting power and also participation in the corporation's profits or losses. Shareholders of common stock might also be paid dividends as a result of the company's profits. *Preferred stock* typically allows the right to be first in line for profits, but it may or may not offer the same level of voting rights (if any at all).

By law, a corporation must have a president and a secretary, but neither is required to work full-time for the corporation. A corporation is operated by its board of directors, which is responsible for the hiring and actions of the company's corporate officers.

A corporation is the only type of entity that can sell its shares in public markets, such as the New York Stock Exchange or Nasdaq. However, most corporations are privately held.

One purpose of a corporation is the protection of assets within a separate legal entity. For example, all rights to a particular author's literary works might be acquired by a corporation whose operating rules detail the ways in which these rights may or may not be exploited. Such a corporation would put these rights out of reach of squabbling family members or other kinds of intrigue.

Another purpose of a corporation is the limitation of liability. For example, when an architect designs a building, he individually is not responsible for its utility or safety. Instead, the architect serves as either an employee or a contractor to the responsible corporation. If there are problems later—say, the building falls down—the injured parties would be more likely to pursue claims from the corporation. The injured parties may pursue the architect individually as well, but if the architect's services were rendered on behalf of a responsible entity, then the architect could receive some degree of protection. Some lawsuits successfully "pierce the corporate veil"; others do not. (If the architect was clearly negligent, he might be more liable; if the architect was following standard industry or company practice, the protection is likely to be greater.)

A regular corporation is technically called a *C-corporation*, and it pays federal taxes. An *S-corporation* does not pay federal taxes; instead, it is treated like a sole proprietorship or partnership; profits and losses are treated as personal income. For a small-time operator who desires the protections associated with a corporation but not the paperwork or tax liability, an S-corporation could offer a solution. In recent years, some of these benefits have also made LLCs popular, for many of the same reasons.

Selecting an Appropriate Entity

If you are working alone, you will most likely choose no new entity; a sole proprietorship; or an S-corporation. Your choice will depend on your tax situation; your need for asset protection; and your willingness to accept liability risk.

If you are working with one other person, or a small number of other people, you could opt for no new entity (everyone simply collects revenues and deducts expenses as individuals working together); for a simple one-time project, this is probably fine. If the same group is comfortable doing so, you (or somebody else) could establish a d/b/a and everybody could simply work for one person on the team. In this instance, you can all operate as operational equals, but one person takes the financial and legal responsibility for the team. To me, this sounds like an opportunity to ruin some friendships. If the team is likely to work together on a variety of projects and is thinking in terms of operating a business together, then a general or limited partnership, or an LLC or a C-corporation or an S-corporation are reasonable options.

If the venture is intended to operate for a period of time, and then be shut down or liquidated, then a general or limited partnership, or an LLC, is probably best.

If you are working with a group of people who are serious about building a business together, with a goal of either long-term employment or eventual acquisition, then either an LLC or a C-corporation is likely to be preferable.

Please, please do not accept these brief summaries as anything but the most rudimentary introduction. Laws and tax codes differ by state and change over time. If you are starting any kind of business, be sure to first check with your accountant so that you can make decisions based on the latest information with the guidance of a professional. If you are starting a business with at least one other person, or you are contemplating a business format any more complicated than a sole proprietorship, you should also consult an attorney. It's best to work with both an accountant and an attorney; this will cost more in the short-term, but it will save time, headaches, and potentially some money in the long-term.

One further benefit of a corporation: "If we think of ourselves as a corporation, it gives us a healthy distance on ourselves. We're less subjective. We don't take the blows as personally. We're more cold-blooded; we can price our wares more realistically. Sometimes, as Joe Blow himself, I'm too mild-mannered to go out and sell. But as Joe Blow, Inc., I can pimp the hell out of myself. I'm not me anymore. I'm Me, Inc. I'm a pro."[6]

Stephen Sondheim expressed the idea with a bit more gentility in *Merrily We Roll Along*. In the story, Charley, a lyricist, an average guy caught up with a composer (Frank) who has become a show-business phenomenon, sacrifices his humanity as his life becomes an entertainment powerhouse:

"He flies off to California
I discuss him with my shrink
That's the story of the way we work
Me and Franklin Shepard, Inc."[7]

Freelancing

According to Laurence Boldt, "The term freelance has come down to use from medieval times when knights independent of any lord roamed the country. Because they were unattached, they were known as free-lances."[8] In the *I Ching*, we find a description that fits both the medieval and the modern sense of a freelancer: "one who does not serve either a king or a feudal lord, but in a lofty spirit values his own affairs."

If you work as an independent contractor—and not as a company

---

[6] SOURCE: Steven Pressfield, *The War of Art*, p. 98.
[7] Stephen Sondheim, music and lyrics; *Merrily We Roll Along*, lyrics copyright Revelation Music Publishing Corp. and Riltiing Music, Inc.
[8] SOURCE: Laurence Boldt, *Zen and the Art of Making a Living*, p. 451.

employee—you can work for whomever you please, do whatever projects you please. Not so, apparently, if you work as an employee. According to *Fortune* magazine, "The Bureau of Labor Statistics reports that about seven million Americans now hold some kind of job in addition to their regular full-time employment....Unless you're covered by an employment contract that specifically says you can moonlight with impunity, your legal rights are practically nil. That's because the dominant principle of U.S. employment law is 'employment at will,'"[9] which, boiled down, means your boss is free to fire you and you are free to quit. "Your employer does have the right to impose terms and conditions on your employment, requiring you to work for that company exclusively" says Marica Keegan, a labor attorney at Wiggin & Dana in Hartford, Conn. "As with any of the other terms and conditions—salary, vacation, health insurance—if the employee doesn't like it, he or she can leave."

Agents and Advisors

Every creative professional ought to have an accountant. If you are preparing your own taxes, or you're going to a retail chain for those services, try an accountant instead. You are a professional. You deserve a professional advisor. Compare costs; they vary widely. Try to find an accountant with a fair number of creative clients. It's good to work with a specialist.

You should also have a relationship with a lawyer. Most years, you might do nothing more than send a holiday card or have dinner. Still, it's great to have someone you can call with questions or when you believe your rights have been violated. Once again, find a lawyer who specializes in work with creative professionals. You'll find them in New York and Los Angeles, but if you're persistent, you will find specialists in smaller cities, too. Also, you will do much of your legal work via phone and e-mail, so a lawyer in another city might not be a problem.

---

[9] SOURCE: *FORTUNE*, June 24, 2002.

If you're a successful performer, producer, or director, you might want to have a business manager as well. These are uncommon outside Los Angeles. Be sure you assign very specific responsibilities to your lawyer, accountant, and business manager—but do not surrender the responsibility for your legal or financial life to any of them. Be specific in what these people must do for you and the decisions they can and cannot make. And be careful!

Relationships with agents can be project-based or long-term. "What is a good agent?" is a difficult question to answer. Agents work strictly on commission (10 to 20 percent, depending upon the industry sector). When you work, they receive the money, deduct the commission, and then pay you. Agents are never paid by their clients—if an agent asks for money, even for expenses, upfront, the agent is not operating in accordance with standard industry practice and is best avoided.

Finance & Money Management for Creative Professionals

For better or for worse, Mark Twain had it about right when he said, "There is no security in life, only opportunity."

Do not compare your income, assets, or standard of living with people in non-creative professions. You will drive yourself, your spouse or partner, and your family and friends crazy. We manage our financial lives differently from other people.

For certain types of jobs, we are inordinately well-paid, but we also lay off for longer periods. We are more likely to operate as independent contractors, responsible for our own taxes and benefits and retirement funds. Many creative professionals peak earlier than peers in other professions. If we succeed, we might receive a secondary income stream: royalties. Over an entire career, a creative professional's resumé is likely to include a dozen, perhaps two dozen jobs, plus many more short-term assignments.

You might value the flexible working hours; the average number of laughs we hear during the workday; our intellectual and personal freedom; our passionate relationship with the right job; the opportunity to entertain and amuse the public; the bits of fame that we might experience from time to time; the allowances made when we act like children; the value that we create when we make someone think, or smile. None of these items is relevant to your financial life, regardless of its theoretical value to your heart and soul.

FINANCIAL PLANNING

Although you will find countless books and advisors who can help you with a detailed financial plan, the essence really isn't all that complicated. Use these worksheets and you'll have a reasonably useful high-level plan.

Annual Earnings

Begin by comparing your annual earnings with your annual expenses. In an ideal world, the earnings should be greater than the expenses.

	ANNUAL EARNINGS
Estimate this year's NET income from salaries, fees, and royalties. (Net income = gross income minus taxes and other mandatory deductions).	
Estimate any additional NET income for the year.	
YOUR TOTAL ANNUAL EARNINGS	

Annual Expenses

Everybody pays bills differently. In order to successfully complete the chart below, you'll need all of your monthly credit card statements from the past year, plus your checkbook and other expense-related bank statements.

	ANNUAL EXPENSES
Housing costs, including energy, water, security, insurance, taxes.	

Food and other supermarket costs (check your past few month's totals, then add about 5% for other incidental expenses).	
Car payments, including fuel and insurance.	
Credit card bills (MasterCard, VISA, American Express, all department stores, etc.).	
Other miscellaneous expenses that you paid by check or by cash.	
Charitable contributions.	
Other expenses that don't fit into the above categories.	
YOUR TOTAL ANNUAL EXPENSES	

The Honest Comparison (Your Personal Profit/Loss Statement)

ANNUAL REVENUES	
ANNUAL EXPENSES	
DIFFERENCE	

If the above year is representative, and the difference is minimal, then you're managing your financial life in a barely adequate way. It's barely adequate because you are not saving any money—you are essentially spending every penny that comes in. The chart below assumes that you are not sitting on substantial assets. The asset issue will be addressed momentarily.

If the difference is positive by:	**Then you are...**
0 - 25%	Courting a potentially serious problem.
25% - 50%	Okay for the next few months.
50% - 75%	You're okay for the next half year, and you're taking in enough to save or invest.
75% - 100%	You're in good shape: enough to invest.

Over 100%	Good for you! Let's hope this situation continues for a long time.

If the difference is negative by:	Then you are...
0 - 10%	Courting a potential problem.
10% - 25%	Drifting into a trouble zone.
25% - 50%	In some trouble, unless you seriously reduce expenses or increase expenses.
50% or more	In trouble, and in need of reworking your income and expense structure.

Assets

Ideally, your assets should not be used to pay expenses. Of course, if you're wealthy with substantial assets, you can afford to do just that. For those of us who are not wealthy and who must use assets from time to time to cover expenses, it's comforting to know that the money is available. Either way, it's important to know what you own and what you could use for cash.

To set a value for each of your current assets, think in terms of the actual price that the asset could fetch in today's market. Once again: For purposes of this exercise, an asset's value has nothing whatsoever to do with the price that you paid; instead, the value is determined by the dollars that it is currently worth in the open market. An asset must be liquid—it must be able to be sold—in order to be included here. Or, it must be cash.

If you're unsure about the tax implications of the various sales, simply deduct 30% of the value and then check for a better number with your tax advisor when you have the time.

CURRENT ASSETS

	ASSET VALUE
MONEY	
How much cash is on hand on your home, in your checking, savings, money market certificates?	

What is the current value of your stock portfolio—after you have paid taxes resulting from any sales?	
What is the current value of your bond portfolio (including savings bonds)? Remember: You want current value, not redemption value. And, once again, list the value after you have paid taxes on the interest.	
What other money assets do you have (trust funds, special types of accounts)? Note the current value of each, after taxes.	
What is the current value of your retirement account(s) if you cashed out today, and paid both the taxes and the penalties?	
REAL ESTATE	
What is the value of your equity in your home? Bear in mind that your equity plus the mortgage equals the home's purchase price—but not its current selling price. (Deduct taxes only if the sale generates a capital gain--many home sales do not generate a taxable event.)	
Similar question, this time for any other real estate that you own.	
TANGIBLE ASSETS	
What is the current value of your car or other vehicle(s)?	
What is the value of your office or home furnishings and equipment (again, think in terms of their sale value in today's market—the amount they might fetch on eBay, for example)?	
YOUR TOTAL ASSET VALUE	

If you're surprised by how high your asset value turned out to be, don't run out to buy yourself a new car, at least not just yet. And if you're depressed because the numbers totaled less than you had hoped, bear in mind that it's better to have a realistic view of your base than a misguided assumption.

Pay Your Taxes!

For those with traditional company employment, paying taxes is an automatic process: Federal and state taxes are deducted from each paycheck, and deposited with the appropriate authorities. For independent contractors, taxes can become a nightmare.

For example, let's say you are a freelance writer. Over the course of the year, you work for a variety of clients, and you typically receive several hundred dollars per article. In a single year, let's say that you gross $40,000—reasonable money for a typical freelance writer. The money does not arrive in reliable intervals—some clients pay immediately, some pay within thirty, sixty, ninety or 120 days, or when they get tired of hearing your complaints. You must pay the rent, so when the $800 check comes in and the $800 rent bill comes due, you deposit the check and pay the landlord. This simple act of paying the rent begins your personal financial disaster—just because the check from your client says $800, this does not mean that you are entitled to $800. Part of the $800 payment belongs to the government—roughly 25 percent of the check, in fact. If you manage the entire year's $40,000 this way, you will end the year $10,000 behind on your taxes. Some freelancers figure they'll spend all $40,000 by the end of the year and make it all work out by the following April, when the $10,000 tax bill comes due. Bad idea! When April comes around, if past behavior is any indicator, you will have spent the tax money on rent or other expenses. And the hole gets deeper.

So what do you do? You train yourself to deposit a portion of every check into a tax account (regardless of your current bills) and you *leave that account alone.* You can even work with a local banker to limit withdrawals. Or, you can require a second signature on any check drawn on the tax account—if your father is the second signature, you're going to seem very silly begging him to take money out of the account.

And what if there's not enough money to pay taxes in a given year? You negotiate a payment plan with the IRS (or with the relevant state or municipal tax authority). You will not be the first person to tell this story. Just be careful about telling the same story year after year; their flexibility will fade if you abuse the privilege.

Over the long term, you must live within your means. If you have only $30,000 available to spend, you cannot spend more than $30,000 without making a mess, bringing on stress, and (okay, you're a creative person, you complete the rhyme).

Watch Your Expenses

It's very easy to give this advice, difficult to follow it.

The best way to watch your expenses is to gain more control over your spending. When credit cards became popular in the 1960s, my father thought they were a terrible idea, and he was probably right. He paid by cash or check, and he always knew how much money he owed. With credit cards, financial institutions have been allowed to popularize the "buy now, pay later" habit. They rely on the idea that we regularly forget how much money we have spent—and then charge us interest on the unpaid monthly balance. This is an insidious, devilish con game; they profit from our stupidity and laziness. Few people do anything as simple as writing down every purchase. Instead, we wait for the monthly bill and try to figure out how to pay for the previous month's fun. This is an *insane* system, a near-guaranteed disaster for the busy creative professional who earns variable revenue.

You know the solution:
- If you can't afford it, don't buy it.
- Pay with a debit card or a check.
- Keep one credit card for major purchases, online purchases, and emergencies. Keep track of every expenditure on the card, and as soon as you make a purchase, immediately deduct the payment from your checking account. Pay the balance every

month; never carry a balance and you'll never have to pay the
usurious (15 percent-plus) interest charges.
• Manage your credit: If you require a large purchase, take out a
proper loan with reasonable interest charges.

You *can* run your life this way. Everybody should.

You should also consider your credit rating. If you pay your bills on
time, you will maintain an excellent credit rating—but the financial
establishment might trust you with only a limited amount of credit.
While in college, you should conservatively borrow small amounts and
then pay them back in a timely manner. A car loan is a good place to
begin, provided that the payments are within your means. Do this for two
very specific reasons: to build a history so that you can later get a home
mortgage and because you might someday need to borrow money for a
new business or for an emergency.

Credit and cash management are only part of your overall expense
picture. How do you manage all of your expenses?

Start with the big ticket items, the ones with the most impact. For most
people, the big ticket items are housing, transportation, and supermarket
purchases. These account for half of your monthly expenses.

First up: housing. Buying is almost always preferable to renting. If you
handle this aspect of your finances with intelligence, and good fortune does
not disappear entirely, you should be able to pay off a mortgage in twenty
to twenty-five years. This means: Apart from repairs, maintenance, and
taxes, your cost of shelter could be essentially free for ten to fifteen years
of your professional life, longer if you buy early in your career. What's
more, your equity in a residence can be traded for progressively better
housing. Plus, there are tax deductions to encourage home ownership.
Buying a home is a good investment.

In the short term, rental might be the only viable solution. You might
lack the assets necessary for a down payment on a purchased residence
(if you need help, explore Fannie Mae and other government programs
that promote home ownership). You might be located in a particular city

for a limited period of time. If neither of these is true, do everything you possibly can to get out of the rental market and buy a house instead. When you rent, you are making somebody else wealthy while reducing your asset base. When you buy, you make yourself wealthy, and you increase your asset base. It's as simple as that.

How much house can you afford? Whether you're paying rent or paying off a mortgage, your *total* housing costs should not exceed 30 percent of your net income (your take-home pay). If you are paying more, or you're stuck in a deal that no longer makes sense based on this formula, you should consider either (a) moving or (b) finding some other way to increase revenues or reduce expenses. Long-term, you do not want to live in a place you cannot afford.

Second on the list: transportation. For most people, transportation = car. The first question you should ask yourself is "How much car can I afford?" And again, it's not just the purchase, loan, or lease price, it's the *total* cost of owning, driving, and maintaining the vehicle. For a while, I fantasized about a Land Rover Discovery. When I dug deeper, I realized how much that car *really* cost. Check out this comparison:

	Land Rover	Honda Accord
Purchase price	$36,000	$24,000
Sales tax (assume 6 percent)	$2,160	$1,440
Financing (assume $24,000 financed at 4.5 percent)	$2,624	$2,624
Insurance: four years	$10,000	$8,000
Gas[10] (assume 15,000 miles/year @ $2.50/gallon)	$3,750	$1,875
Maintenance: four years (est.)	$5,000	$3,000
TOTALS	$58,784	$40,564
AVG. MONTHLY COST (48 months)	$1,225	$845

[10] Land Rover Discovery gets 12.5 mpg, Honda Accord gets 25 mpg.

Remember: Advertising and marketing campaigns focus on the purchase price of the car, not on the actual cost of ownership.

Are you prepared to spend as much money on a car as you do on housing? I'm asking because $1,200 per month is a substantial mortgage payment. The differential—$400 per month—could mean the difference between home ownership and a rental. In comparison with a house, a car is a rotten investment: It loses value quickly, has virtually no value after five to seven years, and does not contribute to your asset base in any meaningful way. Let me say this differently: An expensive car is an expensive toy. If you're renting a home while playing with expensive toys, and you have the option to do otherwise, you are a fool.

Third: the supermarket. Do yourself a favor. For the next three months, track your supermarket expenses on a spreadsheet. You will find that you spend less than half of your supermarket dollars on food, and that only about half of that money is related to food that you really need. Don't dismiss this budget line as inconsequential!

Last year, my family (four people) spent $1,000 on club soda (roughly ten bottles per week times $1.00-$1.25 x fifty-two weeks per year), plus another $500 on those convenient little bottles of water (same basic math). This is terrifying! Another $1,000 goes to boxed cereals, cookies, pretzels, and ice cream.

As it turns out, fruits, vegetables, even meats and fish, aren't expensive at all. Two pounds of an expensive cut of meat rarely costs more than twenty-five dollars, and that's enough food to feed a family of four. Add veggies, other side dishes, beverage, and dessert, and you probably won't spend more than ten dollars per person for an excellent meal. The very same meal served in a restaurant will cost about twice as much.

No big deal, you say? Let's say you eat out once or twice a week, maybe seventy-five times per year. Just know that you're paying a $1,500 premium, per year, for restaurant service. Conservatively, add $500 more for take-out meals.

Just an hour with receipts and a spreadsheet can teach you a lot about how you live your life and spend your money. Looking for $5,000? You'll find most of it in supermarket expenses that you've never bothered to think about.

The Occasional Items

It's always entertaining to watch someone order a hugely fattening meal and then order a diet soda to wash it down. It's no less weird to mindlessly waste a few thousand bucks at the supermarket and then obsess about the cost difference between a $250 and $350 leather briefcase (the difference would be ten weeks worth of club soda).

Consider both purchase price and the product's short- and long-term value. A paperback novel, for example, is worth about $15 to me—I'll read it once and enjoy myself for about five hours. A CD at about the same price also seems fair; I'll play it many times.

Occasional items are either (a) small pleasures, like books or CDs or movie admission tickets; or (b) investments in tools that will help me with my work. If I limit my expenses to these categories, I'm fine.

New furniture, trips abroad, expensive gifts or jewelry, or home furnishings are rarely impulse purchases; they are considered in terms of price, utility, desirability, and other factors. Some of us spend money on hobbies—I spend a few hundred dollars per year on art supplies and an equal amount on film and photo supplies. Others spend on cookware or dance classes. If you are unable to afford these simple pleasures, you ought to rethink your financial situation.

Babies and Other Life Events

Children are expensive, and worth every penny. Most young couples are fearful of covering the cost of a child (or several children). One partner's income might be absent, at least for a while. Costs spread over two decades—with a gigantic college expense to end the story (and perhaps a wedding after that). If you are both a creative professional and a prospective parent, you must manage your financial life with the utmost care and sobriety—if you don't, you will probably sacrifice the freedom and joy associated with creativity and find yourself in a traditional job simply because you need the money.

Joseph Campbell said, "I think the person who takes a job in order to live—that is to say (just) for the money—has turned himself into a slave."[11]

Of course, babies are not the only life-changing event that might affect your financial situation. You could inherit your rich auntie's fortune. Hope for the best (and plan for the worst).

Keep both health and life insurance sufficient and up to date. Too many creative professionals—particularly those freelancers who work at home—sacrifice health insurance because it is so very expensive. Instead, try to join some group so that you maintain at least basic coverage. If you have a family, you must provide more than the basic coverage.

Save for the Lean Times

For many of us, annual income fluctuation is a way of life. One year, you're in a senior role with a solid company earning a hundred thousand dollars per year; then the company is sold, and you're back either in job search or freelance mode with half the income. This is a remarkably common situation.

The only sensible way to cope is to live as if you regularly earned fifty thousand to seventy-five thousand dollars per year. If you set up your life on the basis of the higher salary, and you are unable to maintain that income level, you'll quickly drown. If you live on sixty-five thousand per year and earn a hundred thousand, you can save some money.

And you *must* save money.

You must save as much money as you can, year after year. In time, you will have saved enough money for a year without employment—use this either as a gift to yourself (avoid the temptation of a full year because you don't want to end up with nothing) or as a protection against the bad times. There is no greater sense of freedom than knowing that you can support yourself without any outside help.

You might be at the top of your game now, but the market for your talents might change. You could find that your skills, capabilities, talents, or persona are valuable today, but they might lose their value as the marketplace changes. Until you develop a new trick, you might

---

[11] SOURCE: Laurence G. Boldt, *Zen and the Art of Making a Living.*

be sidelined. Also, you might find yourself unable to work. If you're an illustrator, and you break your arm, you might not work for two or three months. And you could get caught up in an unexpected situation: a family member who requires your personal care and attention; a lawsuit that shuts down your place of employment or otherwise prevents you from working. Or, you might simply decide that you want to work on your own project—a work of art or a whole new company. Money in the bank will buy you the time you need for any such endeavor.

One last word about "money in the bank." For this, I turn to the underrated economic scholar, filmmaker, author, and troublemaker Michael Moore, "(The stockbroker) asked me about my 'investments.' I told him I … don't own a single share of stock.… (He) started sending me weekly 'market updates' and other propaganda in the hope that I'd give him my kids' college fund to gamble on the Strip known as Wall Street.…The Nasdaq has lost over 40 percent of its value, and average Americans, snookered into playing the market with their meager savings, have lost billions."[12]

We too-easily forget that money in a bank account is safe, that it is protected from loss by reasonably reliable federal government insurance, and that any money "invested" is *entirely* at risk. For a creative professional whose income fluctuates, this is a reminder that should be posted on the front of any stock portfolio.

Retirement

For those who are unfamiliar with the concept of retirement, or in denial, this would be the part of your life when people no longer pay you for your work. Worse yet, this is the part of your life when you have either no revenue or minimal revenue, but you still intend to spend money, perhaps even travel around the world.

If you're the local postmaster, you might not enjoy the world's most creative job, but you possess something that most creative professionals will never touch: a retirement pension.

---

[12] SOURCE: Michael Moore, *Stupid White Men*, p. xv, xvi.

Once again, for those of us who value interesting work over a real job: A pension changes the above definition of retirement—you no longer work, but you do receive some or all of your salary for most or all of the rest of your life.

Most creative people figure out this pension idea after it's too late to do much about it. And so, we have the free-spending former postman wondering why his buddy with the high-visibility career now thinks twice about every restaurant decision.

In retirement, your expense situation will change: Fewer people live in the house, so there are fewer bags of pretzels to buy each week. If you bought your house, you probably own it by now. It's difficult to project your needs, particularly when economic stability becomes a thrill ride, but it's fair to assume you will need enough money to get you through nearly two decades of retirement—that's *twenty years* without any meaningful salary or fee income (except, of course, a pension).

The only reasonable way for most creative professionals to plan for a comfortable retirement is to put money away on a regular basis and to isolate that money in a retirement fund. A search on the Web or through any book about financial planning for retirement will turn up a series of worksheets that allow you to define: the amount of annual retirement income you will need in order to maintain a particular lifestyle; the likely cash coming from Social Security and any pension funds; the size of your required nest egg; and the amount of annual retirement savings required to achieve these results.

Please do not treat retirement planning lightly. When I take my trips around the world, I want to meet up with you in Kyoto or Copenhagen to talk about art and architecture, not about how you can't really afford the trip (and how nice it would be if I bought you dinner).

RETIREMENT PLANNING

If you're planning income and expenses for yourself, just consider your own financials. If you're planning for a couple, or for more than two people, your calculations should consider the household, not just the individual.

TIMELINE

Current Age	
Expected Retirement Age	
Age When Retirement is Completed	
TOTAL RETIREMENT YEARS (subtract "Expected Retirement Age" from "Age When Retirement is Completed")	

ANTICIPATED INCOME

Salaries and Fees	
Pension	
Interest Income	
Social Security	
Other Income	
TOTAL ANTICIPATED INCOME	

Be sure to consider the likely decline in income over the years. You are far more likely to generate income at age 65 than at age 80. You might wish to average all years or to work out a spreadsheet for each individual year (not just for income, but for expenses and assets as well).

AVAILABLE ASSETS

Based upon the chart of assets on page 297, fill in the chart below:

Money	
25% of Real Estate	
10% of Tangible Assets	
TOTAL of Above	
TOTAL AVAILABLE FUNDS for retirement (assumes you will either keep your house or trade it for a smaller residence; assumes you will not sell most tangible assets)	

ANTICIPATED EXPENSES

Housing (include energy, water, insurance, security, taxes)	
Food and Other Supermarket Expenses	
Car Payments (include fuel and insurance)	
Charitable Contributions	
Health and Medical	
Other Expenses	
TOTAL ANTICIPATED EXPENSES	

RESULTS

Number of retirement years	
Average Annual Income	
Assets Divided by Number of Retirement Years	
Average Annual Funds Available	
Average Annual Expenses	
Add 25% (because you probably under-estimated)	
Average Annual Expenses	
Difference Between Average Annual Funds and Average Annual Expenses	
Number of Years Between Now and Retirement	
Additional Retirement Monies to be Saved Each Year Prior to Retirement	

The above is an oversimplification because it does not consider the time component in determining money's value, nor does it consider tax issues. Therefore, this worksheet should be used as only the most rudimentary retirement planning tool. For a more complete picture, work closely with your financial advisor—and not just once! Do this every five years and you should be in control of your personal retirement plan.

Chapter 8-Your Career

There are two songs from Broadway musicals, each with a similar title. One, from *CHICAGO*, is called "We Just Move On," and the other, from Stephen Sondheim's *Sunday in the Park with George*, is "Move On." The *CHICAGO* song is sung by two chorus girls who acknowledge that life's adventures are temporary. When the situation becomes uncomfortable, there's a whole world out there, and they exit for the next adventure. The Sondheim song is sung by an aging artist's model and her grandson. It's a sad song about the scary unknown world and the difficulty in moving from the comfortable to the unknown.

Nothing lasts forever.

I suspect we all sing a part of each song, not once, but several times in a creative career. Moving on is all about new adventures, but also about a certain sadness because the world will never be the same again. Show people become hardened to this reality. Over the course of several weeks or months or years, a cast and crew spends endless hours together in the intense workshop atmosphere of a movie set or a regional theater; they develop their own language, their own unique sensibility.

On the *Carmen Sandiego* set, I remember when the host, Greg Lee, thought everyone ought to be called by their cowboy names for one taping day. Nobody thought this odd or unusual; we just spent the day calling one another "Tex" or "Sarsparilla Annie," and when the day ended, we went back to our regular names. Silly stuff, but when you know someone's cowboy name, it's difficult to move on.

And yet, that's the nature of our work. The majority of the companies who have provided employment for me are no longer in business. The majority of the people with whom I've worked are no longer reachable by the phone numbers on the old contact sheets. The projects I did in the 1980s are distant memories, useful for the resumé, but irrelevant in today's marketplace. The career of a creative professional is like any other career in that we enter a new role with some trepidation, then master the role and move on to the next stage. Along the way, we learn a great deal. But the opportunities aren't often in the same arena. As a result, we move around a lot. Remarkably, the faces change but the personality types do not. As we grow, we recognize the patterns of who we are and how we work.

Career Stages

Every creative industry is full of *young pups*—they're talented, ambitious, often very verbal, and they try their best to score points by hanging around more experienced players. They make claims about their own projects, but few possess the skills or experience to progress from concept to completion. Still, for every mistake, there's learning. Some young pups are headstrong and insist on attention. In time, and with each new learning experience, they mellow. As these experiences accumulate, the young pup becomes a *young professional*.

The big difference between a young pup and a young professional is the way he plays the game. There are rules, and the young professional follows them. He doesn't draw constant attention, but instead seeks out suitable showcases. A young pup might discount mistakes or blame others; a young professional accepts responsibility and uses the occasional error as a means to build her own knowledge or relationship base and also learns to cope with the reality of things not working out as planned. When a young professional moves on, he maintains strong connections to the world and the people left behind; and these relationships and experiences will be valuable in later adventures.

The *developing professional* operates in a similar manner. She knows the craft and understands the game; self-assurance and consistent output are hallmarks. He knows how to ask for help and understands that such requests are not a sign of personal or professional weakness. The developing professional also knows how to "manage up," no longer accepting the boss's word verbatim, but instead he operates in a cooperative way so that the boss's overall picture is improved. When a developing professional moves on, it's most often because the show closed, the company folded, or a better opportunity has emerged. Developing professionals are valuable, and they know it. Still it's easy for a developing professional to get passed over for a key promotion because the organization cannot imagine finding a suitable replacement.

The *solid professional* is seasoned, credible, comfortable in her skin, suitable to the role, a good leader, and a good manager. She is given considerable responsibility, with good reason. When she decides to move on, the organization shudders. A new solid professional might not provide the same degree of excellence, or leadership, or compassion, or project understanding. Solid professionals do not move quickly or without considerable thought about the consequences of the move. Some stay for a long while. Others recognize the potential for a trap: Stay too long and the next gig is that much more difficult to find. That's why some solid professionals seemingly leave earlier than anyone would expect.

The *aging professional* brings endless experience, often with a knack for teaching, or providing an unusually comfortable work environment. The aging professional has less to prove, and often fewer external options, so they focus—and encourage everyone else to do the same. They are there to do the job. Many aging professionals are capable of stunning output— the work is sometimes done very quickly because they know what they're doing, and because they know what *not* to do. The output might be impressive in terms of speed and amount of production and quality. What's more, many aging professionals are excellent teachers, mentors, and guides—they might have the time and inclination not only to teach the craft but to model behavior as well. If some give the impression that they do the work because they love it, all the better. Creative work is supposed to be fun. The challenge for the aging professional is to find a sufficient range of projects that offer the right combination of money, personal growth, personal satisfaction, and visibility. Some aging professionals are lucky and find their niches. Others are irrepressibly youthful. Others use their age as the mask of experience and credibility.

PRIORITIZING CAREER GOALS

The chart below should be completed every six months. Your goals will change; it's helpful to keep each chart you complete and to refer to them from time to time. If you build the charts in an Excel workbook, you can simply establish a new tabbed worksheet for each new chart and keep all of them in one place.

To fill out the form, simply distribute 100 percent (100 points total) into as many "Focus" categories as you like. (For example, 60 points for "Make a lot of money," 30 points for "Expand your current domain," and 10 points for "Develop a new domain," with zeroes for the others, or a more even distribution, as you like.)

FOCUS	Today	+ 6 months	+12 months	+18 months
Make a lot of money				
Make enough money				
Purchase your freedom				
Laughter / applause				
Be a part of the process and the team				
Expand your current domain				
Develop a new domain				

Career Strategy: Concentrate on the Work, not the Career

Your work is intellectually stimulating. It pays reasonably well. With consistent practice and focus, your capabilities deepen and widen. Mentors, education, hours of practice, and interaction with audiences or clients allow you to continue to improve. There is joy in your art and craft. What you do makes you happy and makes other people happy. In time, you can envision yourself at the top of your craft.

If the money is good, or good enough, the above scenario is sufficient for a lifetime. If this is where you are headed, nothing in this book, nothing anybody says or writes or does to you should cause you to stray. A career is something that *you* define; if you work at something for a long time, that something becomes your career.

Just do not proceed blindly. Do not allow the market to pass you by. Instead attend to your strategy and make adjustments from time to time. Some ideas follow.

Seek Out a Growing Market

Several years ago, designers moved from the world of paper, and paint to Adobe Photoshop and developed a new expertise. They intuited a new market would develop around computer-produced images, and the Web proved them right. Growing markets are not easy to identify; phantoms are everywhere. Is desktop video and its low-cost production a promising market, or will it become so inexpensive and easy that there is no commercial value in the practice?

Seek Out a Fading Market

There's a lot to be said for specialization. With digital photography now dominating both the industry and the hobby, photographers who work with film, paper and chemicals will slowly become a minority. The special quality associated with this type of work will allow a minority of old-style photographers to successfully serve a smaller market. For those who do, their market share might be higher.

More examples of niche workers in faded markets: photo researchers (today, anyone can search for photos via the Web, but a skillful photo researcher brings a trained eye and experience); musical instrument makers (guitars and drums are mass-produced; but high-quality violins and other specialty instruments are made by craftsmen); draftsmen (for the few situations where computer-aided drafting is inappropriate); quilters (old-fashioned ways are best); calligraphers (same reason); cartoonists and illustrators (a small market, but there's always space for the best); tap dancers; and authors (who continue to use the written word, despite the image empire).

Danger Signs

When you're happily at work with a long-term gig, you can lose yourself. Then one day, you wonder why it's so quiet, so you open the blinds and realize that yours is the only building in the neighborhood, that everybody else has left town.

In the 1950s, every television station was built around at least one large studio, sometimes two. The studio was used constantly: There was a daily news show, at least one daily talk show, a children's series hosted by a local clown or a friendly policeman, and more. Each station employed producers, directors, performers, writers, and other staff. It was expensive, but the operation was central to the station's role in the community. By the 1980s, nearly all of the children's shows were gone, the TV clowns were either retiring or finding another way to make a living, and local talk shows were being replaced by syndicated talkers. By the mid-1990s, they were gone, and local talk show hosts, who had been local celebrities, either moved to news or left the business. The marketplace changed, seemingly overnight. Stations learned to cut headcount and expenses, replacing original productions by simply writing a check to a syndicator for the right to run *The Phil Donahue Show*. The business moved to New York and Los Angeles, and station managers either filled the old studios with open-plan newsrooms (local news operations expanded during this period) or moved to smaller facilities.

Was this a historical hiccup? For the past few years, the person to ask is a prime-time television writer. Ten years ago, there were plenty of jobs because there were plenty of prime-time dramas and sitcoms. Today, many time slots are filled with news magazines or reality shows—and neither requires the high-priced services of a prime-time drama or comedy writer.

Is the problem limited to television? You might ask the reporter who used to work for a local newspaper—if you can find more than one local newspaper in your town. Or a local radio personality. They're becoming hard to find, too. How about a Web development firm? That gold rush ended fast! Nearly every firm has either closed or sold out to a larger firm before half the staff was fired. No reliable statistics exist, but it's fair to guess than no more than one in three people who were designing Web sites in the late 1990s are doing the same job today. In music: One day, hundreds of studio and live musicians were gainfully employed, and the next, they were replaced by sound samples and racks of digital equipment. One person can compose, score, record, mix, and master a film or television soundtrack, without ever touching a musical instrument (other than a keyboard).

Pay Attention!

If your market is drying up, don't wait to make your move. If you're becoming significantly older than your peers, make a change so that you aren't the oldest guy in the room. You must constantly scan the environment. This is easier for some, a nuisance for others.

How to sense signs of a changing marketplace? Read trade magazines, visit Web sites, and go to lunch or dinner with several peers every month—people who do what you do, but do not work for your company. At least once or twice a week, read *The Wall Street Journal*, *USA Today*, and *The New York Times*—between them, you'll get a good idea of what's happening. Read *Time* or *Newsweek*; these weekly newsmagazines do a good job with trends.

How to Network

The idea of networking is abhorrent to some, a necessary evil to others. I *like* networking. I like meeting new people, talking about ideas, hearing their stories, and figuring out how I can help them or they can help me, or how we might work together.

Certainly, it's no thrill to visit people's offices, hat in hand, looking for work. Then again, that's not what networking is supposed to be about.

Instead, networking is getting out and talking to people who work in creative fields and in related professions. You attend organized events, like cocktail parties and awards presentations. Overcoming any natural shyness or discomfort, you force yourself to become involved in several conversations. You find some common ground, trade business cards. Some of your new contacts will call or send an e-mail; you should do the same and then follow up with the people who most interest you. The purpose of all this is to maintain a steady flow of new people in your life, to hear their stories and learn from them, to help them develop a higher comfort level when you ask for help, and to discuss perceptions of a changing marketplace. You might also share information about clients, rates, projects, and resources. Honestly, I know that networking can be painful, but the results are worth the angst, time, and effort. As you network, be sure to ask for names, phone numbers, and e-mail addresses of others whom you might contact—and do be generous with your own address book. A large network of connected individuals is everyone's best defense against a market slowdown and sudden lack of income. E-mail helps; if you don't talk with everyone in your network of contacts regularly, at least you can keep in touch with short messages.

The Constant Need for Adaptation and Reinvention

Adaptation is a key skill. Some might say that we enjoy changing jobs often. Others would argue that the market causes frequent changes. Steve Bobowski, a senior marketing executive who worked with me at CDNOW, insists that certain people are drawn to jobs that will not last more than a few years. With a resumé that includes stints at Playboy, Fleer (baseball cards), Rawlings (sporting goods), and Iams (pet foods), Steve believes we are challenge junkies—attracted to, and therefore attractive to, high-visibility companies that are likely to change. He believes we *prefer* to work this way, that adaptability comes *naturally* to our style of working.

How do creative professionals develop essential adaptation skills? Read constantly. Pay attention. Refrain from doing only things you know how to do. Learn something new every year—start as a novice and work your way up—so that you never forget how to learn, and maintain confidence in mastering new domains. This is not idle advice. If you do not provide yourself with a constant flow of learning opportunities, your brain will assume that you no longer participate in this behavior and will gradually shut down those services, at least for a while. (For more, see chapter six.)

Career Strategy: Explore Alternative Paths

It's often interesting to attend a corporate meeting with some relatively senior executives. A creative issue comes up, and remarkably, the head of technology takes the lead. Dig a little deeper and you find that the woman who is currently a technology executive came up through the creative ranks—she used to be an illustrator but changed careers when she realized the money was better in tech. Not all creative professionals stay for the entire ride—some of us shift into careers that allow for some creativity while also providing security and a more manageable career.

The Leap to Marketing

Maybe it's because creative people and marketing people spend so much time together. Maybe there's a natural affinity between the creative communication process and the marketing process—the idea of reaching an individual's heart is common to both fields.

Whatever the reason, many pure creatives move into the business side through marketing. It's not unusual to read about a company president who came up through the creative and marketing side. After college, she designed pages at a New York City magazine. She became aware of the advertising side of the magazine, then left to make more money as an artist at an advertising agency. The ad agency life appealed to her, especially as she spent more time with clients and with the account staff. She merged the account and creative sides on her first small team. A mid-level management job opened up, and she worked her way up at the agency, then became VP, marketing, for a client company. Already accustomed to the advancement game, she became Senior VP, marketing and sales, and because she did the revenue thing so well, the board elected her president.

Foundation skills served her well: a strong instinctual understanding of the audience and the customer; a well-developed sense of how to communicate through design and in person; and a clear view of the marketplace, both for herself and her products. She concentrated on the essence of her foundation skills, but she was not concerned whether those skills would be exercised by designing magazine layouts, advertisements, broader campaigns, or higher-level marketing strategies. She was flexible enough to use her skills with consistent, powerful impact.

Of course, she picked up other skills along the way. A designer does not become a company president without a lot of natural talent, ability, and training. Still, designers do become executives. And sometimes, they wonder why they were so darned anxious to leave the creative satisfaction of a design job.

The Leap to Technology

There's a strong kinship between scientific invention and creative innovation. Until fairly recently, however, the amount of training required for any technical endeavor was too great for most creative professionals to make the shift.

The Web changed that. Most Web sites were either developed by individuals or in small shops where designers and programmers worked side-by-side. Out of curiosity, or in response to a crunch, one began helping the other; the programmer is making buttons in Adobe Photoshop. Suddenly, the designer is building html pages. With some training and some user-friendly, page-building software, the designer realizes she can control both the look and the functionality of a Web site. The designer digs deeper into source code and learns some Java or Flash. There's a beauty to coding and an art form emerging in interactive media design. It's not all technology, it's not all design, it's a mix.

Here, foundation skills include holistic thinking; attention to detail; a knack for making things or for invention. The expression of those skills finds a wide open field in Web design and other facets of software architecture and applications development. In addition, there is professional room to grow into creative, technical, and project management. For a creative person who wants to stay close to the audience and the toys, this is a wonderful path.

The Leap to Teaching and Education

The novice teacher assumes that classroom education is about learning. More experienced teachers recognize the experience for what it is: students plod through period after period waiting for someone to capture their attention and imagination. That connection can be made through words, pictures, music, magic, performance, video, audio, kinetic activity—all in a teacher's portfolio.

Many creative professionals are born teachers—they want to communicate ideas, and the classroom provides a basic way to do just that. Stand in front of a class and explain why a building stands up, or how animation fools the eye, and some members of the audience hang on every word. Several students ask for your autograph! Imagine being a fashion photographer for a little-known full-figured women's apparel catalog, spending an hour with a rapt junior high class, and meeting a teenager who wants to be who you are today. It's a heady experience.

If you've been using these skills doing an almost-funny routine for an audience that drinks too much on Friday or Saturday nights, teaching might be more satisfying. Boundless curiosity and a passion for new interests (this week, acoustic bass; next week, Japanese brush painting) find a fertile environment in the right schools.

All teachers are not the passionate, creative souls that you might believe yourself to be. Teaching is about plowing through endless curriculum, regardless of relevance, utility, or interest, because that's what you are paid to do. Teaching can also be a fallback profession for intelligent people who prefer tenure to corporate adventure. You might find school confining. The good news is that you get to spend every day with some terrific kids; the bad news is, you'll spend your time with some not-so-wonderful humans, and there's almost nothing you can do about that (except wait for the school year to end).

Roles in higher education provide considerable flexibility for creative and scholarly endeavors. My attorney is a both a creative person (we've written a book together), and a law professor. His scholarly endeavors are both scientific and creative: He is studying the relationship between biological development, human behavior, and the rules that humans make, which we call laws. He also sings. Many filmmakers, authors, artists, musicians, and other creative professionals work as full-time or part-time college or university instructors, professors, even administrators. Gary Burton, one of America's finest jazz vibraphone players, is the executive vice president of Boston's Berklee College of Music, a leading music school.

The Leap into Entrepreneuring

An entrepreneur constantly scans the environment in search for connections between concepts and business opportunities. Some creative people possess the entrepreneurial combination of self-confidence and stubbornness. Do you? Don't say no too quickly! Creative professionals are famous for making something out of nothing and for working around obstacles with conviction. Perhaps you are not yet ready to become the founding entrepreneur of a multinational biotechnology startup. Start with what you can achieve. Develop your people skills, so you're comfortable working with a variety of personalities under pressure. If you're interested, learn the financial and legal aspects of startups and as much as you can about marketing. Then get a job with an entrepreneur. Observe the single-mindedness, the unwillingness to give up, the strong survival instinct, the adversity to foolish risk (most entrepreneurs are notoriously risk-averse, despite what you may have heard). Go through this cycle at least three times before setting out on your own. Learn from other mistakes—startups are filled with lessons.

TIME FOR A CHANGE?

Answer each of these questions, then look at the scoring information. Answer honestly. And if you're a freelancer or someone else who doesn't quite fit the 9 to 5 mold, do your best to reword the questions before answering them.

1. When is the last time you interviewed for a new job at a new company?
      A. This year
      B. Last year
      C. Two years ago
      D. More than two years ago

2. When was the last time your job title changed?
      A. This year
      B. Last year
      C. Two years ago
      D. More than two years ago

3. Write down your salary as of two years ago. Is your current salary…
      A. The same
      B. Up to 5% higher
      C. Up to 10% higher
      D. 15% higher, or better

4. Make a list of the ten people you work with most often. Now make a new list of the ten people who you worked with most often two years ago today. How many names are the same?
      A. 0-2
      B. 3-4

C. 5-7

D. 8-10

5. List five of the most recent projects that you've done, or will do, this year. What's your honest feeling about them?

A. They're not challenging, but they're enjoyable

B. They're the kinds of projects that I've always done well

C. They're familiar, but contain some interesting puzzles

D. They're mostly new and challenging

6. If you were to choose one person from your work group as a mentor, what might you learn from him or from her?

A. Different ways of thinking

B. Better ways to plan and execute projects

C. Better ways to deal with problem personalities

D. Not much to learn

7. Think about all of the people who have graduated from your work group or department in the past two or three years. Focus on just one person, the person whom you consider to be most successful in his or her new role. Would you say that he or she:

A. Wildly exceeded the real potential of others in your group

B. Exceeded within reasonable bounds

C. Made more money doing essentially the same job

D. Made a lateral move, albeit a positive one

8. Time to make another list. This time, list all of the people who used to work for your company—in any department—whom you could call for a new job or for job leads. How many people?

A. 5 or less

B. 6-11

C. 12-18

D. Over 18

9. If your job evaporated, what would you do once you got your head on straight?
    A. Call the many people in your personal network
    B. Call a few trusted friends in your personal network
    C. Target a few potential employers in your field
    D. Search the Internet and the classified for suitable jobs

10. Are you paying enough attention to your overall career? Be honest.
    A. I do my work, but career is always in the background
    B. I'm always networking, always interested in new opportunities
    C. I think about it every day
    D. I think about it from time to time, but don't really do much about it

11. How old are you?
    A. 20s
    B. 30s
    C. 40s
    D. 50s
    E. 60s

12. Are you doing what you want to be doing?
    A. Yes
    B. Usually
    C. Sometimes
    D. On occasion
    E. Rarely, or no

Comments and Analysis:

First, score yourself:

1: A=4; B=3; C=2; D=(-1)
2: A=4; B=4; C=1; D=(-1)
3: A=(-1); B=1; C=3; D=5
4: A=4; B=3; C=2; D=1

5: A=1; B=2; C=3; D=4
6: A=5; B=2; C=2; D=(-1)
7: A=3; B=4; C=1; D=1
8: A=1; B=2; C=3; D=4
9: A=5; B=3; C=2; D=(-1)
10: A=3; B=5; C=1; D=1
11: A=10; B=8; C=6; D=4; E=2
12: A=(-10); B=5; C=2; D=5; E=10

Second, add it up. Here's the horoscope:
If you scored in the 40s (or higher), it's probably time to make a change, or to start making plans. I said "probably" because there is a population that consistently scores in the 40s—people who never settle in, for whom change is constantly desired. Most people, even creative professionals who live on the edge, don't do well with constant change. What's more, their resumés tend to frighten potential employers.

If you scored in the 30s, it's time to move on. Maybe not immediately, but within the next 6 to12 months.

If you scored in the 20s or below, you're either in a safety zone or you're feeling a bit too complacent. Think about a five-year plan: do you want to be doing the same thing, for the same company, five years from today? More than likely, that's the path you're on today.

Third, some specific comments about the questions:

Obviously, the first five questions deal with where you are, and the velocity of movement around you. Too much velocity can be negative, but in the creative world, you want more than the average amount of activity in a "normal" business setting.

Questions 6, 7, and 8 are focused on the people whose work affects you: role models, co-workers, people whom you might learn from. Bear in mind that the learning might not be directly related to the creative craft, but to ways of working, succeeding, and dealing with people. In question 6, the A answer, "Different ways of thinking," is most valuable long-term, but for many, the more tactical B and C answers provide valuable short-term answers. Finally, if you're finding yourself mired in learning better ways of dealing with problem personalities (answer C), you might ask yourself why you are spending your time on that kind of problem. A change of company might allow you to spend your time more productively.

Questions 9 and 10 place you in the job market. In today's employment marketplace, networking rules. The size and depth of your network will provide a far higher likelihood of new employment than a small number of trusted friends or a short list of desirable employers. Internet advertisements often pull thousands of resumés, making them no more useful than classified ads.

Age plays a role. If you're in your 20s, you must move around some. Three jobs are good, four is better, five is acceptable. Meet new people, learn, try new roles. The 20s are the time to do all of that and more. If you're in your 30s, you want to demonstrate some flexibility and willingness to change, and you want to continue learning and expanding your network. Figure three jobs. In your 40s, 2 to 3 jobs is good and, more often than not, one will be a short-term clunker. Ditto for your 50s. Hard to say what the 60s might hold as millions of baby boomers overpopulate the market of available creative jobs in the next decade or so.

Finally, if you are not doing what you want to be doing, then you should seriously consider moving on. Certainly, there are real-life factors to hold you back, but those real-life factors should always be considered temporary. If you can't move on now, then develop and start executing a plan to move on at a particular point in time. Don't just stay in one place if you're unhappy— that's the worst thing that can happen to a creative professional and his or her magical powers.

When It Stops Working

Sometimes even when you're doing everything right, the universe collapses.

The Force-Out

Often creative people are perceived as specialists. Do a good job and you'll be valued by your boss and your company. Do a good job for a long time, and you'll make it difficult for your boss or your company to conceive of you in any other role.

There's a wonderfully sad scene in the Albert Brooks film, *Lost in America*, in which Brooks expects to be promoted to vice president. Instead, he is introduced to his new boss and told that the company kept him in his old job because they needed his creative skills. Brooks quits. This event quite logically causes Brooks to sell everything he owns to buy an RV and travel across America. Things don't work out as planned, so—what else—he grovels and gets his old job back.

Creative people are in a tough spot. Talent is difficult to replace, so we get passed over for promotions because we're needed in the studio. Our only hope is to demonstrate skills beyond the creative toolkit, to demonstrate that we are good not only at inventing campaigns, but also at managing clients, budgets, and people, too.

The Uncomfortable Interim

One job is done, and the next is nowhere in sight. You could take some time off, clear your head and deal with the problem when you return. You could also call everyone you know, let them know you're available, and then take some time off, remembering to check for messages at least once a day. You could finally start writing that novel, or developing the new product. But what you really want is for someone to call and say, "I think we may have something for you." When that call doesn't happen soon enough, we get a little crazy. Fortunately, the gods watch out for most of us and, despite the occasional gap, the phone does ring, and we find ourselves working more often than not.

When Things Aren't Working Out At All...

The phone didn't ring today.

I spent four hours writing e-mails and placing phone calls to drum up work, but nobody responded to the e-mails or picked up the phone.

This has been going on for weeks.

Is it over?

Let me first answer with the paragraph I want to write....

A true creative professional doesn't give up. A professional knows no fear because he believes in himself, his talent, and the contribution he know he can make. He is valuable to any organization, and given both time and focus, he can find a role anywhere and succeed mightily.

Here's the version that my left brain made me write:

If you're really creative, you will come up with something. Competent, talented people rarely starve. You might not do precisely what you want to do, at least not for a while, but you will find employment or some gigs to keep money coming into the house. What you've lost is momentum. Get yourself out there, build up your confidence, make yourself more public and you'll find work. I've seen this cycle time and again. The key is to interact with people who can provide or recommend you for work—and not to sit in your home waiting for the phone to ring or for someone to answer a random e-mail.

And now the paragraph that you probably ought to read...

Maintaining a career as a creative professional over multiple decades is mind-numbingly difficult. You start out young and hopeful, then you get hired and you work hard, hit a few bumps, maybe a few more, and you're not working as much as you did before. You develop your own projects, but that turns out to be a short-term adventure, not a long-term solution. You grow concerned about money, so you begin to take whatever work you can find. Like the MBA working as a cashier, you tactfully leave the creative highlights off the resumé. You must present yourself to the world as an ordinary person, not a superhero.

Go Away! (A Temporary Solution)

Every creative person should travel. Certain places attract creative professionals. Others are simply essential stops along the way for anyone involved with the arts, media, or the beauty of the planet. Among the big cities, New York City, Paris, London, and either Hong Kong or Tokyo are essential stops; it's best if you can actually live in one of these cities for a few years. Washington D.C., San Francisco, and Boston are also places you should know, along with Dublin, Florence, Rome, Marrakech, and Beijing. Among smaller cities, I'd include New Orleans, Santa Fe, Kyoto, and Jerusalem as essential stops, with Copenhagen, Prague, and Amsterdam also high on the list. Regionally speaking, you should make time to explore Tuscany in Italy, Provence in France, and the Rocky Mountains. Life would be incomplete without Yosemite, the Himalayas, and some tropical islands, perhaps Hawaii, Tahiti, or Fiji. These, plus a favorite beach or mountain town where you can lose yourself.

Going away is something that every creative professional must do at least once a year. And, when things aren't going so well, a bit of money socked away for a month in Japan or Tibet or Italy can be just what the doctor ordered.

Why the Traditional Job Market Doesn't Work

These days, the traditional job market doesn't seem to be working for anyone. Non-creative workers are learning what creative workers have known all along: You don't get a job like they do in the movies. It's not about resumés, classified ads, Internet ads, employment agencies, or search firms. It's about getting out there and meeting people. Personal referrals generate jobs. In our profession, there is almost no other way. This has been true for years. (There are exceptions, but we'll deal with them later.)

The Employer's World

A job opening is born when: (a) somebody leaves and the company seeks a replacement; (b) the workload increases and the existing staff needs help (sometimes extra hands, sometimes leadership or management); or, (c) the company requires staff to pursue an emerging market opportunity.

In (a) and (b), the company will first consider existing employees. There's a job opening, but only for those who have been told, or who happened to hear about it. Sometimes, a formal job description is posted on a bulletin board or the intranet. Sometimes employees are rewarded for referrals.

If the company is entering a new domain (c), it probably lacks the necessary staff. In these situations, a job posting might be required by company policy or law, but it's a formality. The hiring manager starts networking, trolling for candidates. If money is available and the position is sufficiently senior, a search firm might be hired. As a last resort, the company might place an advertisement online, in a local newspaper, or a trade magazine. Most jobs are filled through personnel referrals.

The Creative Job Seeker's World

Most people begin the job search process by revising a resumé. Creative professionals also update their demo tapes, portfolios, etc. Next comes an environmental scan, perhaps some phone calls to friends.

When nothing happens, panic sets in. How do you find out about a job?

That's when the foolishness starts—time spent on work that is very unlikely to produce a return on investment.

Classified advertisements in daily or weekly newspapers are nearly useless for creative professionals. You're not going to find an advertisement for a television program executive or a speechwriter in a local paper (yeah, you might get lucky...). Trade magazines are better because they're focused on your business. Every week, a few dozen advertisements in the TV trades advertise jobs in far-away cities (where talent pools are thin). The classifieds in *Publishers Weekly* include some jobs in book publishing, but most available jobs aren't advertised at all. Still, sending a resumé via e-mail costs nothing, a paper resumé and cover letter are inexpensive. Most likely, you are not going to get a job through a classified ad, so don't obsess about pretty paper or perfect wording.

Web advertisements are worse. There are postings for creative jobs on the Web: a designer for a pharmaceutical company's direct marketing group; a music director for a college program. Jobs posted on monster.com pull hundreds, even thousands of e-mailed resumés. If I think back, I might have once hired one person via a Web ad. From the employer's and candidate's perspective, they're cheap. Neither side puts effort into the process. The result is an overload of marginal resumés for the employer and a big nothing for most job seekers. Postings on industry-specific sites should not be overlooked, but odds are, you are not going to get a job this way.

The way to get a job is to meet someone with a need and the power to hire. The way to find that person is to find someone who knows him or the company. Networking is most productive when the process is ongoing: Don't construct your network when you need a job. You're more likely to help people you've known for a while; other people work the same way. Nurture your network. People will help you, but maybe not immediately.

Visibility matters. Write for magazines and get your work published or profiled. Do volunteer work for community organizations—guaranteed, there's a local theater group not ten miles from you that would welcome your volunteer assistance. Get out of your office, home, or studio and teach. Do seminars. Organize something that gets your name in the paper and does good for the community. Do not work quietly in your office waiting for the phone to ring, even (or especially) if you scored a high I on the MBTI scale.

The best defense in today's market and the *only* strategic combination that works is:

- Long-term planning
- An adaptive style
- A strong network
- High visibility
- Perseverance

Hiring Creative People – Secrets of the Hiring Manager

How do I hire a team? Like most people, I start by laying out job functions, write some job descriptions, and make phone calls to people who might be interested, or who know someone who's interested. The first source is always personal referrals. If that doesn't work, then I might place an advertisement or sort through any resumés that might have been filed away. More often, though, I'll simply make more phone calls and send more e-mails until I find the people I need.

For most creative jobs, there are a sufficient number of qualified candidates. Supply almost always exceeds demand, and this is especially true in cities where creative professionals congregate. It's not difficult, for example, to find a designer in San Francisco or a television producer in Los Angeles. Still, it might be challenging to find just the right person for a particular job, or there might be other obstacles, such as budget, a notoriously temperamental star, or a company with a reputation for not paying its bills. Inevitably, every job search becomes more difficult and complicated than anticipated, so every hiring manager tends toward a wider net and options that remain open as long as possible. It's not easy to be on the receiving end of that process, but that's the way it works. Your best defense: an equally wide net and enormous flexibility.

When I review resumés, I toss out those with insufficient experience and typically interview between three and five people for the job. The ones I like I keep, mainly as a meeting agenda for part of the interview. When interviewing creative people, I follow Jack Keil's advice: "Ask to see copies of their work—but not just the completed efforts, because these will have been altered by clients and budgets and all sorts of other considerations. Ask to see the work that was turned down…"[1]

Most candidates are interviewed by me and by several associates. We discuss our feelings about each one, obsess a bit about our choice, and

---

[1] SOURCE: John Keil, *How to Zig in a Zagging World*, Wiley book on audiocassette, draft script.

then make an offer. My goal in hiring has nothing whatsoever to do with your goal in building a career. I'm simply hiring someone to get a job done. Pretty much, you can keep your dreams to yourself and just focus on convincing me that you can do the work.

The Formula for a Successful Creative Career

My younger son's "career day" provided the opportunity to first tell a group of fourth graders about my work. I asked them whether I had "a bunch of jobs" or "a career." They felt a job was a temporary construct, regardless of its duration. They also agreed that a career reflected the cumulative impact of a series of jobs, while not necessarily bounded by the specifics of any single job or role (yeah, these kids were smart and I helped them a little).

They detected the creative professional pattern that flows throughout my life and throughout this book: Creative careers tend to define themselves at a somewhat higher level than the job description. They identified key characteristics and recurring themes: leadership and motivating others toward good work; ability to move from concept to completion; constant scanning of the environment; an entrepreneurial tendency; perceiving work and fun as closely related; a desire to teach and guide others.

Admittedly, I am jealous of the creative professional who will be remembered as a great musician, artist, writer, architect, or director because I am no one thing. And, in this regard, when I speak with friends who are musicians or artists or writers, they often comment on my good fortune and my flexibility; they cannot imagine a career for themselves that contains so much variety.

- Nothing happens by accident.
- Nothing happens just because you're lucky.
- Nothing happens without interacting with other people.
- Something happens when you're a part of the world, part of the community, making noise that other people can hear.

So what's the formula for a successful career? Try this one:

    (jobs) x (time) x (growth) = career

In detail: (a) A single job does not make a career, regardless of your tenure; (b) a career materializes over time; (c) growth is the transformative; it's the byproduct of relationships, projects, disappointments, deadlines, learning, listening, thinking, taking action, being right sometimes, being wrong a lot, self-confidence, and self-delusion. Growth is the nurturing environment that enables the formula to be calculated; without growth, it's just job after job, and that does not equal a career.

So how do you grow? Some answers are below; be sure to come up with more of your own.

At least once a month	At least once every three months	At least once every six months
Attend a networking event.	Complete a piece of work for your personal or professional portfolio.	Go on a job interview, if for nothing more than to stay in practice.
Participate in an activity with peers who are not part of your company.	Get your name in front of people who can help you (whether inside the company or your industry group).	Update a list of the ten companies where you would most like to work.
Meet somebody new in a company that interests you.	Attend an event showing a peer's work.	Update a list of two dozen people to call when you want a new job.
Read all of the relevant trade magazines that were published that month.	Attend an event by a creative wizard or someone who inspires you.	Update your daydream. (see page 201)
Read a magazine you've never read before, on a topic you know nothing about.	Go to an art museum.	Either leave the country, or make plans to leave the country within the next six months (or if not possible seek out the contrast in a place you can visit).
Read a book that feeds your intellect.	Go to a concert.	Spend an entire day taking pictures—from before dawn until after dusk.

At least once a month	At least once every three months	At least once every six months
Read a wonderful book with a wonderful story.	Go to a play.	Make a new friend.
See a movie that causes you to think differently.	Visit a place that's at least a hundred miles from your home, one you have never visited before. Spend a day walking, talking to people.	Try drawing—even if you can't draw.
Spend at least fifteen minutes in a serious discussion with someone less than half your age.	Read a book or see a movie about a country or culture that's foreign to your own.	Try singing, or playing a musical instrument—even if you can't.
Spend a half hour with someone twice your age (or, if you're over forty, with someone who's over seventy)—parents don't count, and it must be a different person each time.	Get into a passionate discussion on a subject you care deeply about.	Browse through this and other creativity books, one more time.
Visit a classroom, tell them how creative people work, tell them what you do, and then develop a concept with their help.	Spend a few hours on site observing someone whose career is entirely different from your own—a doctor, lawyer, police captain, fishing boat captain.	Arrange to spend a day at an elementary, middle, or high school. Teach the kids who want creative careers.
Go to a restaurant with a cuisine you've never tried before (or one you decided you did not like).	Volunteer your time for a community project.	Read a science or history book.
Buy something that you will use as a creative tool.	Don't eat anything for a whole day.	Learn something about Eastern or Western Philosophy.
Study—really study—a great work of art or music; learn about the creator's life and times.	Engage someone you don't know in a long conversation. You listen.	Learn a dozen words in a new language.
Wake up several hours before you usually do, and/or go to bed several hours later than usual. Get out and see what you're missing.	Plan a wonderful trip. Whether you go or not.	Make a list of everything you really want to do, but can't or won't.

You own your time, and you own your future. If you do not plan ahead, however, you cede control over your time and your future to your employer (or to your few clients). This is a profoundly stupid thing to do, and yet most employees do it anyway—they wait until the last possible moment to ignite a job search and then accept any job that comes along because they need short-term cash. As a result, many people suffer in the wrong jobs, limiting growth and causing oddball results when the career formula is calculated.

It's unreasonable for you to work this way. It's far more reasonable to envision your career path as a journey that you control. You must decrease your reliance on others, so that you determine which jobs you do, and you control how you grow. This is as essential as health insurance or money in the bank.

Achieving the Dream

There is no guarantee that you and the dream will ever meet. Here's how you can tilt the odds in your favor:

- Develop a new domain for yourself with a new job, volunteering, or freelancing.
- Regularly meet new people who can help you, or who you can help (yes, part of your job is to help make other people's dreams come true).
- Use your resumé, credentials, and personal network to pitch projects into a new space. Even if projects don't sell, the exposure might help you.
- Just do it. Just 'Nike' your way into a new domain by putting together people and projects. Sometimes your lack of knowledge will result in novel approaches and novel results. Even a modest project is better than none at all.
- Assume you will fail. Repeatedly. You will learn more by making mistakes than you will by doing nothing.
- For a project of superior strength, surround yourself with a superior team.
- Find a friend or a trusted business associate who completes you,

one who is equally committed to the journey.

• Put out the word about your dream (or about the general direction you want to take). Be diligent, almost to the point of being relentless (the market respects diligence, but relentless pursuits frighten people).

• Talk up the project. Eventually, the right person might hear you. (Didn't the "Think System" work for Professor Harold Hill in *The Music Man*?)

• Become a journalist in your new space. After several years of legitimate reporting, you will know enough about the space to establish yourself in a new role in the new space.

• Work with a mentor or teacher to learn about the field.

• Work with a therapist to develop a better understanding of yourself and greater confidence in your abilities.

• Pray. Use creative visualization. Visit the spiritual domain for greater understanding, confidence, and natural wonder.

Confidence

What, exactly, is confidence? It comes in two forms. There's self-confidence, the irrational but somehow reasonable sense that you are correct in your assessment and decisions. And there's confidence that others invest in you, perhaps because your personality and style seems to warrant this trust, or perhaps because they've seen you in action before. When confidence in yourself is supported by confidence from others, the result can be a very positive spiral.

Still, insecurities creep in. What if you are less than you believe you are? What if others find out that you aren't as worthy of their invested confidence? From time to time, you will mess up. You will lose confidence in yourself, and others will lose confidence in you or simply lose interest in you. When that happens, it's important to regain a firm footing. This is best accomplished by briefly analyzing what went wrong, then taking a break and returning to the action with somewhat reduced expectations.

If you've got the real stuff, you will be back to yourself in no time. And if you've been guilty of overconfidence, you will find your own level. It's important to stretch—to reach beyond what you believe your capabilities to be, but it's also important to maintain a support system that allows you to fail without dire consequences.

Giving and Taking Credit

Artists and photographers sign their work; without the signature, the work is not nearly as valuable. When a new building is going up, a wooden sign lists the architect, contractor, and financier. A chef sometimes adds his or her name to the restaurant name. Broadcasters say their names aloud; journalists take bylines; production staffs get screen credit; songwriters are credited on liner notes.

Few other industries credit employees or contractors. An inventor or entrepreneur might name a company or a product for himself (David Oreck's vacuum cleaners). A screen or print credit might be a source of pride for you and your family, but it might also cause resentment. In television the production staff gets credit, but the executives and managers who work for the network are equally deserving of a credit, and they might not get it. Saying a public "thank you" can go a long way toward good relations.

Be generous, but be truthful. Be sure to say thank you, as often as possible and as publicly as possible to those who deserve the acknowledgement. However, when you acknowledge an undeserving person, you minimize the value of your words for those who deserve thanks.

Be Patient

Reference Matt Lauer, the popular host of NBC's *Today Show* since 1997 and the show's news reader from 1994 until 1997. It took him fifteen years to get there—fifteen years of hosting local news and talk, of going to auditions for just about any available job in New York City (he auditioned several times for me in the 1980s, and mine were not big projects). In fact, when he was wrapping up a job in Boston, he was thinking about leaving the business. Then, the *Today* call came in.

Many people have the talent and the ability, but the slots simply aren't available. Soledad O'Brien, who hosted *Weekend Today* for NBC, left the network to join CNN, where a morning anchor slot opened up. She'll gain experience there, but mostly, she seems to be waiting for the next broadcast network opportunity. Now in her mid-thirties, she could become a major network personality over time.

If you have the talent, it's important to gain the exposure. If people do not know who you are, you will not get the opportunities that you deserve. So, patience becomes a career virtue only if you are doing everything else right. If you're patiently waiting to be discovered without putting your work out there for all to see, you are dreaming. It comes back to the Gypsy Rose Lee advice: Just keep working. People will notice.

Remember Where We Came From

We're not the first generation of creative professionals. Any progress we've made is on the shoulders of giants. Learn the history, read about the legends: Houdini, Michelangelo, Franz Schubert, Robert Johnson, Fred Allen, DaVinci, Rembrandt, Ernie Kovacs, Hokusai, Isaac Bashevis Singer, Bob Hope, Mark Twain, Al Jolson, Enrico Caruso, Frank Lloyd Wright, Louis Armstrong.

You should know who Bert Williams was, and why he matters.

Spike Lee, on *Bamboozled*: "The reality of black people putting this stuff on their face was devastating for Tommy Davidson and Savion Glover. It took away part of their soul, it took away part of their manhood, it made us think of Bert Williams. Tommy and Savion did it for a couple of weeks, but Williams had to do that his entire career."[2]

Talent's Intangibles

So you're thinking, "All of this is well and good, but why are my friends

---

[2] SOURCE: Gary Crowdus and Dan Georgakas, 2001 – *Cineaste*, p. 26, No. 2 (January 2001).

opening for the Dave Matthews Band while I'm still stuck in this lousy bar band?"

Or, you're thinking, "I can tell by that guy's attitude why *he's* stuck playing in a bar on Saturday nights. But I'm different. I'm talented, well-educated, motivated, well-connected, and experienced. So why am I out of work half the time? Why am I working on meaningless projects just to pay the rent? When's my turn?"

Fair question. What's the secret?

A certain look in your eyes, a style, character, and charisma that a particular audience finds appealing. Some people are naturals. When I watch Katie Couric, Ted Koppel, or Charles Osgood, I am awed by their ease and their skill as broadcasters. Walter Cronkite was the embodiment of a television news personality. Bill Cosby. Bob Costas. Oprah Winfrey. When I watch decades-old tapes of Dean Martin or Bing Crosby or Bob Hope, I see magic.

Years ago, when David Letterman was on NBC, the show's producer, Robert Morton, introduced me to Robin Williams. I expected the usual "Hi, how you doing?" and maybe a handshake. Instead Robin and I did ten minutes of schtick—we made each other laugh. Morton set up the conversation by explaining that he and I had worked together on a high school radio station. This was all Williams needed; he skillfully imagined the details and asked me the right questions so I could be funny and inventive along with him. What an experience! It was like flying, holding on to someone who really did know how to fly.

While I was writing this book, the actress Lynne Thigpen passed away. She played The Chief on *Where in the World Is Carmen Sandiego?* When Lynne died, the show's host, Greg Lee, remembered what she had done, so often and so well. Lynne generously helped Greg to shape his character on the series so that they could work as a successful and funny team. When they were in a sketch together, it was never about Lynne, and never about Greg. It was about two of them together, working as a single entity.

Is the answer pure, natural talent? Do you really need to practice for hours and hours every day before you can be John Coltrane?

I don't know. (Okay, return the book to the store. The author doesn't know the answer to the most important question in the book.)

I can observe the phenomenon, but there is no single path, no logical set of reasons, no replicable set of instructions that will reliably separate you from others who do what you do. Your personal magic, willingness to work hard and do things right, perseverance, and the desire of other talented and influential people to work with you—all of this goes a long way. And then, there's luck. And maybe something else...

Fame

One of the extraordinary aspects of life as a creative professional is the potential for personal fame. That's right—you could become famous. Is it possible to be a successful mystery or science fiction writer without becoming famous among readers? Probably not. Can you be a successful photographer or director without becoming famous? Certainly. Your name might become known, but little more will be known about your life. For several years, I was a frequent guest on television and radio, and I wrote a newspaper column that appeared in about a hundred newspapers. When I introduced myself to someone I'd never met, they often told me that they knew my name. This frightened me a bit, and in time I slowed down those high-visibility activities. Still, in some corners of the creative world, it's nearly impossible to enjoy great success without also becoming famous. The two actors below, for example, are creative people for whom success and fame have become a single conception.

The actors Denzel Washington and John Goodman have successfully cultivated their careers and their fame for nearly twenty years. Neither set out to become famous; in fact, neither set out to become an actor at all. Goodman was set to become a football player, but he got hurt in college and took up acting instead. Washington considered a career as a doctor, then earned a journalism degree, doing some acting at college for fun. Both found that they were good actors and pursued the craft. Goodman struggled for years in dinner theater and other small productions before he got a break in a Broadway musical (*Big River*). Washington found better work faster, first in the New York Shakespeare Festival, then in an off-Broadway show that became a movie (*A Soldier's Story*). Solid character roles in successful television series set the stage for stardom; Goodman played Rosanne Barr's wife in her first TV series, and Washington became a popular lawyer on *L.A. Law*. Then both men were smart and lucky enough to find distinctive movie roles. In a remarkable seven-year period, Goodman played Fred Flintstone, a Blues Brother, Louisiana Governor Huey Long, and gained credibility among serious film-goers with roles in *Raising Arizona* and *Barton Fink*. Washington became known as a serious, charismatic actor through roles in *Glory*, *Malcolm X*, *Philadelphia,* and *Much Ado About Nothing*. Here was an African-American leading man who did not build a career on comedy or violence.

Washington became a role model, a family man, a member of the comunity who used his fame to set a standard. Goodman was a man who clearly enjoyed a good time and let others join in the fun, an actor who said "yes" to a stunning range of large and small roles—plus he has hosted *Saturday Night Live* more often than just about anyone. When either actor shows up for anything, I'm interested. And it's been that way for a decade or more. That's the use of celebrity fame as its very best.

Whether intended or not, every celebrity becomes a kind of role model. Director and actor Spike Lee probably speaks for many celebrity performers when he claims he's not wild about the idea. Still, he accepts it as part of his life. He said, "I remember at the first LA premiere of *She's Gotta Have It*, a skinny black kid walked up to me and said, 'Hi, my name is John Singleton,[3] and I'm in high school now, but I'm going to make movies just like you.' For me, that's... the reward...." Lee also said, "If I really considered myself to be a role model, it would be a hindrance. It means you can't have anything negative connected with you—Michael

---

[3] John Singleton is a writer and director whose credits include *Boyz N the Hood* and *Baby Boy,* and the 2000 *Shaft* remake.

Jordan can't be photographed drinking a beer. I'm an artist. I can't wear that straitjacket."[4]

Celebrity carries responsibility to fans. If someone stopped you on the street, would do you stop, chat, and sign an autograph? Would you allow your picture to be taken? Where do you draw the line?

Fame also affects family relationships. In the U.S., being in the public eye can be risky, so many celebrities protect their private lives. Would you curb your family activities to avoid interaction with the public? Or would you show up at Little League games and eat at ordinary restaurants because that's what everybody else does? Would you call a restaurant for reservations under your name, knowing that you'll ace someone else out of a table? Are you your public image? When you go out for ice cream, do you dress the part or do you "leave it at the office"?

Fame may or may not last. You could be famous for fifteen or twenty minutes, then forgotten. This has messed up lots of folks. As the wife of jazz legend Charles Mingus told reporter and musician Billy Taylor, "Of course he's resentful, of course he's bitter. He wants fame and recognition for what he's done and he sees other people, not as talented as he is, getting credit for his accomplishments.... His music is so well thought out, and organized, but he doesn't act that way in his personal life. He's very sensitive to rejection and sometimes he feels it when it isn't there."[5]

It might be foolishly idealistic to assume that fame will not affect you. Successful performers are almost always famous performers. Some creative professionals can ride unnoticed; many cannot.

Decision Time: What Are You Really Trying to Accomplish?

Most creative people work: (a) for the money; (b) for the art; or (c) as a way to fill their time.

At the end of the day, it's depressing to envision a tombstone etched

[4] SOURCE: *Spike Lee Interviews*, James Verniere, 1993, *Sight and Sound*, February 1993.
[5] SOURCE: Joe Goldberg, *Jazz Masters of the Fifties*, p. 149.

for eternity with: "She worked for the money."

Money is a scorecard; it provides you with a sense of the market value of your talents or services or products. Some creative professionals have amassed fortunes by building companies around their talents: Walt Disney; Thomas Edison; Stephen Spielberg; Oprah Winfrey; Paul McCartney; Paul Newman; Lorne Michaels.

Those who have not built companies around their talents are hardly the unsuccessful minority. In fact, we're in the majority.

Maybe quality and quantity of the work matters more than the money. This might be personally satisfying, but in today's world, saying, "I'm an artist; I don't care about the money" sounds either silly or dishonest. Besides, it's very difficult to live and work without either revenue or an asset base in today's world.

When the audience laughs or applauds, perhaps the mission has been accomplished. The unique talent that allows a performer to utter words and cause humans to respond with their emotions is something quite special. To say that someone was a fine actor, or a very funny comedian, is a fine epitaph.

Thankfully, most creative professionals don't obsess about their legacy. Being a good parent, a good provider, a good partner, a good contributor—that's enough. Most people don't have a pressing need to be THE CREATOR. Instead, most of us are happy to be a part of a wonderful process, working side by side with clever, motivated, talented people in a pleasant environment where humor, friendship, and magic are commonplace. Look no further, for this is the prize.

Some people aren't happy accomplishing just one thing. Mastering one domain, they develop another. To be remembered as a great Broadway composer isn't enough; the composer is often just a bit jealous of his reliance on the lyricist. Tony Bennett the singer is also Tony Bennett the artist. Jerry Garcia the guitar player was also Jerry Garcia the textile designer. This should not be so difficult to understand: If you start before you're twenty and finish in your eighties, that's more than sixty years, a very long time to be doing the same thing day after day, no matter how much you enjoy it.

The composer and conductor Leonard Bernstein struggled mightily with this issue, particularly in his later years. In the 1950s, Bernstein led the New York Philharmonic; he taught everywhere, including his own CBS series (*Young People's Concerts*); he wrote for Broadway (*West Side Story*) and for the movies (*On the Waterfront*). After eleven thrilling seasons (and nearly 1,000 concert performances) with the New York Philharmonic, he resigned. He was fifty. His intent was to compose serious classical works. Over the next twenty years, he became one of the world's best-known conductors. Original classical works came, but only a Bernstein fan or scholar knows even one of their names.

"Bernstein could not stay away from conducting, no matter how much he thought he should," explains biographer Joan Peyser.[6] Instead, he would mount exhausting international tours, highlighted by strenuous, emotional performances, accolades, adoring fans, political and social activism of the highest degree; then he would spend days or weeks coming down from the high; trying to settle into a state of mind necessary to compose; then become frustrated because his work was not up to his standards. Bernstein the performer was adored; Bernstein the composer, post-1950s, was mostly ignored. His legacy: one of the finest Broadway scores of all time; hundreds of superior recordings of the popular symphonic catalog; endless support for social causes; unflagging, endless support for Israel and for the Israel Philharmonic; *Young People's Concerts*, revered as one of the finest mass market music education projects; and more. All good, Bernstein might say, but he was really hoping to make it as a classical composer, too. (I can't help thinking about the line, "but what I really want to do is direct…")

An Expansive Look at Your Career

Creative professionals tend to be very concerned about personal accomplishment, resumés and the opportunity to do the next great thing— or to just keep the money coming in. Turns out, a career is more than that. From time to time, it's helpful to assess where you are and where you're

---

[6] SOURCE: Joan Peyser, *Bernstein: A Biography*, Ballantine Books, 1988, p. 397.

going. And as you approach the latter parts of your career, there will be more behind you than ahead. This can be a tough idea to accept. Hopefully, the next few pages will help you out.

When Should You Move On?

With a clear idea of where you want to go, and why, the next question becomes when?

In an ideally paced career, you should have about four to five jobs in your twenties; three to four jobs in your thirties; two to three jobs in your forties; two to three jobs in your fifties; and then, whatever you can get or keep in your sixties (there's not much demand for workers in their sixties, so hang on to whatever you've got). Overall, if you are working in more or less traditional jobs, you'll have a total of twelve to twenty different jobs. Ideally two or three of these jobs should be with different companies.

If you stay in a creative job for more than four or five years, you will be perceived as lacking in ambition, coasting, or shutting yourself off from opportunity for some mysterious reason. Then again, if you're happy and well-paid in a great job, why leave?

If you've been working at home for more than two or three years, you will be perceived as a solo act, and some companies might be reluctant to hire you. Be aware of detachment from the traditional job market; spending too much time at home without regular professional comrades isn't always the best strategy. Meeting new people plays a major role in career development: How many new people did you meet at home today?

Given the above structure, and acknowledging that an ideal scenario rarely matches reality, how do you know when it is time to move on? Here's a rundown:

You've reached an appropriate level of competence. You know how to do the job, and the tasks are becoming repetitive. Your work is as good as it's going to get with the available resources, constraints, mentors, clients, and so on. You are ready to do the next job on the ladder.

You have become truly excellent. You are clearly the best architect in the firm, the designer who always gets the best assignments, the performer who always plays the lead. You are beginning to understand how good you are, and others acknowledge your talents and skills. There is more to learn by working somewhere else.

You should now teach others. You realize that your talent and skill set have taken you as far as you are going to go, and teaching provides as much or more satisfaction than doing the work yourself. Besides, teaching comes naturally; associates and friends become students. You want to spend some or all of your time teaching.

You no longer want to teach others. You have spent considerable time and talent in service of other people's talent. Now, you want a break from others; you want to develop your own career or to pursue other interests.

You need more time to try other things. If you're lucky, you've got about sixty-five years of competence to accomplish your life's mission (under twenty, you're still learning, and over eighty-five or so, maybe it's getting tougher). No rule says you must do any one thing for any period of time. You can be a marketing wizard and a bassoon virtuoso at the same time, or you can put together a string of varied activities. Sometimes, though, you might want to concentrate on doing just one thing, or one new group of things, without the encumbrance of your present role. You need more time each week/month/year doing what you want to do, regardless of the impact on a particular point in your career. More often than not, a serious change in direction, accompanied by diligence, will result in a powerful new career trajectory.

You've made enough money. If you've done well, perhaps with a hit, there comes a point where you really do have enough money. You live in a beautiful home that you own. Your kids' college education is fully funded, and you have enough available money to fund your own life and most of theirs. Money is no longer the object of the game; now you want to use the freedom that money should provide, and so, you decide to move on to the next adventure.

You're in conflict with your employer or client's agenda. Regardless of the time you have invested, or the strength of your relationships, or your contributions to an organization, times change. Changes in the market, in leadership, in the company's culture, or changes in the way that you see yourself in the context of the organization— each of these can evolve into conflict that's sufficiently serious to cause a parting of the ways.

You're in conflict with coworkers or the boss. Most often, this occurs as the result of change: You're in a new role, or new team members join up, or the group is led by somebody new. Sometimes, the people are fine with one another, but some external force changes the dynamics and causes conflict. Regardless of the reason why, if you're not comfortable with your co-workers or your boss, you can either cope (a learning experience, sometimes, but without much of an endgame for the employee), or you can leave. You can also choose to wait out the problem— you could endure the pain and outlast the problem person. And, you can choose to fight. Sometimes the lessons learned during the fight are reason enough to stay a while. Sometimes you win and you can take control of the situation. It's worth experimenting; don't just leave because of a conflict. See what you can learn from it, and see if there's a win for you in the midst of the mess.

You've gone as far as you can go. The company does not exist in order to provide you with opportunities. When your goals and the company's needs match up, it's wonderful. Sometimes your journey ends because there is no other place to go. It's invigorating to build some new road yourself, but more often, it's more productive to pick up the story elsewhere. When you find that every opportunity looks similar, and that every path looks like every other path, it's time to make some changes in where you're going and why. Fortunately, most people can find a productive, satisfactory path through a job search.

You've been passed over for the best project(s) or for the choice promotion(s). If this happens once or twice, try to figure out what happened and why. If you've done your best to improve the odds, and it happens again, it's time for a job search. And if this pattern repeats itself time and again, regardless of the organization or your role in it, you ought to be evaluating your overall plan.

You're tired of "development hell." The term is common in television and motion pictures: You pour your heart and soul into early-stage projects, and although some of them reach later stages, none reaches completion. Every creative profession includes some sort of funnel model: lots of ideas at one end of the funnel, and very few completed projects at the other. This phenomenon happens to the best of us, but it's tough to tolerate it for long. Most people maneuver their way out of development-oriented roles and into roles that are closer to the action.

Career Paths and Side Tracks

Back to the idealized world, where most people travel the interstates, making (seemingly) efficient progress from one milepost to the next. Some people choose not to travel the interstates, instead pursuing what author William Least Heat Moon calls "blue highways"[7]—those thin lines on the map that travel through more picturesque towns, each unique to those who are willing to take the time to explore.

Traveling blue highways takes longer and doesn't necessarily get you where you want to go, but the trip itself is always worthwhile.

[7] SOURCE: William Least Heat Moon, *Blue Highways*.

Why pursue a career along the blue highways? The truth is, there aren't enough jobs for creative professionals. As you work your way to and through jobs with progressively greater responsibility, you will find yourself increasingly alone—working with other managers or directors or vice presidents, but you will be unique because your background is creative, not technical or operational or financial or sales.

Initially, visiting a place on a blue highway is intriguing. Maybe you find your way into a college town, and you teach a few classes for a friend. You enjoy interacting with the students, and you're intrigued by your friend, the music professor, and the creative freedom he enjoys. Maybe you ought to find a job like that for yourself.

Or, you're vacationing and you find a wonderful town by the shore with an abundance of people who write, paint, or take photographs. Or, there's a political consultant who lives by the shore but spends three days a week in a city that's a seemingly reasonable two-hour drive from home.

Or, you travel the blue lines in a more metaphorical way. You wake up an hour early every day to work on the novel, or the screenplay, or the painting. You begin to meditate. You set aside time to learn how children think, or for social activism. You drift toward a different place—perhaps you volunteer for an organization you believe will make a difference. You are sidetracking, and there's nothing better in the world for the creative mind.

You could, however, take a wrong turn. You could drive yourself into a dead end, or allow other people to drive you crazy. Many sidetracks are just that and nothing more—unnecessary alternative routes that lead nowhere and just slow you down.

A sidetrack can grow from the family. You want to be a good father, so you become the Little League team's coach. A few hours a week, it feels great to be outside, watching your daughter learn the fundamentals. Baseball's fun, so you add soccer. Hours mount, you're happy, she's happy, life is terrific. It's less stress, too: You're outdoors living a normal life with other normal people, not stuck indoors obsessing over the stupid characters in the stupid rewrite of your stupid book that every stupid agent has already turned down.

A few years later, you're not writing anything at all.

What to do? Certainly, don't miss out on coaching your kid's team. That's real life, and real life *always* wins over our made-up lives, regardless of what we're trying to accomplish for ourselves. Don't kid yourself, either. If your goal is to write a novel, it won't get done if you're out playing with your kid instead of writing. Manage your time, manage your life, make time for what's important.

Why People Pay You

During the early stages of a career, the value proposition is easily defined. You are paid because there is a stack of work to be done, and your skills are suitable to the task. Since there's no scarcity of young writers, artists, musicians, designers, programmers, or other newcomers, it's relatively easy to describe the work and to price it. Over time, most creative professionals (a) develop superior production skills; (b) learn to manage the work and the people who do it; and/or (c) figure out there is more to the story.

Getting Paid to Think

At some point in mid-career, it happens. You realize that you are no longer doing the work! Instead, you are being paid to think about the work that other people do. To some extent, you might manage people or process, but it's your brains and experience, not your hands, that the employer or client wants and needs.

There's an ecstatic pleasure in envisioning a world that does not exist and causing it to exist because you possess personal power beyond what you thought possible. When you speak, people listen. When you say something can happen, people believe you. When you say there is a better way, people support your idea and link their careers to yours.

The role can be mysterious to others who don't completely understand how or why you have achieved this remarkable place in their world; and it can be mystifying because, down deep, you know that you're not doing anything that you haven't been doing for years. You wonder whether you're faking it, whether you've been placed in somebody else's life for a while, or whether any part of you resembles the real thing.

Then you settle in and you begin to understand yourself in your new role, and your value. You operate at a higher level, but because you come from the troops, you understand their world and speak their language; you understand their issues and consider them in your thinking. You gain confidence, and your power of persuasion becomes stronger. Your understanding becomes more global, and you see the business realities. And you wonder, like Frank Baum did when he gave the tin man a brain, what the possibilities might be.

Getting Paid to Guide

When a guide is appropriately and optimally employed, she should design the team, casting not only capabilities but chemistry. A guide well-schooled in the Myers-Briggs personality evaluator and other such ways of thinking will put together a team that's organically right. She will set a cooperative mood but will also teach the others how to make the best of conflict and work together as a single entity.

If the guide is also the primary creative force—and this is not unusual—he can and often does design the project so that it fits not only the market and mission but the capabilities and philosophies of the team as well.

As a guide, you manage neither the work nor the people who do the work. Instead, you influence the entire organism.

Focus becomes primary. Team members bring varied experiences and perspectives; the guide embraces and synthesizes these many unrelated or incongruous ideas and finds ways to create a coherent whole. There is wizardry here—the magic of inclusion.

When a project is properly constructed, each individual can point to his own specific contributions to the end project, but no one will be able to explain how so many different ideas were so successfully glued together. The magic is not in the ideas; the magic is in the structure that allows the ideas to adhere. Most creative projects are not about a single creative professional's brilliant ideas; they are about that creative professional's ability to listen to the entire team, to sort out the ideas that work, don't work, and could work. It's partially sculpture—the final product is concealed inside the block of marble, and it's up to the sculptor to eliminate just the right pieces of rock to find the miracle inside. And, it's partially about quilting—each person sews a small part of the quilt, guided by a grand design that every quilter at the table understands and adapts to their own skills and aesthetics.

Older Creative Professional

This next paragraph is terrifying:

According to *Newsweek* (December 16, 2002), "...In 2000, there were sixty-one million Americans forty-five to sixty-four; by 2010, there will be seventy-nine million, estimates the Bureau of Labor Statistics. Roughly one in three working-age Americans will soon be 'mature.' The trouble is that society doesn't know what to do with us. In 1960, 78 percent of men from sixty to sixty-four were in the labor force, as were 31 percent of those sixty-five and over. By 2000, those figures were fifty-five and 18 percent, respectively.... We need a transformation of work as profound as when women flooded the labor market. More older Americans need to move gradually from work to full-time retirement. They need to mix jobs and leisure in ways that seem natural and aren't embittering."[8]

I am among those sixty-one million Americans. I am doing everything I can to counteract the direction that society is moving, but I am frightened. If you were born between 1935 and 1955, you should be frightened, too. And I wouldn't relax too much if I were born in the 1955-1965 period, either. I'm not sure what to tell the rest of you, but you'd better stay awake....

In my work I don't have much respect for age. Just because someone is older does not mean that they're smart, or capable, or experienced. I do have enormous respect for competence, energy, enthusiasm, trust and

---

[8] SOURCE: Robert Samuelson, *Newsweek*, December 16, 2002.

loyalty, willingness to give and to teach, and a desire to do great things. Give me a good idea and a group of clever people of whatever age, and we'll light up the room with enthusiasm, energy, and magic. Creativity is always about the magic, and I don't much care how old the magicians are. I care about what they know how to do and whether they're willing to take another magical adventure. The fact that some talented writer is a month out of college or an artist is on the cusp of retirement is meaningless. When we're in the midst of the good fight, everybody in the room is the same age, and that's no age at all.

Pitfalls Associated With Aging Creative Professionals

People who are old in their ways and old in their thinking aren't going to be much help. What's more, you don't have to be chronologically old to be perceived as old and in the way.

James Adams wrote, "Old dogs can learn new tricks. However, old problem-solving dogs must also realize that much of their knowledge, attitudes, and abilities are wired-in—controlled by neural networks that have physically and chemically been determined by experience. Old dogs must also understand that there is difficulty associated with learning new tricks...."[9]

Two thoughts from two sages:

"Many people would sooner die than think. In fact, they do." (Bertrand Russell)

"People do not quit playing because they grow old. They grow old because they quit playing." (Oliver Wendell Holmes)

The "been there, done that" school can slow things down and sack enthusiasm. Good creative work requires listening to the marketplace and approaching projects and audiences with enthusiasm. If you can't muster the necessary energy, get out of the way. (Yeah, that was harsh. I don't have much time or patience for those who ramble on without pitching in.)

---

[9] SOURCE: James Adams, *The Care and Feeding of New Ideas*, p. 35.

Various scientific studies note that youth is the most creative period only in abbreviated lifetimes. Of 150 adults studied in one survey, over half had begun their most creative period after age fifty.[10]

"Older adults do seem to experience a decrease in divergent thinking, the ability to generate a quantity of novel ideas.... Adams-Price (1998) concludes that the association of creativity with novelty and innovation is appropriate for the characteristics of youthful thinking, but late-life creativity reflects aspects of late-life thinking: synthesis, reflection, and wisdom."[11]

Think about this. You were born in 1960, and you're now in mid-career. Your first clear memories of the marketplace begin with *The Brady Bunch*. You're working with a young pup, born in 1980. Her memories begin with *Rugrats*. She has no memory of life without cable, video games or a computer in the family room. Born in 1940? Your version of home entertainment was not *I Love Lucy* reruns, but the original series. This is inconceivable for someone who grew up with Nick at Nite.

The mismatch becomes too great. At seventy, it's not easy to reinvent yourself. At seventy, you've either got to adapt, speak to people who are closer to your own age, or make up your own rules. Or, just work for your own pleasure.

But what are you trying to accomplish?

The Final Semesters

At some point, though, you will face the big question:
"If I don't work, what will I do all day?"

For a creative person who never really felt as though she was really working in the first place, this question might not present a challenge. Creativity is, and always will be, an advanced form of play. There are the sense of freedom and discovery, the toys and laughter, and a dreamscape beside the adult interpretation of reality. Without a workplace, the freedom and discovery can continue, along with the toys and the laughter

---

[10] SOURCE: -- ERIC EDO-CE-99-204 – "Creativity in Adults" by Sandra Kerka.
[11] SOURCE: -- ERIC EDO-CE-99-204 – "Creativity in Adults" by Sandra Kerka.

and the dreamscape. Not much changes when employment evaporates, except perhaps access to people and resources. Both of these can be found outside traditional offices.

For the creative person who has been more reliant on structure and the magic of other people's dreams, the transition can be rough. In time, you become self-sufficient. You do what you can with other people, and you involve yourself in a wide range of activities. Still, you cannot rely on the way that other people will choose to spend their leisure time. There is abundant free time, but without money and career advancement as a prime motivator, one or more of your friends or associates might opt for travel or family time or personal pursuits rather than attend rehearsals for your new retirees-only vocal group. The photography club might not meet once a week because members are out visiting their kids.

So you learn to rely on yourself and your own desire to accomplish. If you're living alone, time might be so abundant that it becomes difficult to manage. If you're living with a partner, you are blessed; fit your pursuits into a schedule that works for both of you. In fact, you might try to interest your partner in your own pursuits; it's more fun to go out on a photography expedition as a pair than alone (and, it's even more fun to go out with a group of several like-minded photographers).

There is time to practice, so now, perhaps for the first time, you can slow it down. You can practice playing the cello for hours a day. You can spend hours in the darkroom, or sculpt without stopping at the wrong time. You can sit in classes for no reason except to learn something new, with time to do the homework. These activities might complete you.

A successful creative professional is self-confident, talented, and capable. Some creative professionals develop a strong need for validation and ego gratification, but these needs can create a vortex of detrimental thinking and bad behavior over time.

Just Keep Working

If there is true joy in what you do, then there's no reason not to continue to paint, invent, design, make music, or explore new domains. Don't worry too much about the money— unless you need it because your retirement plan didn't work out. Instead, set aside several hours a day to do your own work. Before long, you will have written a short story or completed a painting, and you'll be on your way to the next challenge. This is how you can stay young and remain interesting to yourself and to others. You'll be proud, and your children will be proud. It's the right way to spend your time after the job market is through with you.

Philanthropic Pursuits

If you have some extra money, now's the time to put some of it to work. Visit several universities and see whether you can make a difference. If you fund even a small scholarship, you'll be helping someone to succeed on the basis of your success. You might find that the occasional visiting lecture is invigorating. You might enjoy the interaction with students. You are giving your money and/or your time for the right reasons.

You might also feel some responsibility to your public. Some authors, and other creative professionals, organize their life's work for a beloved university library. Others lend their names and influence to charitable organizations that can make a difference. These are worthy endeavors, and not enough of us spend our later years in these pursuits. It's up to you to change that: Do it yourself and evangelize the idea among others with whom you have shared a career.

The Ultimate Creation

Being a creative person is being a god. You are a Creator, the central figure in every creation myth. In the beginning, there was nothing. You made something. You made something from nothing. You made someone happy. Or sad or angry. You filled someone with laughter or wonder or questions. You did that. You. Not the team, not the agency, not the tool. At the moment of creation, you were filled with something that few other people on earth ever touch.

The ultimate creation is, of course, your own life. You control it, you shape it, you nurture it and you live with it. You decide what matters, you manage your time and your goals and your future. You determine whether to use your talent to make people laugh at a comedy club or to scare them through a suspense film. You know, and you've probably always known, why you work so hard to win awards, why money is so important, why you work best when you consider your boss to be the enemy of your soul. You operate at several levels: the very practical level where you get paid well because you do good work; the contributory level where you encourage others to be their best; the higher level where you know that your ideas can and do affect other people's minds and spirits.

Your deepest knowledge is captured in the Einstein conundrum: "Imagination is more important than knowledge." You are certain that this statement is true, based mainly on your own knowledge of imagination.

And What if You Didn't Create?

According to the gods, there are 7,777,777,777,777,777,777 morsels of creative talent in the universe. The morsels were generated by the big bang, and the total number has never changed, not by a single morsel.

These morsels are distributed among all living souls; the pool is constantly revitalized as people's lives end and new lives begin. Morsels are energized by usage and by proximity to other energized morsels. Morsels that are not utilized lose their energy. Morsels without energy are likely to disengage, and to adhere to other energized morsels.

So, go find yourself a chocolate chip cookie, and don't worry so much. Just keep doing what you're doing, make the necessary changes along the way, and don't stop creating. You've been given 77,777,777 morsels. Make the best of them.

APPENDIX: The Creative Bookshelf

Certainly, every creative domain enjoys its own literature. No list of suggested book titles is ever going to be complete or comprehensive. Feel free to add your own favorites and to question my choices. Books marked with an asterisk are, in my opinion, required reading for every creative professional.

Creativity:

* *Creativity: Flow and the Psychology of Discovery and Invention* by Mihaly Csikszentmihalyi. This book covers many of the ideas in the author's other excellent book, *Flow: The Psychology of Optimal Experience*, but delves into the way that creative people behave, work, and age. If you own only one book about cognitive science and new ideas about the psychology of creativity, this would be the one.

The Rise of the Creative Class by Richard Florida. An insightful study of social and economic trends that places creative professionals at the center of the new economy.

Jump Start Your Business Brain by Doug Hall. Written by a guy who runs creative workshops for a living, this book stands out because (a) it is useful; (b) it's not filled with the same old ideas; and (c) his stuff works for real companies. The same author's *Jump Start Your Brain* is equally good.

Working with Others:

* *People Skills: How to Assert Yourself, Listen to Others, and Resolve Conflicts* by Robert Bolton, Ph.D. This book should be handed to every employee of every company on the planet.

Emotional Intelligence by Daniel Goleman. Emotions and how they work, written by one of the century's best *New York Times* reporters.

* *Do What You Are* by Paul D. Tieger and Barbara Barron-Tieger. One of the most popular Myers-Briggs books, practical in its orientation.

Type Talk at Work: How the 16 Personality Types Determine Your Success on the Job by Otto Kroeger with Janet M. Thueson. A serious rendition of the Myers-Briggs system at work. Their original *Type Talk* is equally good and popular. No need to buy both.

Atlas Shrugged by Ayn Rand. The description on amazon.com captures the essence: "the astounding story of a man who said that he would stop the motor of the world—and did. Tremendous in scope, breathtaking in its suspense, *Atlas Shrugged* stretches the boundaries further than any book you have ever read. It is a mystery, not about the murder of a man's body, but about the murder—and rebirth—of man's spirit." Creative professionals should also read Rand's *The Fountainhead* for its direct relevance.

Innovation:

Nuts!: Southwest Airline's, Crazy Recipe for Business and Personal Success by Kevin Freiberg, Jackie Freiberg, Tom Peters. An uplifting company profile that demonstrates the power of enlightened management, employment empowerment, and the unabashed power of love in building a business.

Truman by David McCullough. Several creative people recommended this book, in part because it shows what one person can do, and in part because McCullough is such a good writer. *The Great Bridge: The Epic Story of the Building of the Brooklyn Bridge* is McCullough's great story of creation.

Presenting:

Envisioning Information; *Visual Explanations*; and *The Visual Display of Quantitative Information* by Edward R. Tufte are filled with provocative, sensible, and in some cases, quite technical ideas about how people and information interact. (Abundant information available on http://www.edwardtufte.com)

Thinking:

Six Easy Pieces: Essentials of Physics Explained by Its Most Brilliant Teacher by Richard Feynman. A clear, if challenging, explanation of the world and how it works.

Gödel Escher Bach: The Eternal Golden Thread by Douglas R. Hofstadter. A wonderful matrix of essays about thinking, creativity, intelligence, and the interlocked concepts pursued by a mathematical philosopher, a logical artist who trafficked in illogical figures, and a mathematical musician.

The Selfish Gene by Richard Dawkins. A reversal of evolutionary theory; filled with provocative thoughts about how and why the tiniest parts of our bodies survive and flourish.

Bob Dylan—Lyrics & Drawings. Says musician Steve Chrismar: "A large hardcover coffee-table book that I have kept available for fifteen years as a reference point. A book that is exactly what it says it is. No intellectual manipulations, no subjective interpretations, just words and pictures."

The Glass Bead Game by Hermann Hesse. Winner of the 1946 Nobel Prize, and still being discovered for its fresh ideas, the book explores intellectual mastery.

* *A User's Guide to the Brain* by John J. Ratey, M.D. The best of several recent guides to the science of brain and mind.

* *A Natural History of the Senses* by Diane Ackerman. Creative jobs are about exciting the senses. This book explains how senses work. Try also *A Natural History of Love*. Another excellent writer, by the way.

Conscientious Objections: Stirring Up Trouble about Language, Technology and Education by Neil Postman. Academic rants about pop culture, TV, learning, teaching, and communication. Postman's *The End of Education* and *The Disappearance of Childhood* will rock your assumptions about the way society works and ought to work.

* *Flatland: A Romance of Many Dimensions* by Edwin Abbot. Over 120 years old, but still provocative and fun to read. Most of the story takes place in two dimensions, which will mess with your head and cause you to question your own sense of reality.

A World Lit Only by Fire: The Medieval Mind and the Renaissance Portrait of an Age by William Manchester. From these embers, the Renaissance became a blaze. Helpful for historical context and a good read, too.

Learning:

* *Frames of Mind: The Theory of Multiple Intelligences* by Howard Gardner. Change the way you think about learning, school, education, and your own abilities. Gardner's work is the basis for change in classrooms throughout the world.

* *Driven to Distraction* by Edward M. Hollowell, M.D., and John J. Ratey, M.D. Many creative professionals consider themselves to be poster children for what is now labeled ADD, or attention deficit disorder. This book explains life for ADD children, adults, and how its unique patterns affect other people.

Spirit:

Asimov's Guide to the Bible by Isaac Asimov. Easier to follow than the real thing, it covers both the old and new testaments.

The Bible. Any good version will do the job.

The Way of Zen by Alan Watts. One of several good introductions to a complicated network of extraordinarily simple ideas.

A History of God: The 4,000 Year Quest of Judaism, Christianity and Islam by Karen Armstrong. Does God play a role in creativity? Who or what is God? Here's the book of answers from a historical perspective.

Writing:

A Writer's Time: A Guide to the Creative Process, from Vision through Revision by Kenneth Atchity. A classic that should be on every writer's bookshelf. The ideas are also useful for those who work in other creative domains.

On Writing Well: An Informal Guide to Writing Non-Fiction by William Zinsser: Another classic, this one specifically useful for journalists, magazine writers, and, to be honest, most professionals who write.

About Art:

* *Understanding Comics* by Scott McCloud. A practical guide (written and designed in comic style) for comic artists and writers, the book serves

a more important purpose: It explains how stories are told and how audiences perceive what they see (and don't see).

Drawing on the Right Side of the Brain by Betty Edwards. A brilliant implementation of the right brain's power in the form of a course that really will teach you how to draw or to draw better. Inspiring and practical.

Art & Fear by David Bayles and Ted Orland. What's happening in your head while you're trying to make art, and why. Also: how to make art despite burn-out, unpleasant reviews, and other negative forces.

Anatomy for the Artist by Sarah Simblet and John Davis (photographer). Yes, the human body is difficult to draw. No book provides more beautiful photographs and detailed explanations. And no creative exercise rivals a quiet session with a model whose form and beauty must somehow be captured on your drawing pad.

Architecture:

* *A Pattern Language: Towns, Buildings, Construction* by Christopher Alexander, Sara Ishikawa, Murray Silverstein. Web wizard and www.photonet. com founder Philip Greenspun suggested this classic: "Nominally about architecture and urban planning, this book has more wisdom about psychology, anthropology, and sociology than any other that I've read." Nearly every one of this volume's 1,170 pages will make you question an assumption that you probably didn't realize you were making. In a section entitled "Four-Story Limit," Alexander notes that "there is abundant evidence to show that high buildings make people crazy."

HOME: A Short History of an Idea by Witold Rybczynski. The author has written several essay collections that consider the spaces where we live and work, and how they have evolved over time. I also recommend his *Looking Around: A Journey Through Architecture*.

Photography:

(Sometimes, in used bookstores, you'll find copies of the *TIME LIFE LIBRARY OF PHOTOGRAPHY*. These square hard-covers are always worth the money; they occupy more than a running foot on my bookshelf.)

Photography by Barbara Upton and John Upton. An adaptation of the TIME LIFE series in a single volume. A new edition is on the expensive side (it's often sold as a textbook), but you can find older editions that are equally useful and valid.

Quality in Photography by Roger Hicks and Frances Schultz. These two British authors are personal favorites. They care deeply about aesthetics and technique, and they're sufficiently specific in their explanations to truly improve your work.

The Ansel Adams Guide—Book 1—Basic Techniques of Photography by John P. Schaefer. No other single book so successfully covers types of cameras, lenses, films, visualization, exposure, and darkroom work so completely or with such wonderful examples (Adams's own photographs, with explanations of how they were made). Buy the revised and updated edition; you'll refer to it often.

Travel Photography by Richard l'Anson. This handy little paperback, published by Lonely Planet, contains an abundance of smart ideas, useful techniques, and practical advice.

Looking at Photographs by John Szarkowski. Says *Photo Review* editor Stephen Perloff, "Probably the most influential photography curator in the world at the time he wrote it (he was curator of photography at the Museum of Modern Art)—and certainly so after he wrote it—Szarkowski took a number of individual photographs and wrote several stunning, concise paragraphs about each one. In tying together photographic history with social, political, economic, and general art history, Szarkowski's meta-analogies allow one to experience these pictures—and all others—in new and deeper ways. It's a hallmark in thinking about images and their place in our lives."

Animation:

The Animation Book by Kit Layborne is the classic. Be sure to buy the latest digital edition.

Music:

Deep Blues by Robert Palmer. More than a history of the Mississippi Delta, a transformative experience that will place you where much of American music began.

All You Need to Know about the Record Business by Donald S. Passman. Covers all aspects of record labels, managers, artists. A favorite throughout the music business.

Entertainment Industry:

On the Real Side: Laughing, Lying and Signifying by Mel Watkins. African-American humor, from slavery to Richard Pryor. Explains a lot about how Americans think, how we treat funny people, and how the entertainment industry evolved.

This Business of Television by Howard Blumenthal and Oliver Goodenough. Shameless self-promotion. I wanted to understand how the whole business worked, so I wrote a book about it. With my lawyer.

Business:

The Portable MBA Series includes books about finance, marketing, entrepreneuring, and other typical MBA coursework. Each book is an education in itself. If you can't find the time or money for an MBA just now, start with these books.

Harvard Business Review on... is a series of paperbacks about leadership, brand management, and other key topics. Each is a compilation of articles published in the popular business magazine.

And...

Time and Again by Jack Finney. A perfectly realized fantasy.